The
Scientific Study of
Marihuana

The
Scientific

Study of Marihuana

Ernest L. Abel, Ph.D.

Nelson-Hall Publishers
Chicago

Library of Congress Cataloging in Publication Data
Main entry under title:

The Scientific study of Marihuana.

    Bibliography: p.
    Includes index.
    1. Marihuana—Physiological effect.   2. Mar-
ihuana—Psychological aspects.   I. Abel, Ernest L.,
1943-
QP981.C14S34   615'.782   76-4508
ISBN 0-88229-144-0

Manufactured in the United States of America

Contents

Acknowledgments

Grateful acknowledgment is made to the following for permission to reprint previously published material:

The World Publishing Company for permission to reprint excerpts from *Les Paradis Artificiels* by C. Baudelaire. In *The Essence of Laughter,* edited by P. Quennell. Copyright 1956 by Meridian Books, Inc.

"Marijuana Intoxication: Common Experiences" by C. T. Tart. Reprinted with permission of the publisher and author from *Nature,* 1970, 226, 701–704.

"Marihuana Effects. A Survey of Regular Users" by J. A. Halikas, D. W. Goodwin, and S. B. Guze. Reprinted with permission of the publisher and the authors from the *Journal of the American Medical Association,* 1971, 217, 692–694.

"Effects of the Marihuana Homologue, Pyrahexyl, on Food and Water Intake and Curiosity in the Rat" by E. L. Abel and B. B. Schiff. Reprinted with permission of the publisher from *Psychonomic Science,* 1969, 16, 38.

"Inhibition of Normal Growth by Chronic Administration of Delta-9-Tetrahydrocannabinol" by F. J. Manning, J. H. McDonough, T. F. Elsmore, C. Saller, and F. J. Sodetz. Reprinted with permission of the publisher and the authors from *Science,* 1971, 424–426. Copyright 1971 by the American Association for the Advancement of Science.

"Effects of Marihuana on the Solution of Anagrams, Memory, and Appetite" by E. L. Abel. Reprinted with permission of the publisher from *Nature,* 1971, *231,* 260–261.

"Hunger and Appetite after Single Doses of Marihuana, Alcohol, and Dextroamphetamine" by L. E. Hollister. Reproduced with permission from *Clinical Pharmacology and Therapeutics 12:* 44–49, 1971; copyrighted by the C. V. Mosby Co., St. Louis, Mo.

"Effects of Marihuana on Auditory and Visual Sensation" by S. A. Myers and D. F. Caldwell. Reprinted with permission of the publisher and the authors from the *Michigan Mental Health Research Bulletin,* 1969, *3,* 1–3. Courtesy of the Michigan Department of Mental Health.

Reprinted with permission of authors and publisher: D. F. Caldwell, S. A. Myers, D. F. Domino, & P. E. Merriam. "Auditory and Visual Threshold Effects of Marihuana in Man." *Perceptual and Motor Skills,* 1969, 29, 755-759.

"The Effects of Marihuana on Auditory and Visual Sensation: A Preliminary Report" by S. A. Myers and D. F. Caldwell. Reprinted with permission of publisher and authors from the *New Physician,* 1969, *18,* 212–215. Courtesy of the Student American Medical Association.

"Delta-9-Tetrahydrocannabinol: Dose-related Effects on Timing Behavior in Chimpanzees" by D. G. Conrad, T. F. Elsmore, and F. J. Sodetz. Reprinted with permission of the authors and publisher from *Science,* 1972, *175,* 547–550. Copyright 1972 by the American Association for the Advancement of Science.

"Marihuana and the Temporal Span of Awareness" by F. T. Melges, J. R. Tinklenberg, L. E. Hollister, and H. K. Gillespie. Reprinted with permission of the authors and publisher from *Archives of General Psychiatry,* 1971, *24,* 564–567.

"Marijuana and Memory" by E. L. Abel. Reprinted with permission of the publisher from *Nature,* 1970, *227,* 1151–1152.

"Effects of Marijuana on Recall of Narrative Material and Stroop Colour-Word Performance" by Miller, W. G. Drew, and G. F. Kiplinger. Reprinted with permission of the authors and publisher from *Nature,* 1972, *237,* 172–173.

"Retrieval of Information after Use of Marihuana" by E. L. Abel. Reprinted with permission of the publisher from *Nature,* 1971, *231,* 58.

"Marihuana and Memory: Acquisition or Retrieval?" by E. L. Abel.

Reprinted with permission of the publisher from *Science,* 1971, *173,* 1038–1040. Copyright 1971 by the American Association for the Advancement of Science.

"Marijuana, Memory, and Perception" by R. L. Dornbush, M. Fink, and A. M. Freedman. Reprinted with permission of the authors and publisher from the *American Journal of Psychiatry 128,* 1971, pp. 194–197. Copyright 1971, the American Psychiatric Association.

"Comparison of the Effects of Marihuana and Alcohol on Simulated Driving Performance" by A. Crancer, Jr., J. M. Dille, J. C. Delay, J. E. Wallace, and M. D. Haykin. Reprinted with permission of the authors and publisher from *Science,* 1969, *164,* 851–854. Copyright 1969 by the American Association for the Advancement of Science.

"Some Cardiovascular Effects of Marihuana Smoking in Normal Volunteers" by S. Johnson and E. F. Domino. Reproduced with permission from *Clinical Pharmacology and Therapeutics, 12:* 762–768, 1971; copyrighted by the C. V. Mosby Co., St. Louis, Mo.

"Marihuana: Standardized Smoke Administration and Dose Effect Curves on Heart Rate in Humans" by P. F. Renault, C. R. Schuster, R. Heinrich, and D. X. Freeman. Reprinted with permission of the authors and publisher from *Science,* 1971, *174,* 589–591. Copyright 1971 by the American Association for the Advancement of Science.

"Marijuana Intoxication: Interaction Between Physiologic Effects and Subjective Experience" by M. Galanter, R. J. Wyatt, L. Lemberger, H. Weingartner, T. B. Vaughan, and W. T. Roth., originally published under the title "Effects on Humans of Δ^9-Tetrahydrocannabinol Administered by Smoking." Reprinted with permission of the authors and publisher from *Science,* 1972, *176,* 934–936. Copyright 1972 by the American Association for the Advancement of Science.

"Adverse Reaction to Marihuana" by M. H. Keeler. Reprinted with permission of the author and publisher from *American Journal of Psychiatry, 124,* 1967, pp. 674–677. Copyright 1967, the American Psychiatric Association.

"Marihuana Use and Psychiatric Illness" by J. A. Halikas, D. W. Goodwin, and S. B. Guze. Reprinted with permission of the authors and publisher from the *Archives of General Psychiatry, 1972, 27,* 162–165. Copyright 1972 by the American Medical Association.

"Marihuana Psychosis: Acute Toxic Psychosis Associated with the use of Cannabis Derivatives" by J. A. Talbott and J. W. Teague. Reprinted with permission of the authors and publisher from the *Journal of the American Medical Association,* 1969, *210,* 299–302.

"Psychiatric Effects of Hashish" by F. S. Tennant, Jr., and J. Groesbeck. Reprinted with permission of the authors and publisher from *Archives of General Psychiatry*, 1972, *27*, 133—136.

"Changes in Anxiety Feelings Following Marihuana Smoking" by E. L. Abel. Reprinted with permission of the publisher from the *British Journal of Addiction*, 1971, *66*, 203—205.

"Changes in Personality Response Ratings Induced by Smoking Marihuana" by E. L. Abel. Reprinted with permission of the publisher from the *British Journal of Addiction*, 1972, *67*, 225—227.

"The Behavior of Worker and Nonworker Rats Under the Influence of (—)Delta-9-Trans-Tetrahydrocannabinol, Chlorpromazine, and Amylobarbitone" by J. Masur, R. M. W. Märtz, and E. A. Carlini. Reprinted with permission of the authors and publisher from *Psychopharmacologia*, 1972, *25*, 57—68.

"Shock-elicited Fighting and Delta-9-Tetrahydrocannabinol" by F. J. Manning and T. F. Elsmore. Reprinted with permission of the authors and publisher from *Psychopharmacologia*, 1972, *25*, 218—228.

"Factors Influencing the Aggressiveness Elicited by Marihuana in Food-Deprived Rats" by E. A. Carlini, A. Hamaoui, and R. M. W. Märtz. Reprinted with the permission of the authors and publisher from the *British Journal of Pharmacology*, 1972, *44*, 794—804.

"Marihuana in Man: Three Years Later" by L. E. Hollister. Reprinted with permission of the author and publisher from *Science*, 1971, *172*, 21—29. Copyright 1972 by the American Association for the Advancement of Science.

Introduction

Marihuana, hashish, grass, and pot are only a few of the names given to preparations that are made from an annual herbaceous plant called *Cannabis sativa*.

Most authorities claim that the cannabis plant is indigenous to the plains of Central Asia and that from there it spread to the Middle East, North Africa, and Europe. When growing in the hot, dry climate of the Far and Middle Eastern countries, cannabis secretes a resinous substance as a defense against the heat. It is this resinous material that contains the psychoactive principle associated with the consumption of the plant. In the warm, moist climates of Europe, however, the cannabis plant is not threatened by the elements and consequently it secretes very little resin. What it does produce is a trunk and stems with a strong fibrous content that can be used to make clothing and rope. It was as a result of these commercial considerations that the plant came to be known to Europeans as Indian hemp or just plain hemp.

The oldest document in which cannabis is mentioned[1] dates back to 2737 B.C.. and comes from China where it is described as "the liberator of sin." Between 2000 B.C. and 1400 B.C. cannabis spread to India and eventually appeared in the sacred Vedas dated around 1300 B.C.

Evidence for its movement further west is next found in writings from Assyria (700 B.C.), an empire that was located in the valley of the Tigris and Euphrates rivers.

While some writers have seen allusions to cannabis as nepenthes, a drug remedy for grief in Homer's *Odyssey,* this interpretation is rather strained. The first unmistakable reference to cannabis by a Greek is not found until the fifth century B.C. when "kannabis" use in Thrace and Scythia was described by Herodotus. For the most part, however, the Greeks seem to have been ignorant of the plant since the eminent biologist Dioscorides and the influential and equally eminent Galen had little to say about its properties.

The Muslim invasions in North Africa and Spain brought cannabis into those countries, but the majority of Europeans remained almost totally unaware of its medicinal value or inebriant properties until the time of the French conquests and occupations of Egypt in 1798 and Algiers in 1830. On these occasions, French scientists who accompanied the armies were able to obtain firsthand information of the effects of the drug on the inhabitants of those countries. Intrigued by what they observed, they carried hashish back with them to France in order to examine its effects under more controlled conditions.

The French physician Jacques Joseph Moreau first became interested in this substance because he believed it might have therapeutic value in the treatment of cholera, since habitual users of hashish seemed to be less severely afflicted by the disease. While subsequent experimentation along these lines proved negative, Moreau's observation of the peculiar psychological effects of hashish on his patients impressed him as having palliative value in the treatment of mental disorders.

However, it was mainly for its commercial value as a source of hemp that cannabis was introduced into Canada by the French, the North American colonies by the English, and Mexico and the American West by the Spanish. During the seventeenth and eighteenth centuries, cannabis fiber was the main source of raw material for the fashioning of sails and riggings for ships, and, as a result of the commercial rivalry among the various European nations during this period, the cultivation of cannabis came under crown control and support.

With the development of steam power and the invention of the cotton gin in the late eighteenth century, hemp ceased to be a profitable agricultural commodity and its cultivation was all but abandoned in North America. As an aside, it is rather interesting that throughout this entire early period, there is almost no evidence that the plant was ever used for its intoxicating effects in any of the New World colonies.

However, by the turn of the nineteenth century, marihuana was being used on a large scale by Mexican people for its euphoriant effects. When many of these people migrated to the United States in search of employment, they carried marihuana with them and initiated their coworkers and relatives into the habit of smoking marihuana as well. From these people, the use of marihuana spread next to various black communities. By 1910, marihuana was being smoked rather extensively in New Orleans and by 1920, commonly used among musicians, both black and white.

From New Orleans, the use of cannabis spread to the major industrial areas of the United States. It was at this point that the sensational reports of licentious behavior, depravity, and the exploitation of young children began to appear in newspapers across the country. Written by irresponsible and highly imaginative journalists, these stories had the effect of alarming the public and in 1938, Mayor Fiorello La Guardia of New York City commissioned the New York Academy of Medicine to make a detailed study of the physiological and psychological effects of marihuana on humans.

The conclusions of that committee were that: "There is evidence in this study that the marihuana users were not inferior in intelligence to the general population and that they had suffered no mental or physical deterioration as a result of their use of the drug . . . a characteristic marihuana psychosis does not exist. Marihuana will not produce a psychosis *de novo* in a well-integrated, stable person."[2]

By the early 1950s, the use of marihuana was still mainly confined to slum-dwelling minority groups, and except for sporadic incidents, the public showed little interest or concern with its growing use in this sector of the populace. Nevertheless, the war on marihuana still continued to be waged. In 1953, Harry J. Anslinger, the former commissioner of the Federal Bureau of Narcotics, denounced marihuana as a drug which "has a corroding effect on the body and on the mind, weakening the entire physical system and often leading to insanity after prolonged use."[3]

Apparently those who had used marihuana or who were using marihuana at the time of Anslinger's campaign were still healthy and sane enough to arouse the curiosity of friends and relatives concerning its psychological effects. Consequently, the hysteria in Anslinger's warnings did nothing to prevent the ever-increasing spread of marihuana throughout the country. By the 1960s, members of every sector of American society had either used or were aware that marihuana was being widely used.

This trend shows no sign of abating. A survey of marihuana usage among students attending college in 1967 revealed that about 5 percent had used it one or more times. By 1969, this figure had jumped to 22 percent and by 1970, it was 42 percent.[4] A comparable survey conducted in that same year revealed that 30–50 percent of all the high school students in the country had accepted marihuana as part of their lifestyle.[5] In addition to providing information concerning marihuana usage among Americans, these polls indicate that a sizable portion of the younger citizens of the United States have broken, and still are breaking, the laws specifically designed to discourage such usage.

As is the case with most drugs which have an ancient past, cannabis usage has been both vilified and extolled on the basis of, at best, second-hand information. Alleged "authorities" in this controversy more often than not have based their arguments pro or con on anecdotal literature, or on evidence which does not even approach modern scientific standards. Many of these well-known authorities did not conduct any original research involving marihuana nor did they take the time and effort to consult current research reports by those who were studying the effects of this substance.

The collection of scientific reports contained in this volume represents some of the most recent findings in the area of marihuana research. Hitherto, much of this material has been buried in scientific journals generally inaccessible to the nonprofessional. The purpose of this book is to make some of this material available to all interested readers—laymen and professionals alike.

In general, most of the articles in this collection deal with the effects of marihuana on humans. However, some of the socially relevant questions that have been posed concerning marihuana cannot be feasibly or ethically studied with humans. The only recourse has been to observe the behavior of animals under the influence of cannabis or its derivatives and to make inferences regarding comparable effects in man from that behavior.

However, a number of objections can and have been raised against the validity of some of these studies. For one thing, the amount of drug that is typically administered to subhuman species is often one hundred or more times greater than that used by humans. This makes any generalizations from animals to humans highly problematical. A second major consideration is that the route of administration of drugs in animals is often via the peritoneal cavity. This method is never used by humans. Since the action of many drugs is greatly affected by absorption, distribution, metabolism and excretion, differences in the way in which cannabis and its derivatives are administered to animals (compared with humans) could result in completely unrelated responses even if dosage of drug were comparable. Finally, while it is possible to observe the behavior of animals with a certain amount of objectivity, it is obviously impossible to question them about their subjective feelings or motives for engaging in that behavior. Instead, the experimenter is forced to rely on his intuition as to what a particular aspect of animal behavior means in terms of human behavior. While studies of animal behavior can raise important theoretical issues and offer valuable leads in pursuing these issues, the ultimate goal is an understanding of the effects of a drug on human behavior.

The topics and articles that are included here have been selected because to me, at least, they represent some of the more socially relevant approaches to cannabis research taken by various investigators. In the conduct of some of these studies I have had a personal involvement. My selection of material may, of course, be regarded by some readers as a biased one. What is of interest or importance to one individual is not necessarily of interest or importance to another. Still, I trust that my choice of material has been diverse enough so that anyone who is interested in knowing about the effects of cannabis will find at least one topic that piques his curiosity.

REFERENCES

1. The history of the use of cannabis is outlined in many sources, e.g., G. Andrews and S. Vinkenoog (Eds.), *The Book of Grass: An Anthology of Indian Hemp*. New York: Grove Press, 1967; E. R. Bloomquist, *Marihuana*. Beverly Hills, Calif.: Glencoe Press, 1968; R. H. Blum, *Society and drugs*. San Francisco: Jossey-Bass, 1969; J. Bousquet, "Cannabis." *Bulletin on Narcotics,* 1950, *2,* 14–30; R. N. Chopra and G. S. Chopra, "The present position of hemp-drug addiction in India." *Indian Medical Research Memoirs,* 1939, no. 31; J. Rosevear, *Pot: A Handbook of Marihuana*. New York: University Books, 1967.

2. Mayor's Committee on Marihuana. *The Marihuana Problem in the*

City of New York. Lancaster, Penn.: J. Cattell Press, 1944, p. 141.

3. H. J. Anslinger and W. F. Tompkins, *The Traffic in Narcotics*. New York: Funk and Wagnalls, 1953, p. 22.

4. R. Brotman and F. Suffet, "Marihuana Use and Social Control," *Annuals of the N.Y. Academy of Sciences,* 1971, 191, p. 237.

5. *Newsweek,* 1970, Feb. 16, p. 65.

Part 1

Pharmacology of Cannabis Sativa

In the preceding pages, reference was occasionally made to either dosage or potency of marihuana. Until quite recently, there was no standard cannabis plant against which objective comparisons of the potency of different samples could be made. This caused many investigators a certain amount of concern since they had no way of determining the amount of psychoactive material contained in the marihuana they were administering to their subjects. Additionally, investigators also felt that without such information they would have no means of comparing experimental findings from other laboratories in terms of some kind of referent.

A few years ago, however, the properties of marihuana and hashish were identified and given the name, *"cannabinoids."* By specifying the amount of cannabinoids in their samples, experimenters felt they had the referent they needed. Since discussion of these constituents in marihuana figures prominently in several of the articles in this volume, the following summary of the chemistry and pharmacology has been included to acquaint the reader with some of the terminology encountered in these readings, as well as some of the problems which arise when too much attention or concern is devoted to equating subjects solely on the basis of the concentration of drug they receive during an experiment.

Although there are a number of different cannabinoids, such as tetrahydrocannabinol (THC), cannabidiol (CBD) and cannabinol (CBN), the principal cannabinoid believed to be responsible for the psychoactive effects of marihuana and hashish is an isomer of THC referred to as either delta—9—tetrahydrocannabinol (Δ^9THC) or delta—1—tetrahydrocannabinol (Δ^1-THC), depending upon the particular system used to describe the chemical structure of the cannabinoid.[1]

Analysis of the Δ^9-THC content in various samples of marihuana from various parts of the world has shown that there is a rather substantial variation in the amount of this substance in the cannabis plant, depending upon the environmental conditions under which it is grown, stored, and processed. In addition, there are also genetic differences among these plants which contribute to the variability in Δ^9-THC content.

Much of the cannabis currently used in North America is originally grown in Mexico, and though it tends to have a higher Δ^9-THC content than plants grown in the United States, it is still relatively low in Δ^9-THC content compared to that cultivated in the Far and Middle East. For example, comparative assays of Δ^9-THC content of cannabis from Mexico and Thailand were found to contain an average of 1.2% and 5% Δ^9-THC respectively.[2] Experienced users of marihuana in the United States have judged marihuana containing about 0.9% Δ^9-THC as of average quality; a 2.8% content was evaluated as being psychoactively as potent as any of the marihuana that they had ever previously used.[3]

In addition to biological variations, it is not uncommon for illicitly obtained marihuana to be adulterated with such inert materials as oregano, parsley, catnip, and so forth. Sometimes the purchased product contains no active ingredient whatsoever, yet the user will still claim that he or she derives the typical marihuana effect. This reflects the well-known placebo effect that illustrates the fact that the user's expectations often color his or her interpretations of a particular experience. Even chronic users of marihuana have reported becoming intoxicated by smoking marihuana, from which, unbeknownst to them, the active material had been removed.[4] The reason for this placebo effect is also related to the fact that the marihuana used in the United States is typically so low in potency that nonspecific factors such as expectancy contribute to the psychological assessment of its effects. The more potent, that is, the higher the Δ^9-THC content in the marihuana being used, however, the less important is the role of such nonspecific factors. To cite a comparison that is often made in conjunction with marihuana, the effects of small doses of alcohol tend also to be subject to nonspecific factors such as the subject's mood, social setting, reasons for using alcohol at the time he or she is being observed, and so forth. However, as the amount of alcohol increases, such nonspecific factors lose their importance and the effects become highly predictable.

A second consideration which arises in conjunction with the illicit use of marihuana is that instead of being adulterated with inert material, it may contain certain hallucinogenic drugs such as LSD, opium, or even heroin, which has been found in marihuana samples from Vietnam. Possibilities for adulteration raise certain misgivings about the value of anecdotal reports concerning the effects of marihuana and hashish that are often cited in connection with arguments for and against the social use of cannabis.

The fact that most of the marihuana used by North Americans is smoked in the form of cigarettes rather than taken orally means that the actual amount of Δ^9-THC consumed by an individual will depend upon the size of the cigarette and the characteristics of his or her inhalation patterns. In smoking marihuana in this country, the user typically inhales the smoke deeply and holds it in the lungs for as long as possible. This tends to maximize the absorption of the active constituents in the smoke. Even so, about one-half of the Δ^9-THC content is lost during the smoking process.[5]

The average weight of the marihuana cigarette is approximately 1.2 grams and about one to two such cigarettes will be consumed during a single marihuana-smoking session.[3] On the basis of typical patterns of use, it has been stated that the average intake of Δ^9-THC per smoking session is about 20 milligrams[3] or about 0.3 milligrams per kilogram for an individual who weighs around 150 pounds.

When smoked, marihuana has a rapid onset of action of about one to ten minutes and a duration of about three to four hours. Taken orally, or in the case of laboratory studies with animals where the drug is injected intraperitoneally, the onset of action is delayed for about one to two hours and the effects last about six hours. With very large doses, however, the onset can be much sooner and the duration much longer. As an aside, it has been estimated that marihuana containing an equivalent amount of Δ^9-THC is about three to four times more potent when smoked than when taken orally.

It has already been pointed out in conjunction with the placebo effect, that the effects of marihuana on human subjects can be quite variable. It is not unusual for an individual to react differently to the same amount of drug on different occasions. Additionally, it is also not uncommon for the same amount of marihuana to produce a "high" in one individual but no comparable effect on another. This is because there appear to be two factors involved in the intoxicating potential of marihuana, one pharmacological, the other psychological.[4] Consequently, the traditional pharmacological approach of administering known amounts of drug to each individual and correlating results with drug dosage has sometimes given way to procedures in which subjects are allowed to take as much of the drug as they request and the effects are related to their subjective evaluations of their degree of intoxication.[6] This methodology has been taken by several investigators and the subjective ratings have been shown to correlate quite closely with the amount of Δ^9-THC actually present in the marihuana cigarette when such analyses have been made.[4]

The alternative, namely giving subjects known amounts of Δ^9-THC, may be pharmacologically rigorous, but as yet has resulted in no compensatory advantage in correlating drug dosage and effect. Nor has there been any standardization in drug dosage among various laboratories. A cursory examination of the literature reveals that the following amounts of Δ^9-THC have been administered to human subjects: 0.35 mg.[7]; 0.9 mg.[8]; 2.8 to 7.5 mg.[4]; 3.5 to 14 mg (smoked)[9]; 8.4 to 33.6 mg (oral)[9]; 24.5 mg[10]; and 20, 40, and 60 mg.[11]

But even these reported dosages cannot be regarded as the amount of Δ^9-THC actually taken into the subject's body. For one thing, we have already noted that about half the Δ^9-THC content of a marihuana cigarette is lost during the smoking process. Secondly, the amount of Δ^9-THC estimated to be present in the marihuana cigarette is based on information supplied to the investigator by the governmental agency in charge of such matters. Recently, one group of experimenters[12] compared the estimate of Δ^9-THC content reported to be present in a marihuana sample which was provided by the National Institute of Mental Health (NIMH) two years prior to their study, with a similar analysis done by a private laboratory at the actual time of the study. The estimate of the Δ^9-THC content by NIMH was 1.312%; the privately done estimate revealed only a 0.2 −0.5% content. The discrepancy was attributed to differences in storage procedures used by NIMH and the group of investigators. The significance of this study, however, is that it points out one of the inherent problems in interpreting results based on the amount of Δ^9-THC estimated to be present in a sample of marihuana when these estimates are not also in some way corroborated with subjective estimates of the potency of the material being used by the subjects at the time of the experiment.

REFERENCES

1. Y. Gaoni and R. Mechoulam, "Isolation, structure and partial synthesis of an active constituent of hashish." *Journal of the American Chemical Society,* 1964, *86,* 1646—1647; R. Mechoulam and Y. Gaoni, "The absolute configuration of Δ^1-tetrahydrocannabinol, the major active constituent of hashish," *Tetrahedron Letters,* 1967, *12,* 1109—11; R. Mechoulam, A. Shani, H. Edery et al., "Chemical basis of hashish activity," *Science,* 1970, *169,* 611—612.

2. R. T. Jones, "Cannabis," in *Chemical and Biological Aspects of Drug Dependence.* S. J. Mule and H. Brill (Eds.), Cleveland: CRC Press, 1972, p. 66.

3. R. T. Jones, "Tetrahydrocannabinol and the Marihuana-Induced Social 'High' or the Effects of the Mind on Marihuana," *New York Academy of Sciences* (Annual), 1971, *191,* 155—165.

4. J. S. Hochman and N. Q. Brill, "Marijuana Intoxication: Pharmacological and Psychological Factors," *Diseases of the Nervous System,* 1971, *32,* 676—679.

5. J. E. Manno, G. R. Kiplinger, I. F. Bennett, et al., "Comparative effects of smoking marihuana or placebo on human motor or mental performance," *Clinical and Pharmacological Therapeutics,* 1970, *11,* 808—815.

6. E. L. Abel, "Marihuana and memory: Acquisition or retrieval?" *Science,* 1971, *173,* 1038—1040; D. F. Caldwell, S. A. Myers, E. F. Domino, and P. E. Merriam, "Auditory and Visual Threshold Effects of Marihuana in Man," *Perceptual and Motor Skills,* 1969, *29,* 755—759.

7. L. E. Hollister, R. K. Richards, and H. K. Gillespie, "Comparison of THC and Synhexyl in man," *Clinical and Pharmacological Therapeutics,* 1968, *9,* 783—791.

8. A. T. Weil, and N. E. Zinberg, "Clinical and psychological effects of marihuana in man," *Science,* 1968, *162,* 1234—1242.

9. H. Isbell, C. W. Gorodetzsky, D. Jasinski, et al., "Effects of (-) delta-9-trans-tetrahydrocannabinol in man," *Psychopharmacologia,* 1967, *11,* 184—188.

10. J. Tinklenberg, F. T. Melges, and L. E. Hollister, "Marihuana and immediate memory," *Nature,* 1970, *26,* 1171−1172.
11. F. T. Melges, J. Tinklenberg, L. Hollister, and H. K. Gillespie, "Temporal disintegration and depersonalization during marihuana intoxication," *Archives General Psychiatry,* 1970, *23,* 204−210.
12. D. F. Caldwell, S. A. Myers, E. F. Domino, and P. E. Merriam, "Auditory and Visual Threshold Effects of Marihuana in Man: Addendum," *Perceptual and Motor Skills,* 1969, *29,* 922.

Part 2

Common Experiences Reported by Users of Marihuana

One of the first steps in the development of any science involves the listing and classification of relevant information into meaningful categories. Once such information has been organized, experimenters can attempt to formulate testable hypotheses concerning the relationships between specific variables. In conformity with this pattern of discovery, the first three articles in this book describe some of the more commonly reported subjective effects of cannabis in humans.

The first article is by the French poet Charles Baudelaire (1821–1867) and is included because of its status as a classic in the anecdotal literature concerning marihuana. The material is drawn from *Les Paradis Artificiels* which appeared in 1859, and reflects Baudelaire's personal experiences with cannabis while he was a member of the *Club des Hashischins,* founded in 1844 by a friend of the French physician Jacques Moreau. The highly imaginative poet had become intrigued by Moreau's reports concerning the effects of cannabis and offered to help the doctor extend his observations by offering himself and his friends as subjects. The club was founded on this basis, and among the more celebrated members in addition to

Baudelaire were Victor Hugo, Honoré de Balzac, and Théophile Gautier.

Among Baudelaire's observations which have frequently been corroborated by other users of marihuana and hashish, are an increase in the rapidity of thought, an impulse to laugh aloud which is often uncontrollable, feelings of coldness in the extremities and weakness in the muscles, an increase in the perceived intensity of colors, and hallucinations in which the user feels that he or she can hear colors and see sounds. Baudelaire also refers to the importance of environmental surroundings and the subjective mood of the individual prior to taking the drug. Thus, he cautions, "any grief or spiritual unrest, any memory of an obligation claiming your attention at a fixed time, would toll like a bell amidst your intoxication and poison your pleasure. The unrest would become an agony, the worry a torture."

Finally, Baudelaire raises an issue which is still being waged today regarding whether cannabis confers a benefit or a detriment on its users: "Let us grant for a moment that hashish gives, or at least augments, genius—they [those who enthusiastically condone its usage] forget that it is in the nature of hashish to weaken the will; so that what hashish gives with one hand it takes away with the other: that is to say, it gives power of imagination and takes away the ability to profit by it."

The second and third articles in this chapter present a less literary but more representative description of the subjective effects of cannabis typically reported. Among the effects most generally noted in these survey reports and elsewhere are increased appetite, distortions in time sense, intensified perception of colors and sounds, and difficulty in remembering. Euphoria and feelings of confidence and adequacy are also frequently mentioned. However, there are also reports of increased apprehension or anxiety.

In experimental examinations of this contradiction in the subjective literature, I noted that under the influence of marihuana, subjects who tended to be slightly anxious before taking it became less anxious, whereas those who were slightly euphoric prior to using marihuana became slightly more anxious afterwards. In other words, there was a slight reversal on the euphoria-anxiety continuum.

A second interesting aspect relating to these reports concerns the frequently reported increase in subjective feelings of confidence and adequacy. In those experimental studies which have obtained both objective measures of a subject's performance and his subjective estimates of that performance, it is not unusual to find the two measures out of proportion. More often than not, a subject will estimate that his or her performance has greatly improved when in fact there has either been no change or the performance has actually deteriorated.

This finding points out the danger in relying on subjective reports for a valid understanding of the effects of cannabis. What a subject reports concerning these effects, and what these effects appear to be when observed by objective means, do not always coincide.

1

Les Paradis Artificiels

Charles Baudelaire

THE SERAPHIC THEATRE

"What does one experience? What does one see? Wonderful things, eh? Amazing sights? Is it very beautiful? Very terrible? Very dangerous?"

Such are the questions put, with a mixture of curiosity and fear, by the ignorant to the initiated. The questioners seem to have a childish impatience for knowledge, such as might be felt by somebody who has never left his fireside, on meeting a man returning from distant and unknown lands. They think of the intoxication caused by hashish as a land of miracles, a huge conjuror's theatre where everything is marvelous and unexpected.

This is an ill-informed notion, a complete misunderstanding. Since, for the common run of readers and questioners, the word hashish conveys an idea of strange, topsy-turvy worlds, an expectation of miraculous dreams (a more accurate word would be hallucinations—which, in any case, are less frequent than is generally supposed), I shall at once point out an important difference between the effects of hashish and the phenomena of sleep.

In sleep, that nightly journey of adventure, there positively is something miraculous; although the miracle's mystery has been staled by its punctual regularity. Men's dreams are of two kinds. Those of the first kind are full of his ordinary life, his preoccupations, desires and faults, mingled in a more or less bizarre fashion with things seen during the day that have indiscriminately attached themselves to the huge canvas of his memory. This is the natural dream—the man himself.

But the other kind of dream; The absurd, unpredictable dream, with no relation to or connection with the character, life or passions of the dreamer. This, which I shall call the "hieroglyphic" dream, obviously represents the supernatural side of life; and it is just because of its absurdity that the ancients regarded it as divine. Since it cannot be explained as a product of natural causes, they attributed it to a cause external to mankind; and even today, and apart from the oneiromancers, there is a school of philosophy that sees in dreams of this sort sometimes a reproach and sometimes a counsel; a symbolic moral picture, that is to say, engendered actually in the mind of the sleeping person. It is a dictionary that requires study for its comprehension, a language to which wise men can obtain the key.

The intoxication of hashish is utterly different. It will not bring us beyond the bounds of the natural dream. It is true that throughout its whole period the intoxication will be in the nature of a vast dream—by reason of the intensity of its colors and its rapid flow of mental images; but it will always retain the private tonality of the individual. The man wanted the dream, now the dream will govern the man; but this dream will certainly be the son of its father. The sluggard has contrived artificially to introduce the supernatural into his life and thoughts, but he remains, despite the adventitious force of his sensations, merely the same man increased, the same number raised to a very high power. He is subjugated—but, unfortunately for him, only by himself; in other words, by that part of himself that was already previously dominant. *He wished to ape the angel, he has become an animal;* and for a brief while the latter is very powerful—if power is the correct word for an excessive sensibility—because it is subject to no restraining or directing government.

It is right then, that sophisticated persons, and also ignorant persons who are eager to make acquaintance with unusual delights, should be clearly told that they will find in hashish nothing miraculous, absolutely nothing but an exaggeration of the natural. The brain and organism on which hashish operates will produce only the normal phenomena peculiar to that individual—increased, admittedly, in number and force, but always faithful to their origin. A man will never escape from his destined physical and moral temperament: hashish will be a mirror of his impressions and private thoughts—a magnifying mirror, it is true, but only a mirror.

Have a look at the drug itself: a green sweetmeat, the size of a nut and singularly odorous—so much so that it provokes a certain disgust and velleities of nausea; as, indeed any odor would do, however pure or even agreeable in itself, if enhanced to its maximum of strength and, so to speak, density. (I may be allowed to remark, in passing, that this last statement has a corollary, that even the most disgusting and revolting scent might perhaps become a pleasure if it were reduced to its minimum of quantity and effluvium.)

Here, then, is happiness! It is large enough to fill a small spoon. Happiness, with all its intoxications, follies and puerilities. You can swallow it without fear—one does not die of it. Your physical organs will be in no way affected. Later on, perhaps, a too frequent consultation of the oracle will diminish your strength of will; perhaps you will be less of a man than you are today. But the retribution is so distant, and the disaster in store for you so difficult to define! What are you risking? A touch of nervous exhaustion tomorrow? Do you not daily risk worse retribution for lesser rewards?

Well, now, your mind is made up. You have even—in order to make the dose stronger and more diffusely effective—melted your rich extract in a cup of black coffee; you have seen to it that your stomach is empty, by postponing your main meal until nine or ten o'clock that evening, in order to give the poison full freedom of action; perhaps in an hour's time you will take, at the most, some thin soup. You now have enough ballast for a long and singular voyage. The steam-whistle has blown, the sails are set, and you have a curious advantage over ordinary travellers—that of not knowing whither you are going. You have made your choice: hurrah for destiny!

I assume that you have chosen your moment for this adventurous expedition. Every perfect debauch calls for perfect leisure. I have told you, moreover, that hashish produces an exaggeration not only of the individual, but also of his circumstances and surroundings. You must, therefore, have no social obligations demanding punctuality or exactitude; no domestic worries; no distressing affair of the heart. This is most important: for any grief or spiritual unrest, any memory of an obligation claiming your attention at a fixed time, would toll like a bell amidst your intoxication and poison your pleasure. The unrest would become an agony, the worry a torture.

If all these indispensable conditions have been observed, so that the moment is propitious; if your surroundings are favorable—a picturesque landscape, for example, or a poetically decorated apartment; and if, in addition, you can look forward to hearing a little music; why, then, all is for the best.

Intoxication with hashish generally falls into three successive phases, quite easy to distinguish. For beginners even the first symptoms of the first phase will be interesting enough. You have heard vague reports of the drug's marvellous effects. Your imagination has preconceived some private notion of them, something in the nature of an ideal form of drunkenness. You are impatient to learn if the reality will match your expectations. This is sufficient to throw you, from the beginning, into a state of anxiety, which to no small extent encourages the infiltration of the victorious and invading poison.

Most novices, of only the first degree of initiation, complain that hashish is slow in taking effect. They wait with childish impatience for it to do so; and then, when the drug does not function quickly enough to suit them, they indulge in a swaggering incredulity, which gives great delight to old initiates, who know just how hashish sets about its work.

The earliest encroachments of the drug, like symptoms of a storm that hovers before it strikes, appear and multiply in the very bosom of this incredulity. The first of them is a sort of irrelevant and irresistible hilarity. Attacks of causeless mirth, of which you are almost ashamed, repeat themselves at frequent intervals, cutting across periods of stupor during which you try in vain to pull yourself together. The simplest words, the most trivial ideas, assume a new and strange guise; you are actually astonished at having hitherto found them so simple. Incongruous and unforseeable resemblances and comparisons, interminable bouts of punning on words, rough sketches for farces, continually spout from your brain. The demon has you in thrall. It is useless to struggle against this hilarity, which is as painful as a tickle. From time to time you laugh at yourself, at your own silliness and folly; and your companions, if you have such, laugh alike at your condition and at their own. But, since they laugh at you without malice, you laugh back at them without rancor.

This mirth, with its alternating spells of languor and convulsion, this distress in the midst of delight, generally lasts only for a fairly short time. Soon the coherence of your ideas becomes so vague, the conducting filament between your fancies becomes so thin, that only your accomplices can understand you.

And once again, on this question, too, there is no means of ascertaining the truth: perhaps they only think they understand you, and the deception is mutual. This crazy whimsicality, these explosive bursts of laughter, seem like real madness, or at least like a maniac's folly, to anyone who is not in the same state as yourself. Conversely, the self-control, good sense and orderly thoughts of a prudent observer who has abstained from intoxication—these delight and amuse you like a special sort of dementia. Your roles are inverted: his calmness drives you to extremes of ironic disdain.

How mysteriously comical are the feelings of a man who revels in incomprehensible mirth at the expense of anyone not in the same situation as himself! The madman begins to feel sorry for the sane man; and, from this moment on, the notion of his own superiority begins to gleam on the horizon of his intellect. Soon it will grow, swell and burst upon him like a meteor.

Let me now revert to the normal development of the intoxication. After the first phase of childish mirth comes a sort of momentary lull. But soon new adventures are heralded by a sensation of chilliness in the extremities (for some people this becomes an intense cold), and a great weakness in all the members. In your head, and throughout your being, you feel an embarrassing stupor and stupefaction. Your eyes bulge, as if under the pull, both physical and spiritual, of an implacable ecstasy. Your face is flooded with pallor. Your lips shrink and are sucked back into your mouth by that panting movement that characterizes the ambition of a man who is a prey to great projects, overwhelmed by vast thoughts, or gaining breath for some violent effort. The sides of the gullet cleave together, so to speak. The palate is parched with a thirst that it would be infinitely pleasant to satisfy, if only the delights of idleness were not still more agreeable, and did they not forbid the slightest disarrangement of the body's posture. Hoarse, deep sighs burst forth from your chest, as if your *old* body could not endure the desires and activity of your *new* soul. Now and then a jolt passes through you, making you twitch involuntarily. It is like one of those sharp sensations of falling that you experience at the end of a day's work, or on a stormy night just before finally falling asleep.

As the narrator indicates, it is at this phase of intoxication that a new subtlety or acuity manifests itself in all the senses. This development is common to the senses of smell, sight, hearing and touch. The eyes behold the Infinite. The ear registers almost imperceptible sounds, even in the midst of the greatest din.

This is when hallucinations set in. External objects acquire, gradually and one after another, strange new appearances; they become distorted or transformed. Next occur mistakes in the identities of objects, and transposals of ideas. Sounds clothe themselves in colors, and colors contain music.

"There's nothing at all unnatural about that," the reader will say. "Such correspondences between sounds and colors are easily perceived by a poetic brain in its normal healthy state." But I have already warned the reader that there was nothing positively supernatural about the intoxication of hashish. The difference is that the correspondences take on an unusual liveliness; they penetrate and invade the mind, despotically overwhelming it. Notes of music turn into numbers; and, if you are endowed with some aptitude for mathematics, the melody or harmony you hear, whilst retaining its pleasurable and sensuous character, transforms itself into a huge arithmetical process, in which numbers beget numbers, whilst you follow the successive stages of reproduction with inexplicable ease and agility equal to that of the performer.

MORAL

But the morrow! The terrible morrow! All the body's organs lax and weary, nerves unstrung, itching desires to weep, the impossibility of applying oneself steadily to any task—all these cruelly teach you that you have played a forbidden game. Hideous Nature, stripped of yesterday's radiance, resembles the melancholy debris of a banquet.

The especial victim is the will, the most precious of all the faculties. It is said, and is almost true, that hashish has no evil physical effects; or, at worst, no serious ones. But can it be said that a man incapable of action, good only for dreaming, is truly well, even though all his members may be in their normal condition?

We understand enough of human nature to know that a man who, with a spoonful of conserve, can instantaneously procure for himself all the benefits of heaven and earth, will never earn a thousandth part of these by toil. Can one imagine a State of which all the citizens intoxicated themselves with hashish? What citizens, what warriors and legislators! Even in the East, where its use is so widespread, there are governments that have understood the necessity of banning it. The fact is that man is forbidden, on pain of intellectual ruin and death, to upset the primordial conditions of his existence, to break the equilibrium between his faculties and the surroundings in which they are destined to function—to upset his destiny, in short, and substitute for it a fatality of a new order.

These people's hopes form, therefore, a vicious circle. Let us grant for a moment that hashish gives, or at least augments, genius—they forget that it is in the nature of hashish to weaken the will; so that what hashish gives with one hand it takes away with the other: that is to say, it gives the power of imagination and takes away the ability to profit by it. Even if we imagine a man clever and vigorous enough to gain the one without losing the other, we must bear in mind a further and terrible danger, which attaches itself to all habits. They all soon turn into necessities. He who has recourse to poison in order to think will soon be unable to think *without* poison. How terrible the lot of a man whose paralyzed imagination cannot function without the aid of hashish or opium!

2

Marijuana Intoxication: Common Experiences

Charles T. Tart

The widespread use of marijuana, chiefly among college students, has raised important ethical, social and scientific questions and has stimulated some research. There is a risk, however, that studies will be unrepresentative of the effects of marijuana as it is actually used. One pitfall is the attempt to study "pure" effects in which extraneous sources of variation are minimized. Thus the report on one otherwise excellent laboratory study[1] says the ". . . greatest effort was made to create a neutral setting . . . verbal interactions between staff and subjects were minimum and formal. . . ."

An adequate understanding of marijuana intoxication which focuses on particular effects experienced by a particular person must take into account

(1) long-term characteristics of the user—his personal and physiological idiosyncrasies;

(2) immediate expectations and desires about what will happen during intoxication;

Reprinted with permission of the publisher and the author from *Nature* (Macmillan Journals Limited), 1970, *226*, 701—704.

Charles T. Tart is affiliated with the Department of Psychology, University of California, Davis, California.

(3) past experiences with marijuana and other psychoactive drugs as well as learned skills for modifying the drug experience;

(4) immediate emotional state;

(5) the social and physical setting;

(6) the amount of marijuana used; and

(7) chemical variations of the marijuana used.

(Many of the marijuana users I interviewed insisted that certain samples of marijuana were qualitatively different from one another, and brought about different effects—laughter or sedation, for example.) During intoxication, these variables may alter as, for example, a user's companions direct his attention to new effects. Knowledge of how these variables affect marijuana intoxication is meagre, and is based almost exclusively on anecdotal accounts[2-5].

Some of the effects of marijuana may be evident only when the variables mentioned above have certain values. Other effects, which may be called "pure drug effects," may be caused exclusively by the pharmacological action of the drug. Both types are equally "real" and interesting. The traditional "neutral" setting of the laboratory, however, can provide a very limited configuration of determining variables: thus many potential effects will not show up in the laboratory situation, so that the picture of marijuana intoxication obtained there may be only partial. Indeed, it has been argued that the laboratory setting probably inhibits many important human manifestations[6-9].

These disadvantages can be overcome, however, if the investigator knows the entire normal range of effects of marijuana. My purpose here is to record this range for the benefit of future investigations. I designed a questionnaire on the basis of what I had read and learned from informal interviews with marijuana users. The questionnaire was answered by experienced marijuana users with respect to all their experiences over the preceding six months. The variables I have referred to would have been operative throughout their ranges, giving an adequate sample of the potential effects as well as the pure drug effects.

Informal interviews, chiefly with students, were carried out for two years to find out what marijuana intoxication was like. The results were combined with other descriptions of effects (see ref. 10) to give 206 descriptions of possible effects. The descriptions made up the chief part of a large questionnaire. The respondent was asked to say how often he had experienced each possible effect during the preceding six months. (The restriction to the last six months of use was intended to reduce lapses of memory. Respondents were also asked to estimate the smallest degree of intoxication necessary to experience each effect on a five-point scale: these data and more detailed analyses will be presented elsewhere.) If the description made no sense to him, he could skip it; otherwise he was asked to estimate frequency in one of five categories:

(1) never;
(2) rarely;
(3) sometimes (between 10 and 40 percent of time);
(4) very often (more than 40 percent of time); and
(5) usually (almost always).

The rest of the questionnaire consisted of questions on background (age, sex, education and experience with other psychoactive drugs).

The questionnaires were distributed by students, who were asked to pass the questionnaires on until they reached experienced marijuana users; this method was intended to ensure anonymity. A stamped return envelope was attached to each questionnaire and, of about 750 questionnaires, 153 were returned.

A letter that went out with the questionnaire was written colloquially and used the drug culture terminology. It explained the purpose of the study, asked the respondents to be as accurate as possible, and offered to make results available to anyone who wanted them after a year. It asked that only people who had used marijuana at least a dozen times should fill in the questionnaire, to avoid problems of adaptation.

METHODOLOGICAL QUESTIONS

Are the answers valid? For example, can the respondents adequately assess their experiences? Allowing for the difficulty of putting precise words to inner experiences, it seemed from the informal interviews that educated marijuana smokers could give fairly articulate descriptions; and the respondents in this study were highly educated. Comprehensive interviews to determine a more adequate vocabulary are needed, but most of the possible effect descriptions seemed understandable and conveyed what the users wished to express. To check carelessness or deliberately bizarre answers, I added fourteen extra descriptions of possible effects randomly among the original 206. They constituted a validity scale by referring to unheard-of-effects. Any questionnaire with six or more positive responses to them was to be rejected without further analysis; three were in fact rejected, leaving 150 that could be used.

A further objection: might the respondent overstress positive effects in order to justify his drug use? One cannot be certain, but two steps were taken to reduce the possibility. First, the accompanying letter was designed to appear sympathetic to marijuana use, so there was no need to win over the investigator. Second, the letter appealed to the respondents' curiosity about other users' experiences and to their loyalty to other users: because it promised to make the results available, the respondents would benefit by being accurate. Negative, unpleasant effects, are, nevertheless, under-represented in the replies, and interpretations should take account of the lack. By definition, an "experienced" marijuana user is an enthusiast; it would be somewhat perverse to indulge continually in criminal behaviour that is personally unpleasant.

Because my purpose is to ascertain the common effects of marijuana intoxication rather than the effects in specific populations, I describe here only major characteristics of the sample. The respondents were chiefly young Californians (67 percent), with some East Coast respondents (11 percent); 87 percent were under 30 years old. There were twice as many males as females. 67 percent were students, and 71 percent unmarried. Only 7 percent had had no college training, and 21 percent had pursued graduate work or had earned advanced degrees. Only 4 percent had been arrested for possessing marijuana. Many of the respondents were interested in self-improvement: 36 percent reported that they practice some sort of discipline for spiritual or personal growth. 74 percent of the sample had smoked marijuana for between six months and three years; the average frequency of use during the preceding six months ranged from "almost every day" (19 percent) to "once a week or more" (42 percent) to less than once a week (39 percent). 72 percent had tried more powerful psychoactive drugs such as LSD-25 at least once, 47 percent of them in the six months covered by the questionnaire. Few (7 percent) had used hard narcotics or dangerous stimulants (amphetamine or methedrine by injection). The respondents had used marijuana to alter their state of consciousness more than twice as frequently as alcohol in the preceding six months.

I classify the results into three categories: first, a large number of effects that may be considered common; second, a smaller number of effects that occur so frequently that they may be considered characteristic (these are shown by an asterisk in the list of "common effects"); third, some infrequent effects that seem at face value to be very significant. "Common" is here defined as being rated as "Sometimes,"

"Very Often," or "Usually" by at least 50 percent of the respondents; "characteristic" as being rated "Very Often" or "Usually" by at least 50 percent of the respondents.

The descriptions of possible effects within the "common effects" category are given in the wording of the questionnaire, except that the qualifying phrase "the effect is more pronounced during marijuana intoxication ['while stoned'] than normally" is usually omitted to save space, and some parts of the descriptions are omitted if the meaning is not thereby affected. The descriptions are put into sixteen classes, although some are relevant to more than one class. Within each class, the descriptions begin with the most common; the figures given are the total percentages of respondents putting an effect into the "Sometimes," "Very Often," or "Usually" categories.

COMMON EFFECTS

Visual effects: (1) I can see patterns, form, figures, meaningful designs in visual material that does not have any particular form when I'm straight, that is just a meaningless series of lines or shapes when I'm straight, 85*. (2) If I try to visualize something . . . I see it in my mind's eye more sharply. . . , 81*. (3) When looking at pictures they may acquire an element of visual depth, a third dimensional aspect. . . , 72. (4) Things seen are seen more sharply in that their edges, contours stand out more sharply against the background, 72. (5) I can see new colours or more subtle shades of colour. . . , 70. (6) There is a sensual quality to vision, as if I were somehow "touching" the objects or people I am looking at, 59. (7) . . . things in the periphery of my vision look different when I'm not looking directly at them. . . , (8) My visual perception of the space around me is changed so that what I'm looking at is very real and clear but everything else I'm not focusing on visually seems further away or otherwise less real or clear, 58.

Auditory effects: (1) I can hear more subtle changes in sounds, for example, the notes of music are purer and more distinct, the rhythm stands out more, 99*. (2) I can understand the words of songs which are not clear when straight, 85*. (3) When listening to stereo music or live music, the spatial separation between the various instruments sounds greater, as if they were physically further apart, 82*. (4) If I try to have an auditory image . . . it is more vivid. . . , 73. (5) With my eyes closed and just listening to sounds, the space around me becomes an *auditory* space, a space where things are arranged according to their sound characteristics instead of visual, geometrical characteristics, 65. (6) The sound quality of my voice changes, so that I sound different to myself when I talk, 63.

Touch effects: (1) My sense of touch is more exciting, more sensual. . . , 86*. (2) Touch sensations take on new qualities. . . , 85*. (3) Some surfaces feel much smoother, silkier, 77. (4) Some surfaces feel much rougher, irregular . . . and the roughness or graininess forms interesting patterns, 73. (5) The temperature of things . . . takes on new qualities, 69. (6) I can experience vivid tactual imagery. . . , 60. (7) Objects seem heavier, more massive when I lift them, 55.

Taste effects: (1) Taste sensations take on new qualities, 93*. (2) I enjoy eating very much and eat a lot, 93*. (3) If I try to imagine what something tastes like, I can do so very vividly, 69. (4) I crave sweet things to eat, like chocolate, more than other foods, 57.

Smell effects: (1) Smell sensations take on new qualities, 71. (2) Smells become richer and more unique. . . , 69.

Space-time perception: (1) When I walk someplace my experience of the distance covered is quite changed. . . , 96*. (2) Time passes very slowly. . . , 95*. (3) Distances between me and things or me and other people seem to get greater. . . , 69. (4) Events and thoughts flow more smoothly, the succession of events in time is smoother than usual, 69. (5) I get so lost in fantasy or similar trips in my head that I completely forget where I am, and it takes a while to reorient after I come back and open my eyes, 63. (6) Time seems to stop: it's not just that things take longer, certain experiences seem outside of time, are timeless, 63. (7) Events and thoughts follow each other jerkily, there are sudden changes from one thing to another, 59. (8) While something is happening I get the funny feeling that this sequence has happened before in exactly the same way. . . *(deja vu)*. . . , 55. (9) Distances. . . seem to get shorter. . . , 53.

Perception of the body: (1) I feel a lot of pleasant warmth inside my body, 71. (2) If I am paying attention to some particular part of my body, the rest of my body fades away a lot so the part I'm attending to stands out more sharply, 69. (3) I am much more aware of the beating of my heart, 69. (4) With my eyes closed, my body may feel very light or even feel as if I float up into the air, 68. (5) I have lost all consciousness of my body during fantasy trips. . . , 66. (6) I get feelings in my body that are best described as energy, force, power of some sort flowing, 65. (7) I lose awareness of most of my body unless I specifically focus my attention there or some particularly strong stimulus demands my attention there, 61. (8) I become very aware of my breathing and can feel the breath flowing in and out of my throat as well as filling my lungs, 60. (9) Pain is easy to tolerate if I keep my attention elsewhere, 59. (10) I feel a vibration or tingling sensation in some or all of my body that I can tell is not an actual muscle tremor by looking at my body, 57. (11) Pain is more intense if I concentrate on it, 54.

Physical movement: (1) I get physically relaxed and don't want to get up or move around, 95*. (2) When I move about or dance my motions seem exceptionally smooth and well coordinated, 81*. (3) I get physically restless so that I want to move around a lot, 58. (4) I feel much weaker when stoned (regardless of whether you're actually physically stronger or weaker), 51.

Interpersonal relations: (1) I have feelings of deep insights into other people, how they tick, what their games are (regardless of whether they actually check out later), 85*. (2) I find it very hard to play ordinary social games, 83*. (3) I empathize tremendously with others, I feel what they feel, I have a tremendous intuitive understanding of what they're feeling, 83. (4) I talk a lot less, 83. (5) I am less noisy and boisterous at parties, 82*. (6) I am less noisy and boisterous at parties than when drunk or tipsy on alcohol, 82*. (7) When stoned with others I play "childish" games, that is, we interact with each other in ways which are very enjoyable but which people would ordinarily consider "childish," 80. (8) I feel the things I say in conversation are more profound and appropriate to the conversation, more interesting, 79. (9) I become more sociable, I want to be with and interact with people more, 76. (10) When stoned with a group of people, the group takes on a much greater sense of unity, or real social relationship. . . , 75. (11) I become less sociable; I want to be by myself, 73. (12) Being with people who are much higher than I am (as from their being on acid (LSD) or much more stoned on grass) gets me higher, even though I don't smoke any more grass, 70. (13) I talk a lot more, 64. (14) I feel isolated from things around me. . . , 50.

Sexual effects: (1) Sexual orgasm has new qualities, pleasurable qualities, 77*. (2) When making love I feel I'm in much closer mental contact with my partner; it's much more a union of souls as well as bodies, 76. (3) I have no increase in sexual feeling unless it's a situation that I would normally be sexually aroused in, and then the sexual feelings are much stronger and more enjoyable, 75. (4) My sexual drive goes up, I have more need for sex, 61. (5) I feel as if I'm a better person to make love with when stoned, 52.

Thought processes: (1) I appreciate very subtle humour in what my companions say, and say quite subtly funny things myself, 91*. (2) Commonplace sayings of conversations seem to have new meanings, more significance, 87. (3) I give little or no thought to the future, I am completely in the here-and-now, 87*. (4) Spontaneously, insights about myself, my personality, the games I play, come to mind when stoned and seem very meaningful, 86*. (5) The ideas that come to my mind are much more original, 83. (6) I find it difficult to read, 80*. (7) I think about things in ways that seem intuitively correct, but which do not follow the rules of logic, 78. (8) . . . I think much more in (visual) images instead of just abstract thought, 75. (9) I am more willing to accept contradictions between two ideas or two views . . . I don't get uptight because the two things don't make immediate sense, 74*. (10) If I deliberately work on it, I can have important insights about myself, my personality, the games I play, 73. (11) I learn a great deal about psychological processes . . . general knowledge about how the mind works (as opposed to specific insights about yourself), 71. (12) I get so wound up in thoughts or fantasies that I won't notice what's going on around me. . . , 69. (13) I get so wound up in thoughts or fantasies while doing some physical task or job that I lose awareness of doing it, yet suddenly find that I have finished the physical task. . . , 67. (14) I have more imagery than usual while reading; images of the scene I'm reading about just pop up vividly, 67. (15) I do things with much less thought to possible consequences of my actions. . . , 65. (16) If I try to solve a problem, it feels as if my mind is working much more efficiently than usual (regardless of how you evaluate the solution later), 64. (17) If I work on a problem, I work less accurately as judged by later real-world evaluation, 63. (18) I can play elaborate games and get very involved in the games, 60. (19) If I try to solve a problem it feels as if my mind is much less efficient. . . , 56. (20) In thinking about a problem of the sort that normally requires a series of steps to solve, I can get the answer without going through some of the usual intermediate steps. . . , 53.

Memory functioning: (1) My memory span for conversations is somewhat shortened, so that I may forget what the conversation is about even before it has ended (even though I may be able to recall it if I make a special effort), 89*. (2) I can continue to carry on an intelligent conversation even when my memory span is so short that I forget the beginnings of what I started to say; for example, I may logically complete a sentence even as I realize I've forgotten how it started, 72. (3) I can't think clearly, thoughts keep slipping away before I can quite grasp them, 71. (4) My memory span for conversations is very shortened so that I may forget what the start of a sentence was about even before the sentence is finished. . . , 68, (5) I spontaneously remember things I hadn't thought of in years. . . , 61. (6) If I read while stoned, I remember less of what I've read hours later, 61. (7) I think I've said something when actually I've only thought about saying it. . . , 57. (8) My memory of what went on while I was stoned is poor afterwards. . . , 57. (9) My memory of what went on is . . . better than if I had been straight, 55.

Emotions: (1) I feel emotions much more strongly, so they affect me more, 80. (2) I almost invariably feel good when I turn on, regardless of whether I felt bad before turning on, 80*. (3) I am more aware of the body tensions and feelings that are part of emotions, 74. (4) Whatever mood I was in before turning on becomes greatly amplified; so if I felt let down I really feel bad, and if I felt good, I really feel very good, 72.

Self-control: (1) I find it easy to accept whatever happens, I don't need to control it or feel in control of it, 89*. (2) I can "come down" at will if I need to be straight for a minute to deal with some complicated reality problem, 89*. (3) I often forget to finish some task I've started, or get sidetracked more frequently than when straight, 86*. (4) I giggle a lot when stoned, I am silly, even though the situation is not that funny, 74. (5) I have excellent control over my fantasies; I can make them go in whatever direction I want, 73. (6) My inhibitions are lowered so that I do things I'm normally too inhibited to do (Note: this does not apply to antisocial acts but to acts that are generally acceptable but that you normally can't do through shyness or the like), 69. (The immediately following item was, "I lose control of my actions and do antisocial things [actions that harm other people] that I wouldn't normally do." The response was 77 percent never, 22 percent rarely, and one respondent sometimes.) (7) I can work at a necessary task with extra energy, absorption and efficiency, 61. (8) I feel as if I lose control over my thoughts; they just go on regardless of what I want (without reference to whether you like this or not), 52.

Sense of identity: (1) I feel very powerful, capable, and intelligent, 71. (2) Some events become archetypal, part of the basic way Man has always done things. That is, instead of me (John Doe, ego) doing something, it is just Man Doing What Man Has Always Done. . . . , 57. (3) I lose all sense of self, of being a separate ego, and feel at one with the world, 55.

Effects on sleep: (1) I find it very easy to go to sleep at my usual bedtime when stoned, 84*. (2) I get very drowsy even though it's not late. . . , 83. (3) My sleep is particularly refreshing if I go to bed stoned, 81. (4) My dreams are more vivid if I go to bed stoned, 51.

Miscellaneous effects: (1) I feel more childlike, more open to experiences of all kinds, more filled with wonder and awe at the nature of things, 91*. (2) I get more involved in ordinary tasks, 80. (3) Others (who were straight at the time) have not noticed that I've been stoned (applied to other people who were your friends and would have told you if they'd noticed), 69. (4) With my eyes closed my inner visions and fantasies become extremely real, as real as night-time dreams, 68. (5) Some of my inner trips, eyes-closed fantasies, have been so vivid and real that even though I know logically they couldn't be real, they feel real; they are as real as ordinary waking life experience, 57. (6) Sounds have visual images or colours associated with them, synchronized with them, 55.

INFREQUENT BUT SIGNIFICANT EFFECTS

The following effects were not reported often enough to be classed as common, but they seem so powerful and unusual that they might well change somebody's beliefs. The numbers given are the percentages of respondents who have experienced the effect at all.

(1) I feel so aware of what people are thinking that it must be telepathy, mind reading, rather than just being more sensitive to the subtle cues in their behaviour, 69; (2) Getting stoned has acquired a religious significance for me, 69; (3) I have spiritual experiences . . . which have had a powerful, long-term religious effect on me, 65; (4) I feel in touch with a Higher Power or a Divine Being to some extent. . . , I feel more in contact with the "spiritual" side of things, 59; (5) I am able to meditate more effectively, 39; (6) I can foretell the future by some kind of precognition, more than just logically predicting from present events, 32; (7) . . . felt "located" outside the physical body. . . , 32; (8) I can perform magical operations that will affect objects or people, 13.

The way in which items were selected for the questionnaire (informal interviewing) produced a set of items that were almost uniformly positive or neutral in tone; there were almost no "bad" effects. But a few negative effects included in the questionnaire are powerful enough to seem important, even if they are infrequent. Figures are again the percentages of respondents who have experienced the effect at all.

(9) I get somewhat paranoid about the people with me, I am suspicious about what they're doing, 80; (10) I lose control of my actions and do antisocial things (things that harm other people), 23; (11) I have lost control and been "taken over" by an outside force or will which is hostile or evil in intent for a while, 20.

One question asked the respondents how often they had seen other people "freak out," that is, have intense, transient emotional upsets. 62 percent of the respondents said never, 36 percent less than one time in twenty, and 2 percent more often. Fifty-three respondents answered a question about what sort of help was necessary for the person who "freaked out"; usually (64 percent) friends talked to the person and calmed him. Medical or psychological aid was used in 13 percent of cases, with other methods or no special help for the rest. When the respondents were asked how many times they had "freaked out" themselves, 79 percent answered never, 14 percent once, and 7 percent more than once. The respondents themselves were usually calmed down by friends (56 percent) or had the "freakout" subside by itself or through their own efforts (37 percent).

These figures probably represent a higher incidence of "freakouts" on marijuana than actually occurs: because of the method of distributing the questionnaires, many of the respondents may have been reporting on the same cases of emotional difficulties in others.

PLEASURES OF BEING HIGH

124 of the 206 items on the questionnaire may thus be considered common experiential effects of marijuana intoxication. Sense perception is often improved, both in intensity and in scope. Imagery is usually stronger but well controlled, although people often care less about controlling their actions. Great changes in perception of space and time are common, as are changes in psychological processes such as understanding, memory, emotion, and sense of identity.

This is not the place to theorize about the results, but they are quite consistent with an earlier, independent description: ". . . Sensations are enhanced and clarified: sight, hearing, taste, touch. Time perception changes. Attention becomes more unified, and moves more into preconscious material and the state of pure awareness. The many broad processes of association, such as social meanings, memory images, expectancies and plans, are reduced in number and relevance. Inhibitions and suppressions relax, allowing emotions, thoughts, fantasies, and memories to flow more freely. The development and strength of these effects will depend on the individual, the times he has used marijuana, how he has used marijuana, and the environment"[11]. Although the validity of the descriptions cannot be proved, there is at least a great deal of agreement among the respondents. To the extent that the described effects are delusory or inaccurate, the delusions and inaccuracy are widely shared. It is interesting, too, that nearly all the common effects seem either emotionally pleasing or cognitively interesting, and it is easy to see why marijuana users find the effects desirable regardless of what happens to their external behaviour. But it should be remembered that negative effects are probably somewhat under-represented.

This research was supported in part by the US Public Health Service. I thank Mrs. Joan Crawford for her help in data processing and, of course, the respondents, who spent several hours filling in the questionnaires.

REFERENCES

1. Weil, A., Zinberg, N., and Nelsen, J., *Science,* 162, 1234 (1968).

2. Andrews, G., and Vinkenog, S. (editors), *The Book of Grass: An Anthology of Indian Hemp* (Grove, New York, 1967).

3. Bloomquist, E., *Marijuana* (Glencoe, Beverly Hills, Cal., 1968).

4. Simmons, J. (editor), *Marihuana: Myths and Realities* (Brandon House, North Hollywood, Cal., 1967).

5. Solomon, D. (editor), *The Marihuana Papers* (Bobbs-Merrill, Indianapolis, 1966).

6. Jourard, S., *The Transparent Self* (Van Nostrand, New York, 1964).

7. Orne, M., *Amer. Psychol.,* 17, 776 (1962).

8. Orne, M., and Scheibe, K., *J. Abnorm. Soc. Psychol.,* 68, 3 (1964).

9. Rosenthal, R., *Experimenter Effects in Behavioral Research* (Appleton-Century-Crofts, New York, 1966).

10. *A Comprehensive Guide to the English Language Literature on Cannabis* (Student Association for the Study of Hallucinogens, Inc., 638 Pleasant St., Beloit, Wisconsin 35311).

11. Anonymous, in *Altered States of Consciousness: A Book of Readings* (edit. by Tart, C. T.), 355 (Wiley, New York, 1969).

3

Marihuana Effects: A Survey of Regular Users

James A. Halikas
Donald W. Goodwin, and Samuel B. Guze

Regular marihuana use is increasingly prevalent among young people.[1-3] Little systematic information, however, has been obtained from regular users concerning effects and patterns of use.[4] The purpose of this study was to evaluate psychiatrically a random sample of regular users selected from a nonpatient population and to describe this new drug experience of white, young adults.

One hundred regular marihuana users from St. Louis were interviewed by a psychiatrist using a structured interview. Criteria for admission to the study were minimal:

(1) subjects had to be at least 18 years old and white
(2) subjects had to be self-defined as "regular" marihuana users and give a history of using marihuana on at least 50 occasions over at least a six-month period.

Subjects were obtained through word-of-mouth chains of referrals. Three source people known to have access to diverse groups of drug users in the metropolitan area were asked to encourage regular marihuana users to participate in the study. Each volunteer was

Reprinted with permission of the authors and publisher from the *Journal of the American Medical Association*, 1971, *217*, 692–694. Copyright 1971, American Medical Association.

James A. Halikas, M.D., Donald W. Goodwin, M.D., and Samuel B. Guze, M.D., are affiliated with the Department of Psychiatry, Washington University School of Medicine, St. Louis, Missouri.

assured of anonymity and was paid $10 for participation. After each interview, subjects were requested to tell their marihuana-using friends about the study and encourage their participation. Multiple referral chains of from one to nine generations were obtained by this arborization method. This chain referral method tapped most sectors of the white drug-using population in the metropolitan area. Participants ranged from high school drop-outs to PhDs and medical students, from transients to married professionals, from children of millionaires to children of blue-collar workers.

Interviews lasting two to four hours were administered to each subject. In addition, subjects filled out a checklist review of effects of marihuana intoxication occurring when marihuana was the only drug used. Acute intoxication effects as well as "hangover" or aftereffects were included. Aftereffects referred to those which occurred following the disappearance of all subjective feelings of intoxication or to next-morning effects. All effects were self-defined by each subject.

This communication deals with the results of the checklist review. The checklist included 105 items, many previously reported in the literature as marihuana effects. Areas covered included changes in mood, perception, consciousness, and personality, and various psychiatric and medical symptoms. Subjects were asked to note if these effects occurred "usually," "occasionally," or "once-or-never."

TABLE 1		
ACUTE EFFECTS DURING MARIHUANA INTOXICATION (No. = 100)			
	OCCURRENCE*		
Acute Effects	Usually (%)	Occasionally (%)	Once-or-Never (%)
(more than 50%)			
High feeling (exhilarated, euphoric)	82	17	1
Relaxation	79	21	0
Keener sound sense	76	21	3
Peaceful	74	25	1
Increased sensitivity	74	23	3
Increased hunger	72	24	4
Time slowed down	62	35	3
Increased thirst	62	32	6
Dry mouth and throat	61	38	1
(10%-50%)			
Floating sensation	45	49	6
More talkative	37	51	12
Hunger for sweets	37	43	20
Laughing and giggling	36	60	4
Heightened sexual feelings	34	59	7
Increased sexual arousal	33	59	8

Better concentration	32	55	13
Heightened mental powers	32	45	23
Increase in pupil size	32	29	23
More self-confident	30	54	16
Increased alertness	30	59	10
"Red eyes"	29	39	30
Better sexual performance	29	46	18
Lightheaded and dizzy	22	60	18
Silly behavior	19	78	3
Drowsiness	19	77	4
Poorer concentration	18	58	24
Less talkative	17	69	14
Visual distortions, magnifying	16	40	44
Rapid heart beat	16	46	37
Improved memory	13	52	35
Cough	13	46	41
Separation from self	12	49	39
Heaviness of extremities	12	65	23
Unsteadiness of walk	11	66	23
Separating from reality	10	55	35
Frequent urination	10	27	63
(less than 10%)			
Poorer memory	9	54	37
Time speeded up	6	39	55
Anxious or fearful	5	54	41
Confusion and bewilderment	5	47	48
Flushing	5	44	51
"Pins and needles"	5	29	66
Poorer sexual performance	5	20	68
Clumsiness	4	73	23
Can't tell whether happy or sad	4	29	67
Indifferent, apathetic	4	49	46
Aggressive feelings	4	43	53
Visual distortions, shrinking	4	39	57
Hear voices	4	23	73
See visions	4	21	75
Brooding or morose	3	39	58
Sad or despondent	3	36	61
Shortness of breath	3	25	72
Numbness over body parts	3	41	56
Loss of pain sensation	3	27	70
Trembling of hands	3	21	76
Headache	2	28	70
Feverish feeling	2	19	79
Decreased sexual arousal	2	31	67
Less self-confident	2	55	43
Crying	2	12	85

Poorer sound sense	2	20	78
Amnesia	1	4	95
Swollen eyelids	1	21	76
Suicidal thoughts	0	6	94
Irritability	0	37	63
Chills	0	18	82
Nausea	0	9	91
Vomiting	0	2	98
Diarrhea	0	4	95
Constipation	0	4	96

*Percentages do not always total 100 because not every item applied to every subject.

TABLE 2
AFTEREFFECTS FROM MARIHUANA INTOXICATION

Aftereffects	Usually (%)	Occasionally (%)	Once-or-Never (%)
		OCCURRENCE*	
(more than 50%)			
Calm	60	32	8
Mind clear	56	39	5
More restful sleep	52	42	6
(10%-50%)			
Awaken refreshed	44	46	10
Driving well	36	20	37
More sleep	29	51	20
Increased appetite	27	36	37
More dreams	24	37	36
Clearer thinking	18	53	29
More alert and sensitive	17	55	28
Happy or euphoric	16	62	22
Fewer dreams	13	32	52
Improved sexual performance	11	31	50
(less than 10%)			
Awaken tired	9	50	41
Mind foggy	6	51	43
Restless	6	35	59
Less sleep	3	21	76
Less restful sleep	3	16	81
Jittery	3	12	85
Withdrawn	3	40	57
Unreasonable fears	3	18	78
Increased perspiration	2	15	83
Driving badly	2	20	71
Anxiety	2	28	70
Anxiety flashes	2	22	76
Craving for more	1	19	80
Depressed	1	34	65
Overactive	1	41	57

Decreased appetite	1	25	74
Hot flashes	1	5	94
Poor sexual performance	1	15	76
Trembling	1	4	95
Hear voices or see visions	1	5	94
Difficulty swallowing	0	13	87

*Percentages do not always total 100 because not every item applied to every subject.

Results

Sample.—In general, the subjects were well-educated and articulate, although of diverse backgrounds and interests. They ranged from 18 to 31 years of age, with a mean age of 22. Three-fourths were between 18 and 23. There were 61 males and 39 females. Thirty had been raised in Catholic homes, 30 in Protestant, 30 in Jewish, and 10 in homes of no religion. Fifty-eight were full-time students, 24 had permanent jobs or professions, 9 had part-time or transient jobs, and 9 were unemployed. Ninety were single. Four had not completed high school, 5 were high school graduates, 62 had had some college, and 29 had had some graduate level education, including 9 medical students.

Usual Effects.—Tables 1 and 2 list the effects of marihuana surveyed. Nine effects were noted as "usual" occurrences during intoxication by a majority of the subjects: high feeling, keener sound sense, increased sensitivity to others' feelings, peaceful feeling, experience of slowed time, relaxation, increased hunger, increased thirst, and dry mouth and throat. No unpleasant effects were noted as usual occurrences by a majority of subjects. A clear mind, more restful sleep, and a calm feeling after intoxication effects had worn off were reported as usual by a majority. No adverse aftereffects were reported as usual occurrences by a majority.

Of the 105 symptoms, 37 occurred on a usual basis for 10% to 50% of these regular users. A wide variety of effects occurred at least occasionally to a majority of the group.

Adverse Effects.—A large number of adverse symptoms were reported as usual, but generally by a small minority in each case. These included reduced self-confidence, crying, indifference or apathy, aggressive feelings, poor memory, hearing voices, clumsiness, headache, restlessness, and jittery feelings.

Sixteen of the 100 subjects reported the usual occurrence of at least one of the following acute or postintoxication adverse effects: (1) *acute*—anxiety or fearfulness, brooding or morose feelings, sadness or despondency, aggressive feelings, amnesia, confusion and bewilderment, hearing voices, seeing visions; (2) *postintoxication—* depression, driving badly, unreasonable fears, hearing voices or seeing visions, and "anxiety flashes."

COMMENT

This study confirms previous descriptions of marihuana intoxication. Pleasurable effects are "usual" for most regular marihuana users. Of interest is the wide variety of adverse effects which occur usually to some individuals, and to many others on an "occasional" basis. These include hallucinations, anxiety symptoms, impaired mental processes, and symptoms of depression. Other effects, occurring only occasionally in a small minority of subjects, also are significant. Suicidal thoughts, for instance, occurred occasionally in 6% of subjects; amnesia was reported by 5% of subjects.

Volunteers in any study may be different from the population from which they are drawn. These findings are subject, therefore, to the limitations inherent in such studies. It is interesting, nevertheless, that one in every six subjects reported at least one unpleasant usual effect during marihuana intoxication. As Mendelson[5] has noted with regard to alcohol, and Lindesmith[6] with regard to opiates, adverse effects from euphorogenic drugs do not always discourage their use.

REFERENCES

1. *Marihuana: First Report by the Select Committee on Crime* ("The Pepper Report") House Report 91-978. Washington DC, US Government Printing Office, pp 1—114, 1970.
2. Pillard RC: Marihuana. *New Eng J Med* 283:6,924—303, 1970.
3. Manheimer DI, Mellinger GD, Bater MB: Marijuana use among urban adults. *Science* 166:1544—1545, 1969.
4. Kaplan J: *Marijuana—The New Prohibition.* Cleveland, World Publishing Co, pp 73—74, 1970.
5. Mendelson JH, La Don J, Solomon P: Experimentally induced chronic intoxication and withdrawal in alcoholics: Psychiatric findings *Quart J Stud Alcohol* 2: 40—52, 1964.
6. Lindesmith AR: *Addiction and Opiates.* Chicago, Aldine Publishing Co, 1968.

This study was supported in part by Public Health grants MH-09247, MH-05804, MH-47325, and a Research Scientist Development Award MH-47325 from the National Institute of Mental Health (Dr. Goodwin).

Part 3

Effects of Marihuana on Hunger

If there is one subjective impression that nearly all users of marihuana agree upon, it is that marihuana induces or increases the sensation of hunger. The desire for sweets seems to be particularly enhanced, although no investigator has as yet been able to demonstrate that marihuana lowers blood-sugar levels, a factor generally accepted as influencing food intake.

Because there appears to be a general consensus among users of cannabis that hunger *is* increased, marihuana and marihuana-like drugs were once advocated as a means of inducing a desire for food in individuals who normally evinced no such interest. For example, in 1941, Adams[1] commented that this "invariable characteristic of the drugs to stimulate the appetite suggests that they might be applicable in psychoneuroses in which a lack of desire for food exists." In 1950, this possibility was investigated by Parker and Wrigley,[2] who administered the marihuana homologue—pyrahexyl—to a group of psychotic patients and observed that "some of the patients who had previously refused food began to demand it," although there was no concomitant change in the extent of their psychoses. Similarly, the La Guardia commission[3] reported that heroin and cocaine addicts who were given cannabis extract during their withdrawal period "maintained their appetite and in some cases actually gained weight." In contrast, the general trend for individuals undergoing the same traumatic withdrawal is to lose weight during this treatment.

In 1941, Roger Adams[1] reported the results of a study he conducted with a number of his acquaintances relative to the question of hunger, noting that "each individual reacted differently [to the drug, pyrahexyl] with the possible exception of the observed stimulation of the appetite." After ingesting 45 mg., one individual developed "a ravenous hunger which was not satisfied after eating the equivalent of two hearty meals." A second "developed a tremendous appetite which was, if anything, sharpened by eating an enormous dinner and popcorn all through the evening."

These excerpts from Roger Adams' Harvey Lecture[3] are typical of the kind of reactions that are commonly reported by cannabis users under "natural" conditions. Similarly, Ames[4] noted that when food was offered to her subjects, they ate with great enthusiasm. However, Ames also noted that her subjects did not report any increase in their appetites until about three hours had elapsed from the time they first received the drug. However, every attempt to observe this same phenomenon in laboratory animals has failed.

Beginning with the experiment by Abel and Schiff and continuing down to that of Manning and his associates (both included in this chapter), investigators have been singularly unsuccessful in demonstrating an increase in food intake or body weight on the part of animals treated with Δ^9-THC or its synthetic analogues, e.g., pyrahexyl. Death due to starvation in animals has even been reported by some investigators such as Scheckel and his associates.[5]

On the other hand, the research efforts involving human subjects have often substantiated the claims found in the anecdotal literature. Thus, Abel observed a dramatic increase in the consumption of marshmallows by his subjects, while Hollister, in his report, was able to detect an increase in the amount of milkshakes ingested by his subjects.

One explanation for the discrepancy between the animal and the human literature is included in Hollister's conclusions. He states one reason human subjects reliably report increases in hunger is that cannabis is usually taken in social settings. As a result, some members of the group whose sensations of hunger are not directly aroused become indirectly influenced as a result of the behavior or suggestions of those who are hungry. However, this explanation only begs the question since it does not explain why some feel so hungry in the first place.

An alternative possibility is that the comparatively enormous dosages of Δ^9-THC (e.g., 10 mg/kg) that are administered to animals have a depressant effect on the appetite, while the small amounts of Δ^9-THC ingested by humans (e.g., 0.3 mg/kg) during the smoking process, act to stimulate these same mechanisms.

REFERENCES

1. R. Adams, "Marihuana," *Harvey Lectures,* 1941-42, *37,* 189—193.
2. C. S. Parker and F. Wrigley, "Synthetic Cannabis Preparations in Psychiatry: Synhexyl," *Journal of Mental Science,* 1950, *99,* 276—279.
3. Mayor's Committee on Marijuana. *The Marijuana Problem in the City of New York.* Lancaster, Penn.: J. Cattell Press, 1944.
4. F. Ames, "A clinical and metabolic study of acute intoxication with *Cannabis sativa* and its role in the model psychoses," *Journal of Mental Science,* 1958, *104,* 972—999.
5. C. L. Scheckel, E. Boff, P. Dahlen, and T. Smart, "Behavioral effects in monkeys of racemates of two biologically active marihuana constituents," *Science,* 1968, *160,* 1467—1469.

Effects of the Marihuana Homologue, Pyrahexyl, on Food and Water Intake and Curiosity in the Rat

E. L. Abel and B. B. Schiff

The active components in marihuana *(cannabis sativa)* are its isometric tetrahydrocannabinols and to date about 80 derivatives of this substance have been synthesized (McGlothlin, 1965). One of these synthetic components is pyrahexyl (synhexyl) (1-hydroxy 3-n-hexyl-6, 6, 9-trimethy 1-7, 8, 9, 10-tetrahydro-6-diberzoprans). Although pyrahexyl was isolated as early as 1941 (Adams, Loewe, Jelinek, & Wolff, 1941) there have been few descriptions of the behavioral effects of this substance. The experiments described in this report contain our initial observations of the effects of pyrahexyl on food and water consumption and curiosity in rats.

METHOD

Twenty albino rats were divided into two groups which were roughly equivalent with respect to food and water intake and body weight. Fifteen milligrams per kilogram body weight of pyrahexyl dissolved in 5% alcohol were injected daily into one group of animals for 6 consecutive days while the other group received placebo injections. Curiosity was measured in a 3-ft square box. On one wall there were

Reprinted with permission of the authors and publisher from *Psychonomic Science*, 1969, *16*, 38.

E. L. Abel and B. B. Schiff are associated with the University of Toronto, Ontario, Canada.

two small apertures (1.5 in. square) separated by 1.5 ft through which the experimental animal could observe either a hamster or another rat. The number of "pokes" through the openings and total duration of the "pokes" were recorded automatically by electric counters and clocks whenever the S crossed the beam of a photocell. Animals were tested on 5 consecutive days. Testing began 20 min after injection and continued for 15 min.

Subjects were on ad lib diets of Purina lab chow and water. Food and water intake, along with changes in body weight, were measured at time of injection every second day for 6 days.

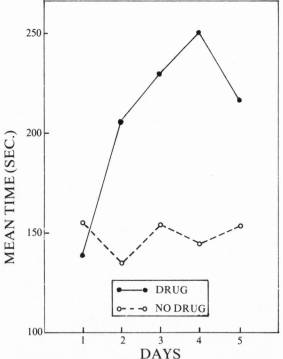

Fig. 1. Mean time spent observing "stimulus" animals on 5 consecutive days of testing.

Results and Discussion

There was no main effect of the drug per se on food intake, but there was a significant Drug by Trials interaction ($F = 3.6$, $p < .05$). There was also no main effect of the drug on body weight, but again the Drug by Trials interaction was significant ($F = 8.1$, $p < .01$). The control animals showed gradual increases in food consumption and body weight, while the drugged animals showed decreased food intake with successive injections and concomitant depression in body weight. Water consumption was not affected by the drug.

There was no difference between groups in the number of times Ss poked their heads through the openings to observe the other "stimulus" animals. But pyrahexyl-injected animals spent significantly more time in the openings than did control animals ($F = 11.1$, $p < .01$). There was also a significant Drug by Trials interaction ($F = 2.7$, $p < .05$). Figure 1 illustrates the nature of this interaction. The drugged animals showed progressive increases in looking on successive days of testing. There were no differences between the groups on within-session habituation.

In summary, pyrahexyl led to a decrease in food intake and an increase in curiosity. On both these measures there was a Drug by Trials interaction suggesting potentiation connected with successive administrations of the drug. This may have been due either to a retention of some portion of the drug which summated with further injections, or sensitization. These alternatives are presently being explored.

REFERENCES

Adams, T., Loewe, S., Jelinek, C., & Wolff, H. Tetrahydrocannabinol homologues with marihuana activity. *Journal of the American Chemical Society,* 1941, 63, 1971–1976.

Chopra, R. N., & Chopra, G. S. The present position of hemp-drug addiction in India. *Indian Journal of Medical Research,* 1939, Supplement No. 31.

McGlothlin, W. H. Cannabis: A reference. In P. Solomon (ed.), *The marihuana papers.* New York: Signet Press, 1968.

The authors would like to express their thanks to Dr. P. Cooper (Department of Pharmacology, University of Toronto) for making this study possible.
This research was supported by Grant No. NRC APB 149.

5

Inhibition of Normal Growth by Chronic Administration of Delta-9-Tetrahydrocannabinol

F. J. Manning
J. H. McDonough, T. F. Elsmore
C. Saller, and F. J. Sodetz

The isolation of marihuana's major active component, Δ-9-tetra-hydrocannabinol (Δ-9-THC)[1], and its subsequent synthesis in relatively pure form[2] has provided the opportunity for better controlled quantitative research in the fields of physiology, biochemistry, pharmacology, and psychology[3,4]. The present study was begun as an attempt to verify under controlled conditions two incidental observations on the effects of Δ-9-THC in laboratory rats. First, rats being given daily intraperitoneal injections of Δ-9-THC very often showed precipitous losses in body weight, despite having free access to both food and water 22 hours of each day. Secondly, six of eight rats involved in a shock-avoidance study died during or shortly after the 2-week period during which they received daily intraperitoneal injections of Δ-9-THC. Postmortem examination suggested that death in all six cases had resulted from complications associated with an irritative or chemical peritonitis. We now report our observations of decreased

Reprinted with permission of the authors and publisher from *Science*, 1971, *174*, 424–426. Copyright 1971 by the American Association for the Advancement of Science.

Frederick J. Manning, John H. McDonough, Jr., Timothy F. Elsmore, Charles Saller and Frank J. Sodetz are affiliated with The Department of Experimental Psychology, Walter Reed Army Institute of Research, Washington, D.C.

body weight and food intake of rats given doses of Δ-9-THC daily for 30 days. Rats receiving intraperitoneal injections of the drug developed peritonitis in every case, while no rat receiving oral doses of the drug developed this condition. Both groups, however, consumed less food than controls over 30 days of drug administration and weighed considerably less even after 30 "recovery" days.

The subjects were 20 male albino rats, weighing between 250 and 300 g at the start of the study. All animals were individually housed in metal metabolism cages, with free access to bottled tap water and 45 mg animal feed pellets (P. J. Noyes Co.). The room was lighted for exactly 12 hours daily and temperature ranged between 20° and 24°C. Body weights were recorded daily, along with food and water intake and feces weight. After 10 days of this regimen, subjects were assigned randomly into four groups. Two groups of six animals subsequently received doses of Δ-9-THC each morning for the next 30 days[5]. These two drug groups differed in both route of administration (intraperitoneal for one, gavage for the other) and dosage (4 mg/kg for the intraperitoneal groups, and 8 mg/kg for the oral group). The remaining eight rats served as placebo controls. Four received daily intraperitoneal injections of vehicle and four received daily vehicle doses via gavage.

Figure 1 shows the effect of daily Δ-9-THC injections on body weight. It is clear that both control groups, which were not significantly different from each other, continued to gain weight throughout the 30 days of placebo administration (mean gain, 53 g). The two drug groups, which also did not differ from each other, showed a notable loss in weight over the first 4 days of Δ-9-THC administration, followed by a very slow recovery up to their initial weights (mean gain, 0.7 g). Analysis of variance on net change in body weight during these 30 days revealed a significant treatment effect ($F = 9.49$; d.f. $= 3,16$; $P < .005$). Individual comparisons indicated that route of administration was not a significant factor in body weight changes. The drug versus placebo control comparison was significant beyond the .001 level ($F = 27.8$; d.f. $= 1,16$) however. After 30 additional days, during which neither drug nor placebo was administered, there was still a significant difference in body weight between the former drug and control groups ($t = 4.13$; d.f. $= 17$; $P < .001$; two-tailed). However, analysis of variance on weight *gain* over this 30-day posttreatment period failed to detect a significant effect of prior drug treatment.

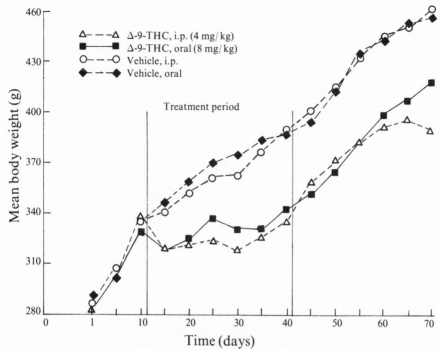

Fig. 1. Mean body weight throughout the experiment of rats receiving Δ-9-THC or placebo by one of two routes (intraperitoneal or oral) daily during the interval marked "treatment period."

Significant changes in food intake were also observed during the course of the study, and the data suggest that the effects on body weight reported above were due predominantly, if not entirely, to these changes, for the four groups of rats were essentially indistinguishable in terms of water consumed and feces weight. The animals in the two groups receiving Δ-9-THC consumed an average of only 522 g of food, while controls averaged 602 g ($F = 22.64$; d.f. $= 1,16$; $P < .001$) The two drug groups did not differ significantly from each other on this measure nor did the controls. In order to assess our hypothesis that this difference in food intake was the primary cause of the observed differences in body weight, an analysis of covariance was performed, with food intake as the covariate or predictor variable. With total food intake controlled for in this way, the significant effect upon body weight disappears ($F = 1.95$; d.f. $= 3,16$). This close parallel between food intake and body weight is substantiated further by the data from

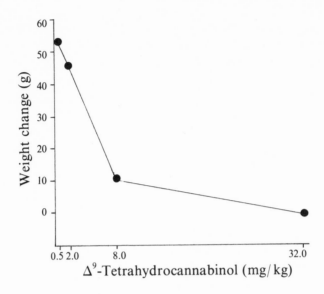

Fig. 2. Mean change in body weight of rats during 30 days of daily oral administration of Δ^9-THC or placebo.

the 30 day posttreatment period. No significant differences between groups were seen in food intake during this period ($F = 2.80$; d.f. $= 3$, 15), just as there were no differences in weight gain. There was still a striking difference in the body weights of former drug and control rats, however, and there was also still a significant difference in total food intake over the entire experiment ($t = 3.36$; d.f. $= 17$; $P < .001$, two-tailed).

At the end of the experiment all animals were killed, and a thorough necropsy was performed. All of the rats given intraperitoneal injections of Δ-9-THC showed evidence of having suffered from chronic diffuse chemical peritonitis. With the exception of one rat that had a large localized abscess of the mesenteric lymph nodes, from which *Pseudomonas aeruginosa* was isolated, no organisms were cultured. Rats are very resistant to infectious peritonitis, and when present it is usually manifested by focal areas of necrosis and acute inflammatory cells. Although the peritonitis seen in these rats was in the healing stage, the diffuse distribution of the chronic inflammatory cells and mild fibroplasia of serosal surfaces is in accord with changes expected from an irritative inoculum rather than a septic injection. The presence of this peritonitis is not surprising, since many other phenolic compounds are highly caustic as well as Δ-9-THC; what is of concern is that intraperitoneal injection has been the predominant route of administration in animal studies of Δ-9-THC. No such damage was found in any animals from the control or oral Δ-9-THC groups. What is puzzling is that only one rat died during the course of this experiment, and from causes unrelated to peritonitis. Yet it was the abnormally high death rate in a shock-avoidance study which led to the study reported here. Apparently the shock-avoidance procedure was an important factor in the earlier study. Preliminary results from experiments currently under way indicate that all three factors, avoidance, peritonitis, and Δ-9-THC, must act in conjunction to produce a high death rate.

We feel that several aspects of these data deserve close attention from those engaged in or planning research with Δ-9-THC. First, despite the fact that it has frequently been used in animal studies, intraperitoneal injection is clearly not the administration route of choice. Severe irritation of the peritoneum may be presumed to have behavioral consequences in itself, perhaps obscuring or distorting those produced by the central nervous system effects. This suspicion has been supported by our difficulties in replicating, with oral administration, certain behavioral effects reliably seen after intraperitoneal injections of Δ-9-THC in the rat. In addition, peritonitis might also play an important role in certain endocrine responses to intraperitoneal injections of Δ-9-THC[6].

A second caveat for Δ-9-THC investigators stems directly from the decrease in food intake shown by our rats. By far the most common finding in work on Δ-9-THC and food-motivated behavior in animals has been dramatic slowing or cessation of such behavior[7]. The depression in food intake observed in our animals suggests that Δ-9-THC may reduce the effectiveness of food reinforcers. This possibility should not be overlooked in attempts to account for decreases in food-motivated behavior following Δ-9-THC administration. It should also be noted that this problem is not obviated by avoiding the intraperitoneal route of administration. Our oral Δ-9-THC rats, all free of notable pathology, showed declines in weight and food intake very similar to those of the rats given Δ-9-THC intraperitoneally, at least during the period of drug administration. An extension of this experiment, encompassing a much wider dose range, revealed that the effects reported here are by no means specific to the particular dose levels chosen. We repeated our observation of body weight and food and water intake on three additional groups of six rats given Δ-9-THC orally for 30 days. Doses employed were 0.5 mg/kg, 2.0 mg/kg, and 32 mg/kg. Figure 2 summarizes the weight changes seen in these animals and combines these data with those of the oral placebo and 8 mg/kg oral groups reported in detail here. It is clear that even at 0.5 mg/kg the drug has a detectable effect on normal weight gain. At the higher dose levels, far more typical of those employed in most reported behavioral studies of Δ-9-THC in animals the effect is striking. Experiments employing the drug at these doses should therefore be approached cautiously.

The persistence of this hypophagia throughout the entire 30 days of drug administration may reduce somewhat the discrepancy between animal data on tolerance to Δ-9-THC and the observations of "reverse tolerance" in human marihuana users. The behavioral effects of Δ-9-THC (or cannabis extract) in animals have most often been reported to subside after two to ten daily doses[8], but among human marihuana users, experienced users tend to require less, not more, marihuana to report effects than do naive users[4, 9]. Our data suggest that the tolerance typically shown by animals is behavioral rather than pharmacological. That is, the physiological reactions to the drug may change very little with repeated doses, but the animal is eventually able to perform despite these actions. It is possible that something similar occurred over the last few days of drug administration in the present study, since all drug groups showed substantial weight gains during this period. However, subnormal weight gains were seen for at least 3 weeks, far beyond the periods required for recovery of rope climbing or bar pressing in other experiments[4, 9]. The pronounced tolerance to Δ-9-THC in animals might then be analogous to the reported ability of experienced human marihuana smokers to perform adequately on some laboratory tests while reporting a normal "high"[10].

REFERENCES

1. Y. Gaoni and R. Mechoulam, *J. Am. Chem. Soc.* 86, 1646 (1964).

2. The Δ-9-tetrahydrocannabinol used in this study was obtained from Dr. J. A. Scigliano of the Center for Studies of Narcotic and

Drug Abuse of NIMH. The material was from batch No. SSC-61516 of synthesized Δ-9-THC and was assayed to be 95 percent pure.

3. F. Lipparini, A. DeCarolis, V. A. Longo, *Physiol. Behav.* 4, 527 (1969); D. Holtzman, R. A. Lovell, J. H. Jaffe, D. X. Freedman, *Science* 163, 1464 (1969); J. C. Garriott, L. J. King, R. B. Forney, F. W. Hughes, *Life Sci.* 6, 2119 (1967).

4. A. T. Weil, N. E. Zinberg, J. M. Nelson, *Science* 162, 1234 (1968).

5. The Δ-9-THC was received dissolved in ethanol in a concentration of 0.20 g/ml and was subsequently diluted with propylene glycol so that each dose was approximately 0.2 ml in volume. Concentrations used, therefore, were 6.6 mg/ml for the intraperitoneal rats, and 13.2 for the oral ones. Placebos consisted of propylene glycol and ethanol in amounts equal to those in the corresponding drug solution. Exact dose volume for each animal was determined from his weight on the first day of drug administration and was held constant in spite of changes in the animal's weight.

6. H. Barry, J. L. Perhach, R. K. Kubena, *Pharmacologist* 12, 258 (1970).

7. C. L. Scheckel, E. Boff, P. Dahler, T. Smart, *Science* 160, 1467 (1968); D. E. McMillan, L. S. Harris, J. M. Frankenheim, J. S. Kennedy, *ibid.* 169, 501 (1970); R. K. Siegel, *Psychopharmacologia* 15, 1 (1969); E. S. Boyd, E. D. Hutchinson, L. C. Gardner, D. A. Merritt, *Arch. Int. Pharmacodyn.* 144, 533 (1963).

8. E. A. Carlini, *Pharmacology* 1, 135 (1968); D. E. McMillan, L. S. Harris, J. M. Frankenheim, J. S. Kennedy, *Science* 169, 501 (1970); M. B. Black, J. H. Woods, E. F. Domino, *Pharmacologist* 12, 258 (1970).

9. D. E. Smith and C. Mehl, in *The New Social Drug,* D. Smith, Ed. (Prentice-Hall, Englewood Cliffs, N.J., 1970), p. 63.

10. D. F. Caldwell, S. A. Meyers, E. F. Domino, P. E. Merriam, *Percept. Motor Skills* 29, 755 (1970).

We thank Mr. Doug Tang of the Statistics Department, Division of Biometrics, Walter Reed Army Institute of Research, for advice and assistance in the analysis of the data; also, Dr. Paul Hildebrandt, Chief, Department of Veterinary Pathology, Division of Veterinary Medicine, Walter Reed Army Institute of Research, for his painstaking pathology reports. In conducting the research described in this report, the investigators adhered to the "Guide for Laboratory Animal Facilities and Care," as promulgated by the Committee on Revision of the Guide for Laboratory Animal Facilities and Care of the Institute of Laboratory Animal Resources, National Academy of Sciences–National Research Council.

6

Effects of Marihuana on the Solution of Anagrams, Memory and Appetite

E. L. Abel

Although anecdotal opinions on the effects of marihuana *(Cannabis sativa* L.) are common, little objective information is available. The following study is concerned with the effects of marihuana on memory, simple intellectual performance, and hunger in humans.

Thirteen adults aged between 22 and 37 served as volunteer subjects. In the marihuana condition there were three men and four women, all of whom had previously had several experiences with marihuana. Six subjects, two men and four women, served as controls. All subjects knew beforehand whether they would be given marihuana. The experiment was run in two parts. The conditions for part A were the same for both marihuana and control subjects. Part B differed only in that one group received marihuana before being tested. Each group was tested separately with two to three subjects per test session. All subjects had eaten a meal 2 h or less before being tested.

Before the experiment began, and at least 30 min before any subjects were given marihuana, each subject was given a plate of marshmallows, "in case someone might get hungry during the experiment." Marshmallows were chosen in the absence of any evidence that marihuana affects preference for this food. At the end of each session,

Reprinted with the permission of the publisher (Macmillan Journals) from *Nature,* 1971, *231,* 260–261.

all plates were refilled and, without the knowledge of the subject, a record was kept of the number of marshmallows eaten by each individual during the session.

At the beginning of part A each subject was tested on the Taylor manifest anxiety scale (MAS)[1]. The results of this study will be reported elsewhere. After the questionnaire had been administered, the subjects took part in an anagrams game. First, the experimenter demonstrated that if the five letters on a 5 × 3 inch card were unscrambled, they would form a recognizable word. The subjects' task was to unscamble the letters in the shortest possible time. Answers were to be written and circled on a pad with the correct solution indicated by a verbal signal such as "OK." A 3 min time limit was given per word and subjects were told that a record would be kept of their solution times. After the last anagram had been tested, all the answer slips were collected and subjects were asked to write down as many of the correct words as they could remember.

Part B followed immediately after the return of the marshmallows to each subject. Subjects were then asked to listen to a "newspaper report," which was in fact a copy of the Babcock memory test described by Rappaport[2]. Subjects in the marihuana condition were then given two marihuana cigarettes to smoke. This took approximately 5 min. Control subjects received no comparable treatment and were allowed to rest for this brief period. Ten minutes after the last cigarette had been smoked, the MAS was readministered. After its completion, subjects were asked to write out as much of the newspaper story as each could remember. The rest of the experiment was exactly like that described for part A except that a different set of anagrams was used.

The data, presented in Table 1, were evaluated using the Mann-Whitney statistic[3]. There were no significant differences between groups in the time to solve the anagrams in either parts A ($U = 19$, n.s.) or B ($U = 23$, n.s.). This result supports Williams's[4] finding that pyrahexyl, a marihuana-homologue, had no effect on performance on the Wechsler-Bellevue intelligence test.

There were no significant differences in the recall of items from the anagrams list in part A. In part B, however, subjects who had smoked marihuana recalled significantly fewer items than did controls ($U = 11$, $P < 0.054$). Inspection of the table indicates that the mean (X) number of recalled items was identical in both sessions for controls. On the contrary, the change from an X of 4.3 to 3.3 items per subject, after smoking marihuana, although small, was a significant decrease ($U = 14$, $P < 0.032$).

TABLE 1
EFFECTS OF MARIHUANA ON THE SOLUTION OF ANAGRAMS, MEMORY, AND APPETITE

Treatment	Mean time to solve anagrams	Mean recall of anagram items per subject	Mean recall of idea units per subject	Mean recall of content words per subject	Mean total words per subject	Mean No. errors per subject	Mean consumption per subject
Part A (Premarihuana condition)							
C	720 s	4.2					34.5
M	630 s	4.3					20.9
Part B (Marihuana condition)							
C	516 s	4.2	8.5	9.6	28.5	7.2	3.8
M	596 s	3.3	3.5	5.3	24.1	10.1	45.6

This effect on memory was corroborated by data from the Babcock test. Three judges were given the recall protocols and asked to rate them for the number of "idea units" based on a prescored protocol which they kept before them. Protocols were also rated for number of errors after the procedure outlined by Rappaport[2] and for the number of content words which appeared in the original. Control subjects recalled significantly more idea units ($U = 3$, $P < 0.004$) and content words ($U = 0$, $P < 0.001$) than did subjects who had smoked marihuana. The fact that the groups did not differ significantly in the total number of words used in their protocols ($U = 16$, not significant) indicates that the greater number of ideas and content words correctly recalled was not a result of control subjects simply writing more than marihuana subjects. Comparison of the error scores also indicates that not only do marihuana subjects remember less than controls, but what they do recall is likely to be less accurate ($U = 7$, $P < 0.026$). Abel[5] has reported that the smoking of marihuana adversely affects the recall of prose material. In that study, however, the material was visually presented. In this study, the generality of this earlier finding is extended by using both visual (anagrams) and auditory (newspaper story) means of presentation.

As for the effects of marihuana on hunger, control subjects ate significantly more marshmallows in part A than did subjects who were given marihuana later ($U = 9$, $P < 0.03$). In part B, this relationship was reversed — marihuana subjects consumed significantly more marshmallows than controls ($U = 4$, $P < 0.004$). Five individuals in the marihuana condition consumed more marshmallows in B than in A. None of the subjects in the control group did so. Although it is possible that control subjects were satiated in part B, it is unlikely that subjects in the marihuana condition would significantly have increased their consumption of marshmallows had marihuana had no effect on some hunger-related variable. It therefore seems reasonable to conclude that marihuana increased the subjects' desire for food, a finding which corroborates the experimental findings of Abel and Schiff[6] with respect to rats.

This study was conducted while I was a postdoctoral fellow at the University of California at Berkeley.

REFERENCES

1. Taylor, J. A., *J. Abnorm. Soc. Psychol.*, 48, 285 (1953).

2. Rapaport, D., Gill, M. M., and Schaefer, R., *Diagnostic Psychological Testing* (International University Press, New York, 1968).

3. Siegel, S., *Nonparametric Statistics* (McGraw-Hill, New York, 1956).

4. Williams, E. G., Himmelsbach, C. K., Wikler, A., Ruble, D. C., and Lloyd, B. J., *Pub. Health Rep.*, 61, 1059 (1946).

5. Abel, E. L., *Nature,* 227, 1151 (1970).

6. Abel, E. L., and Schiff, B. B., *Psychon. Sci.*, 16, 38 (1969).

7

Hunger and Appetite after Single Doses of Marihuana, Alcohol, and Dextroamphetamine

Leo E. Hollister

Marihuana smoking or hashish ingestion has long been reported to increase hunger and appetite. "Marihuana hunger" was described as coming on for 3 to 6 hours following the drug, with a special craving for sweets.[1] Another modern investigation[2] found that subjects did not experience hunger during the first 3 hours despite fasting; but when food was offered, they ate with great relish. Such reports apparently led to the assumption that marihuana lowers blood glucose. Several recent studies[3, 4, 6] have, however, demonstrated that neither smoked marihuana in small doses nor orally ingested tetrahydrocannabinol (THC) in large doses has any significant effect on plasma glucose levels. To test whether or not marihuana stimulates hunger and appetite, food consumption was measured systematically after fasted subjects were treated with marihuana, alcohol, dextroamphetamine,

Reprinted with the permission of the author from *Clinical Pharmacology and Therapeutics, 12:* 44–49, 1971; copyrighted by the C. V. Mosby Co., St. Louis, Missouri.

Leo E. Hollister, M.D., is Medical Investigator with the Veterans Administration Hospital, Palo Alto, California, and Associate Professor of Medicine at Stanford University School of Medicine, Stanford, California.

and a placebo in one experiment and after fed subjects received marihuana, alcohol, and placebo in a second experiment.

METHODS

Experiment No. 1. Twelve normal young volunteers were chosen primarily on the basis of their being in good physical and emotional health and intelligent and cooperative enough to carry out the required procedures. All but one were men. Although most subjects had prior experience with small doses of marihuana and amphetamines, and all with alcohol, except for modest use of the latter, none were chronic or recent users of any of these drugs. Subjects were told which drugs were to be given and that one might be given twice.

Four trials were run at weekly intervals, with random assignment of the following four treatments: (1) marihuana prepared as an extract and calibrated for THC content, 0.5 mg. per kilogram[5]; (2) 95 percent ethanol, 1 ml. per kilogram; (3) dextroamphetamine sulfate, 0.2 mg. per kilogram; and (4) a placebo made by reextracting marihuana from which all cannabinoids had previously been extracted. Subjects varied in weight between 66 and 91 kilograms. Total doses of drugs were: marihuana (as THC), mean dose 32 mg., range 27 to 39 mg.; dextro-amphetamine, mean dose 15 mg, range 13 to 18 mg.; ethanol, mean dose 57 Gm., range 50 to 68 Gm.

Doses of each drug were administered in 180 ml. of a flavored, noncaloric soft drink. To mask taste differences further, doses were given with the subject blindfolded and the nostrils occluded. To the greatest extent possible, double-blind control was exercised, although various circumstances (distinctive taste and effects of alcohol and marihuana) mitigated against this.

Subjects were instructed not to take anything but water by mouth; i.e., no food or calorie-containing beverage after 7:30 P.M. the evening before the trial. They were put at rest in the fasting condition in the test room at 7:30 A.M. A number of preliminary tests were done over the next 30 minutes, including completion of a hunger questionnaire and removal of blood samples for determination of glucose and free fatty acids. Drug was administered at 8 A.M. Offerings of food were first made at 11 A.M. and they were repeated at 11:30 A.M., 12 noon, and 1 P.M. Just prior to the first offering of food, the hunger questionnaire and blood samples were repeated. At the end of the trial, an appetite questionnaire, concerned with enjoyment of food, was completed.

The hunger questionnaire asked subjects to rate on an 8-point scale their current degree of hunger (from "not hungry" to "hungriest ever") and their current feeling of satiety (from "empty" to "uncomfortably full"). A point was scored for each response, from 0 to 7 in the first instance, and 7 to 0 in the second. The appetite questionnaire asked the subject to rate the taste of the food offered at each trial over a spectrum ranging from "much worse than usual" to "much better than usual," using a 5-point scale scored from —2 to +2.

Food was offered in the form of a standard chocolate milk shake made according to the following recipe: homogenized whole milk, 240 ml.; skim milk powder, 60 Gm.; powdered chocolate, 25 Gm.; ice cream, 360 Gm. Ingredients were mixed in a blender immediately prior to use. Total volume was 800 ml. with approximately 1.5 calories and 0.6 Gm. of proteins per milliliter. The subjects knew that they would be offered chocolate milk shake, as it had previously been ascertained that this was acceptable to their tastes. The presentation was made in a covered box from which only a straw protruded, effectively masking any appreciation of the amount offered or consumed. They were instructed to drink to satiety or to the limit of the single offering, with the expectation that more food would be offered over the next 2 hours. The largest amount of milk shake offered at any single time was 480 ml.

Experiment No. 2. The general procedures used in the second experiment were similar to those used in the first experiment with the exceptions cited below. Twelve healthy subjects, all young men, were selected. All had some previous experience with marihuana, but at no greater frequency than twice monthly. Three trials were run at weekly intervals, with random assignment of the following treatments: (1) marihuana prepared as an extract calibrated to a dose of 0.35 mg. per kilogram of delta-1-THC; (2) ethanol, 95 percent calibrated to a dose of 0.7 ml. per kilogram; (3) placebo (marihuana extract with all cannabinoids removed). Total doses of drugs were as follows: marihuana (as THC), mean dose 26 mg., range 20 to 29 mg.; ethanol, mean dose 43 Gm., range 27 to 52 Gm.

In this experiment, unlike the first, subjects were permitted to have their customary breakfast, with the specific instructions that, no matter what it was, it be the same on all 3 test days. Thus these subjects were in contrast to the fasted subjects in the first experiment. Offerings of food were made 2, 2 1/2, 3 1/2, 4 1/2, and 5 1/2 hours after the drug was given. The maximum amount of each offering was 240 ml. of the chocolate milk shake. The hunger questionnaire was completed 1 1/2, 3 1/2, and 6 hours after each drug was given. The appetite questionnaire was completed at the end of each trial.

RESULTS

Experiment No. 1. Ethanol ingestion, in the large amounts given in the fasting state, had an immediate and profound effect, readily recognized as alcoholic intoxication. Most subjects were also able to distinguish the effect of marihuana, which developed more slowly and was characterized by euphoria and sleepiness. The effects of dextroamphetamine were less readily evident. The placebo had no discernible effect, other than its unpleasant taste which resembled the marihuana extract.

The mean total intake of milk shake during the entire trial revealed that marihuana increased it as compared with placebo (731 ml. vs. 503 ml.), dextroamphetamine decreased it (390 ml.), and alcohol produced little change (511 ml.). Data from individual subjects were variable: 7 of 12 subjects consumed more food after marihuana, 2 showed no essential change, and 3 took less food. With dextroamphetamine and ethanol 7 and 6 subjects, respectively, ate less food; 2 and 3, respectively, showed no change, and 3 each consumed more food. These differences were not significant on chi square analysis. The acceptance of food offerings followed a similar pattern for each treatment. Of 48 offerings of food in any given trial, 31 were accepted after marihuana compared to 24 after placebo, 19 after dextroamphetamine, and 25 after alcohol. Despite these trends, the relatively small sample size and high variation between subjects ruled out a statistically significant difference in total food intake between treatments on complex analysis of variance ($F = 2.06$; df, 3). As might have been expected, however, there were significant differences between subjects and between time periods.

The typical pattern of food intake over the four time periods is shown in Fig. 1. Following the 15-hour fast, substantial amounts were taken during the first two offerings of food but declined rapidly thereafter as satiety was reached. The pattern with dextroamphetamine followed that of placebo, except that smaller amounts were required during the first two offerings to attain satiety. The effect of alcohol was a slight decrease during the early stages of acute intoxication followed by increased consumption of food some 5 hours after the drug had been taken. The pattern following marihuana was like that after placebo initially, but at no point was it clear that satiation was complete. Analysis of variance showed a significant interaction between treatments at the last feeding period, in which both alcohol and marihuana were associated with greater intake of food than the other two treatments (F = 2.93; df, 3; p < 0.025).

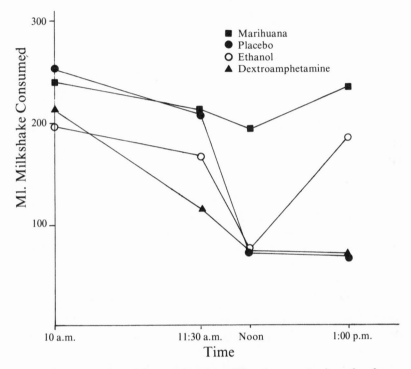

Fig. 1. Pattern of total intake of food at each time for four treatments.

Mean scores on the hunger questionnaire are shown in Table 1. Ordinarily, continued fasting might have been expected to increase hunger slightly from the time of beginning the trial until shortly before the first offering of food. Such was the case for all treatments but dextroamphetamine, which made hunger less intense. The greatest increment in hunger followed marihuana. Following three opportunities to take food, subjects treated with marihuana reported more persisting hunger than did the others. In terms of appreciation of food as judged by the appetite questionnaire and compared with scores obtained after placebo, after marihuana 8 patients reported improved appetite and 4 reported diminished appetite. After dextroamphetamine, 4 reported enhanced appetite, 5 reported diminished appetite, and 3 unchanged appetite. Ethanol produced an equal division, 4 reporting improvement, 4 reporting impairment, and 4 reporting no change.

TABLE 1
MEAN VALUES OF HUNGER QUESTIONNAIRE SCORES,
PLASMA FREE FATTY ACIDS, AND PLASMA GLUCOSE

Treatment	Before	2½ hr.	4½ hr.	7 hr.
Hunger questionnaire				
Placebo	4.8	5.0	3.8	4.1
Dextroamphetamine	5.0	4.3	3.7	3.7
Alcohol	4.6	4.8	3.4	3.5
Marihuana	4.8	5.8	4.5	4.0
Plasma free fatty acids				
Placebo	507	464*		
Dextroamphetamine	602	707†		
Alcohol	416	288*		
Marihuana	479	430		
Plasma glucose				
Placebo	86	85		
Dextroamphetamine	86	90		
Alcohol	87	84		
Marihuana	85	84		

*P less than 0.05
†P less than 0.01; t test, correlated mean, 2 trial.

Compared to pretreatment values, plasma free fatty acids (FFA) fell significantly during treatment with placebo and alcohol, rose significantly with dextroamphetamine, and were unchanged by marihuana (Table 1). Analysis of variance of the plasma FFA values during the drug conditions revealed that levels were significantly higher after dextroamphetamine and lower after ethanol than they were after placebo and marihuana. The correlation in percentage change in plasma FFA levels and total amount of food consumed was undertaken to determine if change in plasma FFA levels might be an indicator of hunger. The correlations were only weakly negative ($r = -0.18$). Absolute levels of FFA in the fasting state, paired to any drug being given, were correlated with reports of hunger only weakly ($r = 0.18$). Plasma glucose values showed little change during any of the four treatments, which were not appreciably different from each other. Inspection of data from individual subjects revealed no clinically significant changes in any instance.

Experiment No. 2. The mean total intake of milk shake during the second experiment virtually duplicated the results of the first one. After marihuana, mean intake was 777 ml. compared with 603 after placebo and 540 after alcohol. Data from individual subjects were variable: 7 consumed more food after marihuana than after placebo, in the other 5 it was about the same in both cases; only one increased food intake after alcohol, 4 decreased food intake, and the remaining 7 subjects consumed about as much as they did after placebo. Of 60 offerings of food in each trial, 42 were accepted following marihuana, 30 following ethanol, and 33 following placebo. These trends were comparable to those in the first experiment.

Analysis of variance of total food intake revealed a significant difference between treatments (F = 10.6; df, 2; p = 0.001) as well as between subjects (F = 6.7; df, 11; p = 0.0005). Correlated t tests (2 tailed) revealed a significant difference between total food intake following marihuana compared with alcohol (t = 4.7; p = 0.001) and placebo (t = 3.3; p = 0.01). The difference between placebo and alcohol was not significant. In this experiment, therefore, the results are clear that marihuana caused an increase in food intake.

The pattern of food intake in fed subjects differed somewhat from that in fasted subjects. Marihuana did not produce a sustained level of food intake but rather a pattern in which satiety tended to be reached after the 3 1/2-hour feeding. The pattern of food intake was similar among the three treatments, although more food was taken following marihuana at each time period except the last.

Initial mean hunger scores were virtually identical for three treatments. Although they rose progressively at 1 1/2 and 3 1/2 hours, the increases were parallel for all three. Following the 5 1/2-hour feeding, subjects reported somewhat less hunger following marihuana, presumably due to oversatiation. Seven subjects treated with marihuana reported enhancement of appetite, 4 no difference, and 1 less appetite as compared to those treated with placebo. Alcohol reduced appetite in 5 subjects, increased it in 1, and had no effect in 6.

DISCUSSION

Marihuana tended to increase appetite and food consumption, while dextroamphetamine and, to a lesser extent, alcohol tended to decrease appetite and food consumption. Marihuana was shown to increase total food intake to a statistically significant degree in experiments which involved the fed subjects. Similar trends were found in relation to the number of offerings of food which were accepted, the greatest number being after marihuana in each experiment. These results confirm the notion that marihuana has a stimulating effect on appetite and food consumption. It is of interest that fed subjects were more sensitive to these effects than were the fasted subjects. One may speculate that the stress of fasting may increase variability, thus making it a relatively poor control measure.

In both experiments there was a great individual variation in response to drugs. Only slightly more than half of all subjects ate more food after marihuana than after placebo. Occasional instances occurred in which results were opposite to expectations. One subject took more food following dextroamphetamine than after either placebo or marihuana. The stimulation or suppression of food intake, at least following single doses of drugs, is variable among different individuals. Allowing for the distinct possibility of a positive bias toward reports of enhanced hunger and appetite following marihuana, due to the fairly easy identification of the drug from its clinical actions, results of the present study scarcely support the stand that the drug reliably stimulates hunger and appetite. But neither did all patients treated with dextroamphetamine respond with appetite diminution, although many do.

One of the reasons for the prevalent belief that marihuana enhances food intake in all persons is the fact that marihuana is often taken in social groups. Assuming that a majority of persons within such groups actually experience an increase in appetite, it is very likely that these effects would spread to other members of the group. Although it has not been clearly documented, it seems reasonable that marihuana may have the effect of increasing suggestibility. In such a case, a group pressure of a majority experiencing a particular effect would be strong for the others.

As in a previous study,[3] marihuana had no effect on plasma levels of glucose and FFA. Since prevailing levels of plasma FFA may in part be a reflection of the degree of the postabsorptive state, it is of interest that changes in the levels during the first 2 1/2 hours following drug did not correlate with food intake. Neither did they correlate with hunger scores as reported in the fasting state prior to any drug given. It would appear that the sensation of hunger is independent of FFA levels.

REFERENCES

1. Allentuck, S., and Bowman, K. M.: Psychiatric aspects of marihuana intoxication, *Amer. J. Psychiat.* 99:248–251, 1942.

2. Ames, F.: *Cannabis sativa* and its role in the model psychoses, *J. Ment. Sci.* 104:972–999, 1958.

3. Hollister, L. E., Richards, R. K., and Gillespie, H. K.: Comparison of tetrahydrocannabinol and synhexyl in man, *Clin. Pharmacol. Ther.* 9:783–791, 1968.

4. Isbell, H., Gorodetzsky, G. W., Jasinski, D., Claussen, U., v. Spulak, F., and Korte, F.: Effects of $(-)\Delta^9$-transtetrahydrocannabinol in man, *Psychopharmacologia* 11:184−188, 1967.

5. Song, C. H., Kanter, S. L., and Hollister, L. E.: Extraction and gas chromatographic quantification of tetrahydrocannabinol from marihuana, *Res. Comm. Chem. Path. Pharmacol.* 1:375−382, 1970.

6. Weil, A. T., Zinberg, N. E., and Nelson, J. M.: Clinical and psychological effects of marihuana in man, *Science* 162:1234−1242, 1968.

Supported in part by Grant MH 03030, National Institute of Mental Health.
Technical assistance was provided by H. K. Gillespie.

Part 4

Sensory and Perceptual Effects

Marihuana is a drug endorsed by some musicians, artists, and writers because they claim it improves their performance and aids their creativity. But whenever these claims have been put to the test, they prove illusory. Instead of there being an improvement, performance usually is worse under the influence of marihuana. Not only does the individual fail to recognize this impairment, but the effects of cannabis are such that the user actually feels that his or her performance has been enhanced. In this regard, Weil and Zinberg noted that: "the greatest puzzle about marihuana is the enormous discrepancy between its subjective and its objective mental effects."[1]

This discrepancy between subjective and objective ratings is illustrated in an article by Aldrich[2] who gave a series of musical tests to a group of twelve individuals after they had been given the marihuana homologue, pyrahexyl, and compared these results with those obtained under nondrug conditions. Some of these subjects were musicians while others had had at least some musical training. When the test was over, Aldrich asked each subject to rate his or her performance on the test. Aldrich found that although nine out of the twelve subjects performed worse when given pyrahexyl than under the nondrug condition, eight of these twelve subjects still judged that their performance had actually improved.

These results were corroborated by Williams and his coworkers[3]. The La Guardia commission[4] likewise failed to observe any improvement in musical ability or acoustic acuity as a result of smoking marihuana.

Williams et al.[3] also conducted several studies in which they evaluated the effects of marihuana on sensory thresholds. Although they provide no actual data, their claims that marihuana had no significant effects in their experiments have been corroborated in the more rigorously conducted studies reported by Caldwell and his coworkers included in this chapter. These studies indicate that marihuana has minimal and mainly insignificant effects on sensory acuity. The third article is included in this section because it summarizes their results and also conveys some of the difficulties that investigators must face in attempting scientifically approved and controlled studies of the effects of marihuana on humans.

The question still remains, however, as to why there is this discrepancy in the subjective and objective effects of marihuana on sensory function. One possible explanation is that because of the euphoria which often accompanies use of marihuana, an individual becomes less critical of his or her performance. Or it may be that because of the drug, the individual sees or hears images and sounds in spatio-temporal relations which he or she has never before experienced and this novelty in some way affects judgment. Obviously, this is a question which cannot be readily answered at present. There is, however, a great deal of evidence indicating that temporal awareness is in fact affected by marihuana. Some of the experiments that have been conducted in this regard are presented in the next chapter.

REFERENCES

1. A. T. Weil and N.E. Zinberg, "Acute effects of marihuana on speech," *Nature,* 1969, *222,* 434–437.
2. C. K. Aldrich, "The Effect of a Synthetic Marihuana-like Compound on Musical Talent as Measured by the Seashore Test," *Public Health Reports,* 1944, *59,* 431–433.
3. E. G. Williams, C.K. Himmelsbach, A. Wikler, and D.C. Ruble, "Studies on Marihuana and Pyrahexyl Compound," *Public Health Reports,* 1946, *61,* 1059–1082.
4. Mayor's Committee on Marihuana. *The Marihuana Problem in the City of New York.* Lancaster, Penn.: J. Cattell Press, 1944.

8

Effects of Marihuana on Auditory and Visual Sensations

Steven A. Myers and Donald F. Caldwell

PROBLEM

Present knowledge of the effects of marihuana on various psychological states is extremely limited and dependent on subjective reports. Foremost among the effects reported following the use of marihuana are enhancement of auditory and/or visual sensation and perception. The Lafayette Clinic is presently engaged in a broad-range program aimed at delineating the effects of marihuana on psychological function. Initially, the effects of smoking natural marihuana will be studied as they relate to primary sensory systems. Data from this initial phase are then being utilized in studies of the effects of marihuana on a range of perceptual problems.

Both of these phases are being conducted on subjects (Ss) both with and without previous marihuana-smoking experience. Results of both

Reprinted with the permission of the authors and publisher (Michigan Department of Mental Health), from the *Michigan Mental Health Research Bulletin,* 1969, *3,* 1-3.

Steven A. Myers, M.D., is in the Division of Psychiatry, and Donald F. Caldwell, Ph.D., is in the Division of Psychobiology at the Lafayette Clinic, Detroit, Michigan.

sensory and perceptual experiments will be utilized in formulating new measures aimed at determining the role of social and physical environment for the marihuana "high."

METHOD

The present research was designed to ascertain the effects of smoking crude marihuana on auditory and visual activity in Ss who had *no* previous experience with the use of marihuana and who were made aware of the substances which they were about to smoke, i.e., suggestibility maximized. Twelve male volunteers with a median age of 29 yrs. were tested from among the Lafayette Clinic employees.

Ss were randomly divided into two equal groups. The control group (N = 6) received one 300 mg. alfalfa cigarette immediately prior to testing and the entire procedure was repeated after a 15-min. rest interval. Ground alfalfa has a remarkable similarity in taste, smell and appearance to marihuana and served as an excellent control substance. The experimental group (N = 6) received one 300 mg. alfalfa cigarette prior to testing and then was given one 300 mg. crude marihuana cigarette and re-tested. The marihuana used in this project contained 1.3% of what is believed to be the active ingredient of marihuana, i.e. delta-9-tetrahydrocannabinol. This amount yielded a cigarette of intermediate potency by "users'" standards.

Testing consisted of the ability to match a one-inch diameter white light of ten predetermined foot candle (ft-c) illuminance values (mean = 2.79 ft-c, range = 1.12-4.00 ft-c) to a fixed white light standard of 2.40 ft-c. The procedure was immediately repeated for a new series of ten light intensities (mean = 4.76 ft-c, range = 2.80-7.00 ft-c) to be matched to a fixed standard of 4.80 ft-c.

Next, each S was tested for his ability to discriminate between a pair of monaurally presented tones differing only in intensity, i.e., loudness. The sound intensity measures were conducted using the method of limits. The first member of each sound pair, i.e., the standard, was a 1000 Hz-15 db. attenuated pure tone. This tone was compared to a second 1000 Hz tone 30 msec. later which was adjusted in 1 db. steps from 5 db. below to 5 db. above the standard. Ten ascending and descending series were administered during each treatment condition.

RESULTS

The light matching results are presented in Table I. It should be noted that none of these group comparisons reached a level of statistical significance.

For the sound-intensity test, a reduction of 0.10 db. was observed in the mean difference limen (x_{DL}) for Ss receiving marihuana ($X_{DL} = 1.00$ db.) compared to their initial alfalfa treatment ($X_{DL} = 1.10$ db.). Control Ss had a mean change in X_{DL} of 0.18 db. from a value of 1.42 db. to 1.24 db. for the first and second alfalfa test series, respectively. These differences were not statistically significant.

TABLE 1
LIGHT MATCHING RESULTS

Condition	Control				Experimental			
	Before		After		Before		After	
	Mean	S2	Mean	S2	Mean	S2	Mean	S2
2.40 ft-c standard	2.24	.010	2.29	.030	2.28	.004	2.26	.010
4.80 ft-c standard	4.80	.240	4.62	.060	4.66	.040	4.63	.010

Table 1. Light matching performance of control and experimental groups before and after smoking. None of the differences are statistically significant.

The point of subjective equality (PSE) shifted away from the standard, i.e., 15.00 db., for the marihuana group from an initial value of 14.80 db. during alfalfa smoking period to 14.64 db. in the marihuana session. In contrast, control Ss shifted toward the standard during their second alfalfa session (14.92 db.) when compared with the first (14.53 db.). Amount of change for either group did not attain, however, a level of statistical significance.

The mean constant error (CE) increased in a negative direction ($X = -0.16$ db.) for the experimental group from the alfalfa ($X = -0.19$ db.) to marihuana ($X = -0.35$ db.) test periods. Control Ss decreased in amount of constant error from an initial value of -0.28 db. to the second alfalfa session value of -0.08. Group differences did not prove to be statistically significant.

CONCLUSION

Overall performance in both the visual and auditory acuity tests indicated a trend, although not statistically significant, toward superior performance for Ss in the control group. In some cases this improvement was reflected in a greater degree of improvement from first to second test sessions even though the marihuana group may have attained superior second session scores, e.g., mean difference limens for groups on the sound intensity measures. In other cases the superior performance of the control group was of a nature that failure to improve was less than for the marihuana treatment, e.g., group means for performance on the bright light standard of the visual acuity measure.

More important is the failure to find evidence for an *improvement* in either visual or auditory performance following the use of marihuana. In a study presently underway, 20 marihuana users are being tested by the methods described and additional visual and auditory measures. By comparing the performance of users and nonusers it is hoped that further directions for research will be indicated.

The delta-9-THC assayed marihuana used in this study was provided by the National Institute of Mental Health, Chevy Chase, Maryland.

9

Auditory and Visual Threshold Effects of Marihuana in Man

D. F. Caldwell, S. A. Myers
E. F. Domino and P. E. Merriam

Psychological and physiological changes following marihuana smoking in a neutral setting have recently been reported (Weil, Zinberg, & Nelson, 1968). Marihuana-naive Ss did not manifest a strong subjective experience for either of two dose levels (viz., 4.5 or 18.0 mg. tetrahydrocannabinol), although measures indicated a dose related performance impairment. In contrast, experienced marihuana users, who received only a high dose, improved on two of three behavioral tasks and showed no change for the third. Previous research in our laboratory (Myers & Caldwell, 1969a, 1969b; Caldwell, Myers, Domino, & Merriam, 1969), with a group of marihuana-naive Ss had failed to find changes in either visual or sensory threshold following the smoking of one 300-mg. cigarette (3.936 mg. Δ^9-THC).

The present investigation was an attempt to measure auditory and visual acuity in a group of experienced marihuana smokers using standardized psychophysical techniques (Guilford, 1954, pp. 101-117). Furthermore, to allow for a more natural set, Ss were fully informed of

Reprinted with the permission of authors and publisher: Caldwell, D. F., Myers, S. A., Domino, E. F., & Merriam, P. E. Auditory and visual threshold effects of marihuana in man. *Perceptual and Motor Skills*, 1969, 29, 755–759.

D. F. Caldwell, S. A. Myers, E. F. Domino and P. E. Merriam are associated with the Divisions of Psychobiology, Psychiatry, and Pharmacology at the Lafayette Clinic, Detroit, Michigan.

the substances they were about to receive and were allowed to smoke until they experienced their own subjective "high." The element of artificiality (neutrality) was introduced through the administration of psychological tests in a "sterile" laboratory test room.

METHOD

Subjects

Ss were 20 college students, with a mean age of 23.3 yr. and were all experienced users of marihuana and signed a subject release form specifying this fact. Each *S* received a psychiatric interview and physical examination prior to assignment to either the experimental or control group. *Ss* smoking marihuana remained in the laboratory over night.

Material

The marihuana for this investigation was provided by the N.I.M.H. who assayed it to contain 1.312% Δ^9-tetrahydrocannabinol. Each cigarette contained 300 mg. of crude marihuana (3.93 mg. Δ^9-THC). Alfalfa cigarettes (300 mg.) were used for the control substance.

Procedure

The following test battery took approximately 1 hr. to administer. *Visual Brightness Test* (VBT) determined *S's* ability to match a 1-in. diameter white light of 2.40 ft-c intensity located at a distance of 6 ft. to a second light of one of 10 predetermined foot-candle illuminance values (M = 2.79 ft-c, range = 1.12 to 4.00 ft-c). The procedure was repeated for a second series of 10 light intensities (M = 4.76 ft-c, range = 2.80 to 7.00 ft-c) to a fixed standard of 4.80 ft-c. Testing was done in a totally dark room with 15 sec. between presentations of each stimulus pair. *S* was able to adjust the intensity of the variable light by means of a hand-held toggle switch. There was no time limit for light matching. Illuminance-foot candle values were computed by use of a photoconductive cell (Clairex, Model CL505L) positioned at *S's* field of vision.

Auditory Threshold Test (ATT) was the standard hearing test. A monauarally presented 100 Hz tone (Hewlett-Packard Model 200 CD Oscillator) was presented in five ascending and five descending 2-db step intervals from above and below hearing threshold. This sequence was repeated 10 times.

Auditory Intensity Differential Threshold Test (AIDT) required monaurally presenting *S* with a sequential pair of 500 msec., 100-Hz tones separated by 30 msec. of silence. The first member of the tone pair was of constant intensity (80 db, re 0.0002 dyne/cm^2) and was compared to the second tone of the pair. All tone-intensity calibrations were done with a sound-level meter fitted to the earphone (General Radio Co. Type 1551-C Soundlevel meter). Five louder tones differing in 1-db steps (range = 81 to 85 db) and five quieter tones (range = 79 to 75 db) were alternately presented in each test series. Ten series were presented alternately beginning above and below the standard and beginning from different starting points. *S* reported after hearing each tone pair whether the second tone was louder, equal or quieter compared to the first tone.

Auditory Frequency Differential Threshold Test (AFDT) followed the same basic procedures as for the AIDT test, except that intensity was held constant (viz., 80 db) and frequency was varied against a standard tone of 1000 Hz. The variable frequency tone changed in 3-Hz units from 15 Hz above to 15 Hz below the standard (Hickock Model DP150 Digital Counter). *S* reported after hearing each tone pair whether the second tone was higher than, equal to or lower than the first tone. In addition to difference limens, point of subjective equality and constant error were computed for each *S* for both the AIDT test and AFDT test.

For the experimental group, the procedure consisted of (a) smoking one 300-mg. alfalfa cigarette, (b) a 15-min. waiting period, (c) administration of the total visual and auditory test battery, (d) administration of as many 300-mg. marihuana cigarettes as *S* needed to obtain a subjective "high," (e) a 15-min. rest period, (f) a second administration of the total test battery. Procedure was the same for control *Ss* except that during the second smoking period, namely (d), *Ss* received a second 300-mg. alfalfa cigarette. Testing commenced at either 6:00 p.m. or 9:00 p.m. and no participant knew of his treatment assignment until the actual time of testing. *Ss* were given 15 min. to smoke either the alfalfa or marihuana cigarette and no attempt was made to interfere with *S's* personal technique of smoking marihuana, although our observations indicated a high degree of consistency in smoking technique.

Four separate statistical analyses were performed for each of the five threshold measures. Initial mean performance scores were compared for experimental and control groups for the presence of performance differences during the first test session. Next, first-test performance for control *Ss* was compared with second-test performance to determine practice effects. A comparison of second-test performance for experimental and control groups provided the test for the effects of marihuana on thresholds. A comparison of the experimental group's first- and second-test periods was made to examine the effects of marihuana performance if significant practice effects could not be demonstrated.

RESULTS AND DISCUSSION

The mean amount of crude marihuana smoked to reach a subjective "high" was 483.0 mg.; $\pm$ 1 SD = 92.9 mg. (M = 6.337 mg. of Δ^9-THC). One of the consistent findings for all marihuana smokers was the abrupt cessation of smoking when S experienced the onset of the drug effect. Onset of the "high" experience occurred for *all Ss during* the smoking period.

Table 1 presents the group mean performance scores for all measures obtained in this study. Student t tests (Walker & Lev, 1953, pp. 151-156) for repeated or independent measures, where appropriate, were used. Analyses showed groups met the criterion of random sampling for treatment assignment. Furthermore, practice effects were not a confounding variable. Only the measure for auditory intensity DL differed between control and marihuana groups (M = 0.94 db and 1.51 db respectively, .025 > p > .01, two-tail test). All group comparisons for point of subjective equality and constant error were statistically nonsignificant.

TABLE 1
MEAN PERFORMANCE SCORES FOR CONTROL AND EXPERIMENTAL MARIHUANA GROUPS FOR VISUAL AND AUDITORY DISCRIMINATION MEASUREMENTS

Measure	First Test Session		Second Test Session	
	Cont.	Exp.	Cont.	Exp.
I. Visual Brightness Test (ft-c)				
2.40 ft-c standard	2.25	2.51	2.21	2.46
4.80 ft-c standard	4.09	4.93	4.60	4.91
II. Auditory Intensity Threshold Test (db)				
Difference threshold	1.46	1.71	0.94*	1.51*
Point of subjective equality	14.56	14.40	14.59	14.41
Constant error	−1.44	−0.66	−0.40	−0.63
III. Auditory Frequency Threshold Test (Hz)				
Difference threshold	3.64	4.06	2.53	3.79
Point of subjective equality	1001.67	1001.24	1000.88	1000.02
Constant error	+1.67	+1.24	+0.88	+0.02
IV. Auditory Threshold Test (db)	75.11	73.83	75.87	76.74

*t = 2.25; .025 greater than p greater than .01.

The results of this investigation indicate that marihuana minimally affects those measures of sensory acuity tested in this study. This was of interest in light of Ss' expressed feelings of superior performance following the marihuana test session. Although a significantly lower intensity DL was recorded for control *Ss* when compared to the marihuana *Ss* for the second test session, the absence of a significant difference between first- and second-test performance for marihuana *Ss* makes difficult an interpretation of this finding. Neither the position of this test in the battery nor its nature appears to account for this result. However, since the intensity DL decreased from first to second test session for the marihuana *Ss*, another interpretation would be that marihuana *Ss* failed to improve *as much* as control *Ss*. This view suggests the possibility of a specific task-related, dose-response phenomenon.

Several directions for further research were raised from *Ss'* comments following their participation in the study. First, the degree to which suggestibility functions in the experiencing of a marihuana "high" arises from *Ss'* statements that, "I could have become 'high' from smoking the alfalfa cigarette if I hadn't been told what it was." This point emphasized to us the importance of informing *S* of the substance being smoked in order to obtain a *valid* measure of the marihuana "effect" and to reduce the placebo "effect." However, a large proportion of the experimental *Ss* reported that the "high" experience, although pleasant, was reduced in intensity by the sterile laboratory environment (viz., bright lights, plain tile walls, test equipment, people in laboratory coats, etc.). The most provocative comment was the frequent report of the ability to "turn-off" the "high" at time of stimulus presentation, thus enabling *S* to perform as in a normal or nondrugged state. Some *Ss* attributed this to not being excessively "high" because of the sterile environment, while others reported the "turn-off" phenomenon to be a *normal* concomitant of the marihuana experience. This apparent ability to turn-off the marihuana "high" during periods requiring short attention spans raises the issue whether such tests (which comprise the majority of those used in studies reported to date) are valid indicants of the marihuana experience or simply measures of an interesting concomitant of the drug's effect, namely, the ability to respond normally at will? Whether this phenomenon is possible only for tasks of short-term duration or would be manifest in sustained performance tests is partially answered in the Weil, *et al.* (1968) study where marihuana users *improved* from baseline levels on digit-symbol substitution and pursuit rotor tests, both being more sustained performance tasks than any used in the present study. Furthermore, no performance decrements were observed for a 5-min. continuous performance test following marihuana smoking for either naive or experienced Ss. Moreover, Crancer, et al. (1969) have reported no impaired performance for marihuana-intoxicated Ss in a simulated driving condition. All tests, however, were basically measures of eye-hand coordination, whereas the present study measured pure sensory response data. Since simulated driving is a relatively complex motor-coordination task and since Crancer's Ss were administered large doses of marihuana (viz., 1700 mg. of 1.312% Δ^9THC concentration), the relationship of task type and complexity to level of intoxication warrants further study.

Data obtained under both the neutral and the "psychedelic" setting with purified substance administered both to "effect" as well as on a milligram per kilogram basis are needed to elucidate the marihuana experience. Studies should concern not only the pure pharmacologic effects of the compound but also the psychologic factors involved.

REFERENCES

Caldwell, D. F., Myers, S. A. Domino, E. F., & Merriam, P. E. *Effects of marihuana smoking on sensory thresholds in man.* Irvine, Calif.: N.I.M.H., 1969, in press. (Psychotomimetics Workshop Series)

Crancer, A., Dille, J. M., Delay, J. C., Wallace, J. E., & Haykin, M. D. A comparison of the effects of marihuana and alcohol on simulated driving performance. *Science,* 1969, 164, 851—854.

Guilford, J. P. *Psychometric methods.* New York: McGraw-Hill, 1954.

Myers, S. A., & Caldwell, D. F. The effects of marihuana on auditory and visual sensation. *Mich. Ment. Hlth Res. Bull.,* 1969, 3, 20—22. (a)

Myers, S. A., & Caldwell, D. F. The effects of marihuana on auditory and visual sensation: a preliminary report. *New Physician,* 1969, 18, 212—215. (b)

Walker, H. M., & Lev, J. *Statistical inference.* New York: Holt, 1953.

Weil, A. T., Zinberg, N. E., & Nelson, J. M. Clinical and psychological effects of marihuana in man. *Science,* 1968, 162, 1234—1242.

[1]We express our gratitude to the National Institute of Mental Health, Washington, D. C. and to Dr. Scigliano, Secretary *ad hoc* Marihuana Committee for providing us with marihuana for this research and for their Δ^9-THC assay. This research was supported, in part, by Grant MH-11846, USPHS.

10

The Effects of Marihuana on Auditory and Visual Sensation: A Preliminary Report

Steven A. Myers and Donald F. Caldwell

The subjective reports of those who enjoy the use of marihuana are generally well-known. Among the many "salutary" effects, enhancement of auditory and visual sensation and perception are frequently described. Morrow[8] (1944) was unable to demonstrate any significant alteration in auditory acuity or musical aptitude in subjects who were under the influence of various natural and synthetic marihuana preparations. Similarly, Williams, *et al.*,[10] (1946) observed no marked alterations in musical talent in subjects smoking crude marihuana. Three of 12 subjects, however, were felt to demonstrate a definite enhancement of auditory acuity while in a state of marihuana intoxication. To date, we have found no reports in the literature of attempts to definitively measure alterations in visual perception.

The tetrahydrocannabinols (THC) have long been considered responsible for the psychological effects of marihuana. Adams and Baker[1] (1940) synthesized a THC which reportedly possessed marihuana activity. Loewe[7] (1944) has written an extensive review of investigations reporting the cannabinols as the active principals in

Reprinted with permission of the authors and publisher from the *New Physician*, 1969, *18*, 212–215.

Steven A. Myers, M.D., is with the Division of Psychiatry, and Donald F. Caldwell, Ph.D., with the Division of Psychobiology at the Lafayette Clinic, Detroit, Michigan.

hemp. In the search to identify the exact structure of the active compound, both (-)-delta[9]-trans-THC (Gaoni and Mechoulam,[3] 1964) and 1-delta[8]-trans-THC (Hively, et al.,[5] 1966) were found to occur in hashish. The marihuana activity of delta[9]-THC has recently been demonstrated in man (Isbell, et al.,[6] 1967). This is believed to be the first demonstration of such activity of a THC of known chemical structure. The possibility of a conversion by heat of delta[9]-THC to a delta[8] isomer (Taylor, et al.,[9] 1966) has been disputed (Claussen and Korte,[2] 1967). This matter remains unsettled.

Our initial interest in research on marihuana was sparked by a flood of requests from parents, high school and college students, church groups, medical societies, and police departments to speak authoritatively on the psychological effects of marihuana. Unfortunately, knowledge of the effects of marihuana on various psychological states is extremely limited and is, in a large part, dependent upon subjective reports. In light of this, one suspects, perhaps even concludes, that current "authoritative" commentary consists in large part of the subjective bias of supposed "experts." It is the rare individual, indeed, who when questioned about marihuana does not generally reflect his own strong feelings. Seldom in recent times has so much been said, by so many, about a subject for which so little is known.

In point of fact, if only one-half of the effects attributed to marihuana could be substantiated, it would indeed be a miraculous drug. With the opportunities for research on this compound seemingly limitless and of immediate sociological consequences, one is amazed by the paucity of work being conducted in this field. With this in mind we naively embarked upon an enthusiastically broad-range program aimed at delineating the effects of marihuana on psychological function. Our basic aim was to attempt to translate the subjective experiences reported by subjects into experimental situations which would lend themselves to clear laboratory measurements acceptable to the scientific community.

Surprisingly, we encountered considerable resistance and criticism from a number of our colleagues. To those of a psychological orientation a frequent implication appeared to be the suspicion that we were attempting to demonstrate that marihuana was physiologically and psychologically harmless and thereby somehow we constituted a threat to the structure of society. In reality, our own bias, which we attempted to suppress, was one of considerable concern that marihuana was, in fact, a drug of potentially dangerous properties both psychologically and physiologically. To those pharmacologically-minded, our design was unforgivably nonscientific in that we proposed to use crude marihuana as opposed to crystalline delta[9]-tetrahydrocannabinol; we felt it should be taken by inhalation, as opposed to parenterally and administered in psychologically effective levels, as opposed to toxic doses.

Our rejoinder to criticism leveled at our decisions was that in the innumerable instances of marihuana usage in the social context, delta[9]-THC is not taken in pure form, nor is crude marihuana parenterally administered, and seldom is it smoked to a point of pharmacological toxicity. In our thinking, such studies would be analogous to attempting to determine the sociological and psychological effects of wine by the parenteral administration of a toxic dose of absolute ethyl alcohol. Such information would hardly be a valid test. That we are interested in determining the effects of marihuana as it is found in *common* usage will be apparent from our experimental design. Although our approach was not aimed at obtaining answers to those questions typically asked by the pharmacologist (viz, changes in blood pressure, BMR, heart rate, specific parenteral dose levels of delta[9]-THC in micrograms per kilogram, etc) it was believed to be of more immediate social relevance. We propose that marihuana be studied primarily in the social context as opposed to a pharmacologic frame of reference.

Thus determined, our first step was to secure approval of our protocol from both the Wayne State University School of Medicine and the Lafayette Clinic Human Experimentation Committees. We were then required to obtain an investigational drug number for the use of an "experimental drug" on human volunteers from the Bureau of Medicine, Division of Pharmacological Drugs, Food and Drug Administration. Next, we were instructed to apply for approval from the Center for Study of Narcotic and Drug Abuse, the National Institute of Mental Health, approval of which was dependent upon a favorable decision by a special committee. If approved, they would then appeal to the Treasury Department to authorize the release of a specified quantity of marihuana by the local District Director.

Having successfully hurdled these barriers, we were informed that the Federal Narcotics Regulations (revised) would not allow for the possession of a quantity of marihuana sufficient for our study. For purposes of consistency of the delta[9]-THC content we requested a 1 kg brick of marihuana. The directive from the District Director's office stated that the safe presently housed in the Lafayette Clinic pharmacy, used to safeguard narcotics such as morphine and Demerol, did not provide adequate safety for the storage of marihuana—not for the quantity requested! Thus we were faced with an additional outlay of several thousands of dollars if we were to proceed with the project. At this point, quite frankly, we were ready to abandon the whole project in total frustration and despair. Happily, NIMH made available to us an analyzed batch of marihuana suitable for our immediate purposes from which we could draw further and for which our present storage facilities were judged to be adequate.

We then addressed ourselves to the task of obtaining volunteer subjects meeting the criteria of male, 19 to 25 years of age, and enrolled in college. We felt the need to use only "confessed" marihuana users and required that they sign a statement to this effect . . . imagine the distraught mother accusing us of making her son a "drug addict." Some subjects balked at signing, fearing that these records could be subpoenaed by the authorities. This apprehension is understandable in view of the fact that they were being asked to confess to a felony punishable by imprisonment. Despite reassurances that this project had been sanctioned by the Clinic, by the University, and by various appropriate federal agencies, there was still a considerable apprehension on the part of some to participate in the absence of further guarantees that the experiments would not be "raided" resulting in their conviction on possession of marihuana. The procedures of having subjects sign a release form is standard practice in the conduction of any human research at the Lafayette Clinic. Still, even with these problems, subjects volunteered in droves, frequently suggesting that they could bring their own marihuana if ours was not available from the establishment.

As a further safeguard to this project, the cigarettes smoked by control subjects (viz, alfalfa, which is virtually indistinguishable from marihuana in taste, smell, and appearance) were made by the Clinic pharmacist, numbered, and recorded. Each subject was requested to sign for the cigarette he received, thus guarding against the possibility of a subject making claim to having received a marihuana cigarette when, in fact, it was alfalfa. To many subjects it seemed superfluous that we required a physical examination. However, we felt that this was necessary in that they were using a compound classified as an "experimental drug." They also questioned the fact that we insisted on their remaining overnight in the Clinic following the completion of the testing. We had to explain that our study would certainly be endangered if following their participation they committed any antisocial act for whatever reason. Subjects were not given any remuneration for their participation in this research because of what we felt to be the obvious implications of paying subjects for smoking marihuana!

In an attempt to gain a better understanding of the effects of marihuana on auditory and visual systems, we believed that a logical first step would be to determine whether intoxication with the drug measurably altered these primary sensory functions. A demonstration of either facilitation or inhibition (as measured by changes in threshold) for either of these sensory systems would call for a thorough investigation of those specific factors involved. A failure to demonstrate significant alterations may imply a need to investigate the influence of psychological factors which may be operative in the perceptual phenomena reported by marihuana users. Test measures consisted of a determination of (a) alterations in auditory threshold, (b) ability to discriminate between paired tones of fixed frequency and varying amplitude, (c) ability to discriminate between paired tones of fixed amplitude and varying frequency, and (d) ability to match a light of variable illuminance to a standard light of fixed illuminance.

Numerous questions remained to be answered before testing could commence. For example, were the tests to be used of a nature that the subjects would be able to attend to them while under the influence of marihuana? . . . would the subjects fall asleep? . . . would they become uncooperative? . . . might some subjects experience something akin to a delirious or psychotic state? . . . would there be pronounced physiological manifestations for which we should be prepared? To answer these and other questions, it was decided to undertake a preliminary study utilizing two of the above measures (viz, the amplitude discrimination and light matching tests) with a group of volunteers from among the Lafayette Clinic professional staff. These subjects had no previous experience with use of marihuana and were made aware of the substances which they were about to smoke. Twelve male volunteer subjects with the median age of 31 years were tested.

Subjects were randomly divided into two equal-sized groups. The control group (N = 6) received one 300 mg alfalfa cigarette which they were instructed to smoke by deep inhalation within a period of 15 minutes. Predrug testing then began. At the end of the predrug testing period, a 30-minute rest period was allowed and the entire procedure repeated except on this occasion the cigarette for subjects randomly assigned to the experimental group (N = 6) contained 300 mg of crude marihuana. The marihuana used in this project contained 1.3% of what is believed to be the active ingredient of marihuana, that is, delta^9-tetra-hydrocannabinol. The cigarettes used in this research compare favorably in potency with those used in the community. All test measurements were accomplished with the subject in a sitting position in a totally dark, sound-proof, air-conditioned room.

Each subject was fitted with earphones and tested for his ability to discriminate between a pair of monaurally-presented tones differing only in intensity (loudness). The first member of each tone pair (the standard) was of constant frequency and loudness and was compared to a second tone of the same frequency but of different loudness values from the standard. Each subject was asked to report whether the second member of the tone pair was "louder," "equal," or "quieter" compared to the first tone of the pair. Ten ascending and descending series were administered during each treatment condition. Measurements of the difference limen, point of subjective equality and constant error were obtained using the method of minimal change (Guilford,[4] 1954).

Light intensity discrimination was next tested. The subject was presented with two small white lights situated in front of him and about 17 inches apart. One light was set at a predetermined foot candle illuminance value. The second light was set at each of ten different illuminance values. The subject was instructed to vary the intensity of this lamp by means of a rheostat control until he perceived the intensities of the two lights as being identical. After he had made his adjustment the intensity of the lamp was measured and recorded.

It has frequently been stated that the first encounter with smoking marihuana is without noticeable effect. Our subjects generally reported no appreciable change in mood or perception. Several subjects reported a sense of hunger, sleepiness, or relaxation. The subjects generally seemed to be more at ease and a little more verbal. These general observations cannot be considered entirely valid since no attempt was made to control for the importance of suggestibility in either the subjects or experimenters arising from being aware of the identity of the substances being smoked. A frequent comment was that inasmuch as they had no previous experience with the marihuana "high" they had no idea of what they should experience. Their sensoria certainly remained clear and there was no evidence of gross motor impairment. The subjects remained uncertain as to the nature of this experience and the general consensus was that if indeed there was any effect, perhaps it was comparable to a "martini on an empty stomach." Of primary interest was the finding that subjects were able to attend to the tests, were cooperative, and manifested no pronounced physiological signs.

Our data analyses failed to reveal significant differences in performance between groups for either of the visual or auditory measures and may reflect, in part, the limitations set on the amount of marihuana smoked by each subject (viz, 300 mg). With this point foremost in mind, and because it represents a practice at variance with the use of marihuana by the "user," our studies with the college population have been conducted under more realistic and revealing conditions. Each subject is allowed to smoke to a "biological endpoint," that is, to smoke *ad libitum* to the point of his own subjective "high." All subjects appeared to reach a rather clear endpoint. Although an unlimited supply of marihuana was available, each would stop smoking at a specific point, stating that he had "arrived." Generally this required 350 to 400 mg of marihuana. These subjects, while reporting a "high," failed to demonstrate objective changes other than those observed in our initial group. These data are presently in the stage of analysis.

At this writing we have completed the collection of data for measures of both auditory and visual acuity on approximately 40 experimental and control subjects, accounting for more than 100 hours of testing. In retrospect, the agony of initiating such research seems grossly disproportionate to the effortless ease in data collection. We have experienced no raids, no reported addiction, no irate mothers, not even an irritated subject at the revelation that he had been randomly selected to partake of only alfalfa . . . that is, be a control. In short, the eventual conduction of marihuana research was remarkably uneventful. The next phase of our study is directed toward a determination of the role played by group participation and the element of suggestibility in producing the marihuana "high." We must, of course, obtain appropriate agency approval.

The social pressures to learn more of the effects of marihuana are great . . . as they should be. However, one cannot but be impressed with the amount of verbiage being paid to this need, relative to the amount setting forth findings from the laboratory. Perhaps this is, in part, due to the frustration experienced by well-meaning researchers in their attempts to initiate their research. If so, our experiences should serve to indicate that caution is necessary, as with any experimental compound, but overcaution as exists today may permanently "stunt the growth" of research in this area . . . and after all—haven't we already dispelled that rumor?

BIBLIOGRAPHY

1. Adams, R., and Baker, B.R.: Structure of Cannabinol. VII. A Method of Synthesis of a Tetrahydrocannabinol Which Possesses Marihuana Activity. *J Am Chem Soc* 62:2405–2408, 1940.

2. Claussen, U., and Korte, F.: Uber das Verhalten der Cannabes-Phenole beim Rauchen Tetrahedron. *Letters* 2067, 1967.

3. Gaoni, Y., and Mechoulam, R.: Isolation, Structure and Partial Synthesis of an Active Constituent of Hashish. *J Am Chem Soc* 86:1646–1648, 1964.

4. Guilford, J.P.: *Psychometric Methods*. II Ed. New York: McGraw-Hill, 1954.

5. Hively, R.L., Mosher, W.A., and Hoffman, F.: Isolation of Trans-delta[6]-Tetrahydrocannabinol from Marihuana. *J Am Chem Soc* 88: 1832–1833, 1966.

6. Isbell, H., Gorodetsky, C.W., Jasinski, D., Claussen, U., Spulak, F.V., and Korte, F.: Effects of Delta-Trans-Tetrahydrocannabinol in Man. *Psychopharmacologia* (Berl.) 11:184–188, 1967.

7. Loewe, S.: Pharmacological Study. In: *The Marihuana Problem in the City of New York. Mayor's Committee on Marihuana, 1944*. Lancaster, Pa: Jacques Cattell Press, pp 149–212.

8. Morrow, R.S.: Psychological Aspects. In: *The Marihuana Problem in the City of New York. Mayor's Committee on Marihuana, 1944*. Lancaster, Pa: Jacques Cattell Press, Abstracted in: *The Marihuana Papers*, Bobbs-Merrill Press, pp 285–290, 1966.

9. Taylor, E.D., Leonard, K., and Shvo, Y.: Active Constituents of Hashish, Synthesis of Dl-delta[6]-3, 4-Trans-Tetrahydrocannabinol, *J Am Chem Soc* 88:367, 1966.

10. Williams, E.G., Himmelsbach, C.K., Wikler, A., and Ruble, D.C.: Studies on Marihuana and Pyrahexyl Compound. *Public Health Reports* 61:1059–1082,

Part 5

Marihuana and Time Distortion

Distortions in time perception are among the most frequently reported effects produced by marihuana. When asked to judge the amount of time that has elapsed between two signals, subjects invariably overestimate actual clock time. This overestimation has been observed for time periods ranging from seconds to hours. For example, in an experiment reported by Weil, Zinberg and Nelson,[1] subjects receiving a placebo were able to estimate a 5-minute period within ± 2 minutes. After receiving marihuana, these estimates were raised to 10 ± 2 minutes. Similar findings have been reported by Jones and Stone.[2] These effects on subjective time estimation have been interpreted by some investigators as evidence that marihuana produces a speeding up of an "internal clock."[2]

In the article by Conrad, Elsmore, and Sodetz which follows, monkeys were trained to push two buttons in order to obtain food. However, there was a condition attached to this work-reward contingency—the second button had to be pushed no sooner than 60 seconds and no longer than 90 seconds after the first. This procedure thus enabled Conrad and his coworkers to study the effects of marihuana on time perception in the monkey. Although their method of analysis is difficult to follow for those who are not acquainted with their terminology, their results basically showed that doses of marihuana which did not affect the rate of button-pushing, did affect the timing behavior of monkeys in such a way that they were no longer able to make the temporal discrimination. In other words, they were no longer able to pace themselves so that they could earn the reward by responding within the 60-90-second interval after pressing the first button. In general, the monkeys tended to overestimate the time, that is, they pressed the second button before the 60 seconds had elapsed. These results have been corroborated by other experimenters using monkeys[3] and rats[4] and seem to reflect a genuine impairment in the mechanisms by which organisms are able to estimate time.

An interesting extension of marihuana's effect on time sense included here is reported by Melges and his coworkers. After administering Δ^9-THC to humans, they subjected them to two questionnaires. The first, called the "Present Concentration Inventory," is assumed to measure "the degree to which a person focuses on the present to the relative exclusion of the past and future." The second questionnaire, called the "Temporal Extension Inventory," is assumed to measure "an individual's extension of awareness into the past and future by asking him to indicate how far back or ahead he is thinking at the time of testing."

The results of their study suggest that under the influence of marihuana, attention is concentrated on the here-and-now to the exclusion of the past or future. Melges et al. hypothesize in their report that this focusing on the immediate present may in some way account for the difficulties subjects have in estimating clock time and may also be associated with subjectively reported changes in the perception of sound and visual stimuli.

REFERENCES

1. A. T. Weil, N. E. Zinberg, and J. M. Nelson, "Clinical and psychological effects of marihuana in man," *Science,* 1968, *162,* 1234–1242.

2. R. T. Jones, and G. C. Stone, "Psychological Studies of Marihuana and Alcohol in Man," *Psychopharmacologia,* 1970, *18,* 108-117.

3. D. P. Ferraro and D. K. Billings, "Comparison of Behavioral Effects of Synthetic (-) Δ^9-Trans-Tetrahydrocannabinol and Marihuana Extract Distillate in Chimpanzees," *Psychopharmacologia,* 1972, *25,* 169–174.

4. C. D. Webster, M. D. Willinsky, et al., "Effects of $1\text{-}\Delta^1$-Tetrahydrocannabinol on Temporarily Spaced Responding and Discriminated Sidman Avoidance Behavior in Rats," *Nature*, 1971, *232*, 498–501.

Delta-9-Tetrahydrocannabinol: Dose-related Effects on Timing Behavior in Chimpanzees

Donald G. Conrad
Timothy F. Elsmore, and Frank J. Sodetz

One difficulty encountered in interpreting results from animal studies of Δ^9-tetrahydrocannabinol (Δ^9-THC), the presumed principal psychoactive constituent of marihuana, has been the high doses generally needed to produce behavioral effects. This drug, in oral doses of about 0.200 mg/kg, has been reported to produce marihuana-like effects in humans[1]. As part of an investigation of its behavioral and toxicological effects, oral doses ranging from 0.125 mg/kg to 4.0 mg/kg were administered to three chimpanzees[2] with highly efficient and stable schedule-controlled timing behavior, and dose-related behavioral effects were observed within the human dose range. A food reinforcement schedule requiring performance based on passage of time was selected because there is a known tendency of humans to overestimate passage of time during marihuana intoxication[1-3].

The three adult chimpanzees had been maintained for the last five years in a multianimal environment for primates with their behavior under control of reinforcement schedules almost identical with the one

Reprinted with permission of the authors and publisher from *Science*, 1972, *175*, 547—550. Copyright 1972 by the American Association for the Advancement of Science.

Donald G. Conrad, Timothy F. Elsmore and Frank J. Sodetz are affiliated with the Department of Experimental Psychology, Walter Reed Army Institute of Research, Washington, D.C.

described below. Each subject was semiisolated in its living-work compartment, the front wall of which served as a work panel. Each contained a clocklike self-identification device, a pair of trans-illuminated pushbuttons (A and B), red and green cue lights, and food and water delivery mechanisms.

A multilink chained schedule of food reinforcement was in effect approximately 20 hours per day. Each response chain required opera-tion of the self-identification device by moving the clock arm to an assigned position for 5 seconds. Then a contingency requiring tem-porally spaced responses was imposed. The animal first had to respond on pushbutton A, and then wait at least 60 seconds, but no longer than 90 seconds, before responding on pushbutton B in order to obtain food upon completion of the whole response chain. If a correct A-B interresponse time (A-B IRT) occurred (between 60 and 90 seconds), the first B response turned on a green cue light and the 500th B response resulted in food delivery and reinitiated the chain. However, when the preceding A-B IRT was incorrect (less than 60 seconds or greater than 90), the first B response produced a red cue light, and the 500 B responses were required to reactivate the self-identification device and hence to reinitiate the chain; there was no food delivery at the completion of the 500th response. Session durations were lengthened by imposing a 30-minute "timeout" period after comple-tion of every tenth response chain regardless of food deliveries obtained. Data were collected to ascertain daily work outputs, response rates, reinforcement frequency, accuracy of timing perfor-mances, and the onset and time-course of Δ^9-THC activity.

Δ^9-Tetrahydrocannabinol, in a vehicle of absolute ethanol, was injected into slices of orange or banana for oral administration at the start of the first 30-minute timeout period of a daily session. Doses in a geometric series from 0.125 to 4.0 mg/kg were given in mixed order at intervals of 1 week or longer, but never before baseline performances had been recovered for all three chimpanzees. Each subject received two administrations at each dose level. Placebos of 1.0 ml of ethanol and fruit were given on days between Δ^9-THC administrations.

Effects of Δ^9-THC on reinforced interresponse times (IRTs) are illustrated by the open symbols and broken-line curves in the lower portion of Fig. 1. Mean frequencies of reinforced IRTs obtained on drug days have been divided by the averaged frequencies of reinforced IRTs for the three placebo-control days prior to each day at that dose level. Values of these drug-placebo ratios of reinforced IRTs are shown on the right-hand axis of Fig. 1. Reinforced IRT frequency was

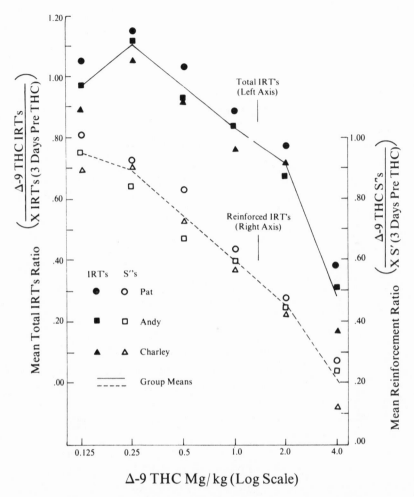

Δ-9 THC Mg/kg (Log Scale)

Fig. 1. Dose-related effects of Δ^9-THC on total number of A-B interresponse times (that is, daily work output) and on frequencies of those A-B IRTs, between 60 and 90 seconds' duration, which resulted in food reinforcements (S's) for each of the three chimpanzees. Dose levels of Δ^9-THC are shown on the log scale of the horizontal axis. The ratio values for total IRTs (left-hand axis) and for reinforced IRTs (right-hand axis) were obtained by dividing the averaged number occurring on 2 days of Δ^9-THC administrations at a given oral dose by the averaged number occurring on three placebo-control days prior to each of the drug administrations at that dose level. Ratio values for individual subjects are marked by symbols. Group mean ratio values for all three subjects are connected by the solid lines (total IRTs) and the broken lines (reinforced IRTs). The left- and right-hand axes are offset to separate the two sets of ratios.

suppressed increasingly as a function of drug dose. The group mean drug/placebo ratio decreased from 0.95 at the low dose, 0.125 mg/kg to about 0.20 at the high dose, 4.0 mg/kg. Highly similar dose-dependent effects of Δ^9-THC on number of reinforced IRTs for timing performances were obtained from each of the three subjects.

These decrements in reinforced IRTs were due, in part, to suppression of daily work output by the chimps. The total number of response chains initiated—that is, total A-B IRTs regardless of duration—was taken as a measure of daily work output. Mean work output on days of drug administration at a given dose level was compared with averaged output for three prior placebo-control days in the same manner as described above for the reinforced IRTs. Effects of Δ^9-THC on work output are illustrated by the darkened symbols and the solid line in the upper portion of Fig. 1. Values of these ratios of work output are shown on the left-hand axis. Little, if any, effect on work output was observed at doses under 1.0 mg/kg, other than possibly a slight increase in total IRTs with the 0.25 mg/kg dose. Decrements in work output, increasing with dose, did occur with doses of 1.0 mg/kg and larger. The group mean drug/placebo ratio of total IRTs dropped sharply from the high of 1.10 at the 0.25 mg/kg dose level to a low of about 0.30 at the highest dose. Prolonged breaks in performance were observed when the higher doses of Δ^9-THC took effect. The chimps appeared just to sit quietly in their cages for several hours before returning to work, if they did so at all. These breaks in performance occurred both as long intervals between response chains and long delays in completing the 500 response terminal link of the chain following an inappropriate A-B IRT. Similar effects of Δ^9-THC on work output at each dose were obtained from the individual subjects, as was the case with reinforced IRTs. However, the lower doses, as well as higher ones, resulted in decrements in number of reinforcements, but the lower doses did not decrease work output.

In addition to the decreased work output, decreased reinforced IRTs resulted also from decrements in accuracy of the timing performance. Some effects of Δ^9-THC on accuracy of timing are illustrated in Fig. 2, which shows an increasing tendency to overestimate passage of time with increasing dose of Δ^9-THC. Frequency of short A-B IRTs relative to total A-B IRTs—that is, relative frequency of A-B IRTs less than 60 seconds—was taken as a measure of the overestimation error. The three top panels of Fig. 2 illustrate the relative frequencies of overestimation errors produced by the individual subjects, and the bottom panel combines the errors in a group average, at each dose level of Δ^9-THC. Black dots connected by solid lines mark relative

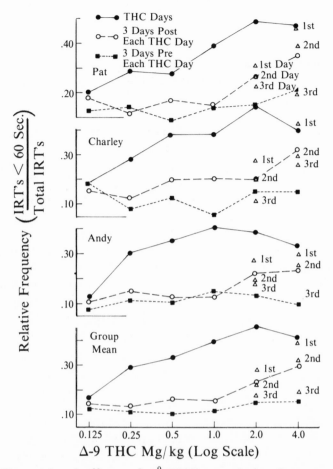

Fig. 2. Dose-related effects of Δ^9-THC on relative frequency of A-B interresponse times (IRTs) less than 60 seconds in duration (that is, overestimation errors), in the timing performances of three chimpanzees. Dose levels are shown on the log scale of the horizontal axis. The numbers of IRTs under 60 seconds in duration are divided by total IRTs regardless of duration. Relative frequencies of these overestimation errors occurring on days when oral doses of Δ^9-THC were administered (black circles connected by solid lines) are compared with relative frequencies occurring during placebo-control sessions 3 days before (black squares connected by dotted lines) and 3 days after (open circles connected by dashed lines) each day of drug administration. Relative frequencies occurring on individual first, second, and third days after administrations of the two highest dose levels are marked by numbered open triangles. Results obtained from individual subjects are shown in the three top panels. Results obtained with all three subjects are combined for the group mean results shown in the bottom panel.

frequencies of IRTs less than 60 seconds in duration which occurred on days when doses were administered. Relative frequencies of such short IRTs during placebo-control sessions are shown for 3 days before (black squares connected by dotted lines) and for 3 days after (open circles connected by dashed lines) each administration of Δ^9-THC. Open triangles mark the relative frequencies of short IRTs which occurred on individual first, second, and third days after administration of the two highest doses. The combined results shown in the bottom panel of Fig. 2 are representative of the results obtained with the individual subjects shown in the upper panels. Relative frequencies of overestimation errors were low and stable on placebo-control days prior to Δ^9-THC administration (black squares). When Δ^9-THC was given, overestimation errors increased in relative frequency with increasing dose level (black circles). This effect of Δ^9-THC on accuracy of timing performance diminishingly perseverated on days following drug administrations (open circles). Relative frequencies of overestimation errors were elevated up to 3 days after administrations of the higher doses of Δ^9-THC (numbered open triangles). The other timing error, A-B IRTs longer than 90 seconds in duration, were typically low in relative frequency, never exceeding 10 percent of the work output. The drug had no observable effect on this type of timing error.

These data are important for several reasons. The fact that doses of 1.0 mg/kg and larger decreased the frequency of food-reinforced operant behavior confirms effects that have been observed with other species[4]. The finding that high doses of the drug continue to exert an effect for up to 3 days also is of interest in view of the biochemical data indicating that metabolites of Δ^9-THC persist in the body for up to a week after ingestion[5]. Finally, the fact that drug effects were obtained at the 0.25 mg/kg dose level, well within the effective dose range for humans, and the fact that the change in timing behavior appears to confirm data on humans, both suggest that the chimpanzee may be a useful animal in studies of marihuana.

REFERENCES AND NOTES

1. H. Isbel, G. W. Gorodetzky, D. Jasinski, U. Claussen, F. Spulak, F. Korte, *Psychopharmacologia* 11, 184 (1967); L. E. Hollister, R. K. Richards, H. K. Gillespie, *Clin. Pharmacol. Ther.* 9, 783 (1968); I. E. Waskow, J. E. Olsson, C. Salzman, M. M. Katz, *Arch. Gen. Psychiat.* 22, 97 (1970); L. E. Hollister, *Science* 172, 21 (1971).

2. In conducting this research, we adhered to the "Guide for Laboratory Animal Facilities and Care," as promulgated by the Committee on Revision of the Guide for Laboratory Animal Facilities and Care of the Institute of Laboratory Animal Resources, National Academy of Sciences-National Research Council.

3. E. G. Williams, C. K. Himmelsbach, A. Wikler, D. C. Ruble, B. N. Lloyd, *Public Health Rep.* 61, 1059 (1946); F. Ames, *J. Ment. Sci.* 104, 972 (1958); T. Petrzilka and C. Sikemeier, *Helv. Chim. Acta* 50, 1416 (1967); A. T. Weil, N. E. Zinberg, J. M. Nelsen, *Science* 162, 1234 (1968); L. D. Clark, R. Hughes, E. N. Nakashima, *Arch. Gen. Psychiat.* 23, 193 (1970); L. E. Hollister and H. K. Gillespie, *ibid.*, p. 199; R. Mechoulam, *Science* 163, 1159 (1970); Secretary, Department of Health, Education, and Welfare, *A Report to the Congress: Marihuana and Health,* 31 Jan. 1971 (U.S. Government Printing Office, Washington, D.C., 1971), document 0-415-832.

4. E. S. Boyd, E. D. Hutchinson, L. C. Gardner, D. A. Merritt, *Arch. Int. Pharmacodyn.* 144, 533 (1963); E. A. Carlini, *Pharmacology* 1, 135 (1968); D. E. McMillan, L. S. Harris, J. M. Frankenheim, J. S. Kennedy, *Science* 169, 501 (1970); J. M. Cole, W. A. Pieper, D. M. Rumbaugh, *Commun. Behav. Biol.* 8, No. 1 (July 1971).

5. L. Lemberger, S. D. Silberstein, J. Axelrod, I. J. Kopin, *Science* 170, 1320 (1970); L. Lemberger, N. R. Tamarkin, J. Axelrod, I. J. Kopin, *ibid.* (1971).

6. Synthetic Δ^9-THC was obtained from J. A. Scigliano (Center for Studies of Narcotics and Drug Abuse, National Institute of Mental Health, Chevy Chase, Md.). It was dissolved in absolute ethanol in a concentration of 0.2 g/ml, and was assayed to be 93 percent pure. It was administered as received or, for a dose of 1.0 mg/kg or lower, it was diluted with ethanol with the dose volume varying from a minimum of 0.07 ml up to 1.08 ml.

12

Marihuana and the Temporal Span of Awareness

Frederick T. Melges, Jared R. Tinklenberg
Leo E. Hollister, and Hamp K. Gillespie

Changes in time sense are frequently experienced by users of marihuana.[1] These temporal distortions consist of (1) changes in the sense of duration, (2) a confusion of past, present, and future; and (3) changes in temporal perspective—that is, alterations in the focus and span of awareness directed to the past, present, or future. Changes in the sense of duration have been demonstrated experimentally by time-estimation tasks.[2] At low to moderate doses of marihuana, the general effect is a speeding up of subjective (internal) duration such that clock (external) time seems to pass more slowly than in the nondrug state; at higher doses, a feeling of timelessness and an uncertainty as to how much time has gone by often takes place. The confusion of past, present, and future has been shown to interfere with goal-directed thinking.[2] This inability to keep track of goal-relevant information is termed temporal disintegration. Increased doses of

Reprinted with permission of the authors and publisher from the *Archives of General Psychiatry*, 1971, *24*, 564–567. Copyright 1971, American Medical Association.

Frederick T. Melges, M.D., and Jared R. Tinklenberg, M.D. are with the Department of Psychiatry at Stanford University School of Medicine in Stanford, California. Leo H. Hollister, M.D., is Associate Professor in the Department of Medicine at the Stanford University School of Medicine, Stanford, California, and Medical Investigator for the Veterans Administration Hospital in Palo Alto, California. Hamp K. Gillespie is affiliated with the Veterans Administration Hospital in Palo Alto, California.

marihuana extract, calibrated to content of tetrahydrocannabinol (THC), have been shown to progressively impair both subjective report and cognitive measures of temporal disintegration.[3, 4] Although the effect on marihuana on judgments of duration and on temporal disintegration have been studied systematically, there have been no experimental reports that deal with changes in temporal perspective. The latter is the focus on this paper.

Our pilot studies with high oral doses of marihuana extract raised the following questions about changes in temporal perspective: Does marihuana induce a narrowing of attention to the present with less regard for the past and future? If so, is the increased concentration on the present related to the euphoriant properties of the drug?

METHODS

The data on temporal perspective changes were obtained during an intensive study of marihuana-induced temporal distortions. The findings on temporal disintegration have been reported recently in the ARCHIVES.[4] Since the latter report describes the experimental and statistical procedures in detail, they will be outlined only briefly here.

Using double-blind controls, we gave eight normal male graduate students three oral doses of marihuana extract or placebo in randomized order on four different test days separated by at least one week. The doses were quantitatively calibrated according to content of (-)-Δ'-tetrahydrocannabinol (THC).[5] The placebo was identical in taste and color to the 20-, 40-, and 60-mg doses of THC used in this study. The 40-mg and 60-mg oral doses are probably higher than the amount of THC obtained from the usual custom of smoking marihuana in social situations.[6] The oral route of administration was used since, at least at present, it offers a far more precise way of regulating dosage.

On each of the four experimental days, a subject was tested before drug ingestion (base line) and then 1 1/2, 3 1/2, and 5 1/2 hours after drug ingestion. This allowed for the study of correlated changes between different measures from one test session to the next during the time course of action of the drug. By using this change-correlation method,[4] it was possible to determine what changes with what for each individual under the influence of marihuana. In addition, through a technique for averaging the individual change correlations, we computed an "average Pearson r," which summarizes the magnitude of relationships between changes for all eight subjects. In this way, individual and aggregate processes (related changes) relevant to temporal perspective and emotion were examined. To determine overall effects of the marihuana doses, analysis of variance was used. The tests used for studying temporal perspective and emotion were presented to the subject in randomized order and are described below.

Present Concentration Inventory

This inventory measures the degree to which a person focuses on the present to the relative exclusion of past and future. It consists of five statements: (1) "I seem to live from minute to minute, with little attention to the past or future." (2) "My past seems remote and far off." (3) "I feel cut off from my past." (2) "My future seems remote and far off." (5) "My future seems blocked." Subjects responded to each statement on a six-point scale ranging from "not at all" to "extremely." The more attention is focused on the present and denied to the past and future, the higher the score on present concentration. In 30 normal subjects tested ten days apart, the test-retest reliability of the Present Concentration Inventory was substantial ($r = 0.82$; $P < 0.001$).

Temporal Extension Inventory (TE)

The TE measures an individual's extension of awareness into the past and future by asking him to indicate how far back or ahead he is thinking at the time of testing. On the TE Future, from a list of time categories ranging from minutes to decades, the subject selects the appropriate one to complete the following statement: "For the way I feel right now, my general tendency would be to think about things that will happen to me in the future _____." The list reads as follows:

Minutes ahead (1-10-20-30-40-50-60 minutes ahead).
Hours ahead (1-3-6-9-12-15-18-21-24 hours ahead).
Days ahead (1-2-3-4-5-6-7 days ahead).
Weeks ahead (1-2-3-4-5 weeks ahead).
Months ahead (1-2-3-4-5-6-7-8-9-10-11-12 months ahead).
Years ahead (1-2-3-4-5-6-7-8-9-10 years ahead).
Decades ahead (1-2-3-4-5-6-7-8-9-10 decades ahead).

The subject is asked to choose one of the temporal categories at the left, and then circle the number of units within that category which most precisely located the focus of his attention in the future.

The TE Past is identical to the TE Future, except that the "future" is replaced by "past" and "ahead" by "ago." The TE Future and TE Past instruments are scored in a semilogarithmic fashion conforming to the foreshortened way that extension of time appears to be experienced subjectively.[7] That is, events further away in "real" or geophysical time seem closer to the present than they actually are. An event one month away, for example, does not seem to be 30 times as far away as an event one day distant. In 30 normal subjects tested two weeks apart, the test-retest reliability of the TE Future was 0.73 and that of the TE Past was 0.72.

Mood Adjective Check List

The 40-item Nowlis-Green Mood Adjective Check List (MACL) was used to measure changes in emotion.[8] Subjects respond to each word by choosing one of the following answers: "definitely applies to me at this time," "slightly applies," "cannot decide," or "definitely does not apply."

In addition to the above inventories, subjects responded on a six-point scale to two statements which asked how "interrelated" or "unrelated" the categories of past, present, and future seemed to them at the moment. Similarly, they were asked to express the degree to which they were experiencing the past, present, and future as "continuous" or "discontinuous."

RESULTS

Compared to placebo, extracts of marihuana induced significantly greater concentration on the present (Table). Of the items of the Present Concentration Inventory, marihuana particularly enhanced the feeling of living "from minute to minute, with little attention to the past and future" and also the feeling that the "future seems remote and far off." Temporal extension into the future was also reduced by THC and there was a significant interaction between dose level and time of testing (Table). The latter indicates that the greatest reduction of future temporal extension took place at the time of peak drug effect ($1\ 1/2$ hours after ingestion) and was enhanced by higher doses. The degree of temporal extension into the past, however, was not significantly affected by THC.

Under the influence of marihuana, subjects also reported that their experience of the time line extending from past to present to future seemed discontinuous and that the past and future seemed unrelated to the present ($P < 0.05$).

These findings on temporal perspective thus indicate that marihuana induces a greater concentration on the present to the relative exclusion of past and, in particular, future references. This greater focus on the present appeared related to the euphoriant

TABLE 1
EFFECT OF THC ON TEMPORAL PERSPECTIVE MEASURES

Inventory	Placebo	THC 20 mg	THC 40 mg	THC 60 mg	F	Significance*
		Mean Drug Effect				
Present concentration	9.5	12.3	13.3	12.8	3.2	0.050
Future extension**	202.7	165.1	133.2	168.7	2.9	0.055
Past extension	214.5	236.5	177.5	232.4	1.7	NS

*Significance was determined by analysis of variance (df = 3.21).
**For future temporal extension there was a significant interaction between dose level and time of testing ($F_{9.63}$ = 2.40; $P < 0.05$).

properties of THC. That is, in terms of within-subject change correlations averaged across subjects, changes in scores on Present Concentration correlated significantly and positively with changes in the following positive MACL mood factors: Egotism (0.38), Pleasantness (0.36), Nonchalance (0.35), and Social Affection (0.27). The average Pearson r's for correlations between changes in Present Concentration and negative mood factors (MACL Anxiety, Depression, Aggression, Skepticism, Startle, and Deactivation) did not reach significance at the 0.05 level. These findings indicate that, for all subjects considered together, marihuana-induced increases in concentration on the present were associated with increases in euphoric moods.

Not all subjects, however, experienced increased concentration on the present as euphoric. For example, by inspecting individual within-subject change correlations, it was found that the correlations of changes in Present Concentration with MACL Pleasantness was substantially positive in four subjects (0.75, 0.72, 0.61, 0.55), but in one subject the correlation was substantially negative (−0.41). Moreover, whereas one subject experienced changes toward greater concentration on the present with decreases in MACL Anxiety (−0.51), another subject experienced increases in anxiety with greater present concentration (+0.62). These individual differences appeared to stem from personality predispositions about losing self-control and normal awareness during the drug experience.

COMMENT

The increased concentration on the present and the foreshortening of the span of awareness into the future found in this experiment has also been reported by smokers of marihuana in social situations. In a survey of subjective experiences during marihuana smoking, Tart[1] found that 87% of marihuana smokers reported the following experience: "I give little or no thought to the future, I am completely in the here-and-now."

Quotes taken from open-ended interviews during our initial studies with high oral marihuana doses (calibrated to 60 mg of THC) also indicate this "here-and-now" focus. For example, one subject stated: "I don't understand it. I don't—there seems to be no transition, no changes in time. It's just *it*. I'm just here . . . right this moment, and I can't—I know I'm moving along, and yet—I'm not. I have no sense of time, I'm just floating along." Another subject claimed that he could not think of the future because he was unable to "keep an idea long enough—I can't remember my future." When prompted to give an example of a future event, he looked at a chocolate bar in his hand and said, "I'm going to take a bite of candy." This foreshortening of future time perspective was in marked contrast to his predrug and postdrug interviews during which he talked about getting his PhD and his career plans for the next six years. Another example comes from a subject who said that he was "completely in the present. . . just savoring the present."

The "here-and-now" perspective during marihuana intoxication may be likened to a childlike temporal view in which each moment appears fresh and vivid since it is experienced without the context of extensive memories and expectations of adult consciousness.[9] Some individuals apparently enjoy such an altered state of consciousness, while others do not. These individual differences were evident in our experiment, yet the overall trend suggests that the euphoriant effects of marihuana are related to an increased concentration on the present. In addition, our clinical interviews with habitual marihuana smokers indicate that many of them use the drug in order to achieve this "here-and-now" orientation.[10] With a greater focus on the present, they claim they are less troubled by past and future concerns and more open to immediate experience.

Vividness of perceptions, reported as common during marihuana intoxication,[1] may also be related to a more exclusive focus on the present. That is, current experiences may seem more intense when they are relatively isolated from elements of the past and future. This isolation of current experiences may stem from marihuana-induced difficulties with impaired immediate memory which hinder the individual's ability to juxtapose and compare current perceptions with memories and expectations.[3, 4, 11] Perceptions may thus seem fresh and new, never experienced before, and unexpected. An alternative hypothesis would be that marijuana induces a greater intensity of perceptions which prompt the individual to become more focused on the present. Studies of peripheral sensory thresholds do not, however, indicate significant changes with THC and thus further research is needed.[12]

Increased concentration on the present, along with remoteness of the past and future, are features of altered consciousness which are not restricted to marijuana intoxication. They have been reported to occur during hypnotic and meditative states as well as during intoxication with mescaline and lysergic acid diethylamide.[13, 14] Indeed, Aldous Huxley[15] highlighted temporal changes as central to his experience with mescaline: "My actual experience has been . . . of an indefinite duration or alternatively of a perpetual present made up of one continually changing apocalypse." Since the sense of duration and of past, present, and future relationships are important aspects of normal adult consciousness, it is possible that time distortions underlie many types of altered states of consciousness. Differences in the type and degree of altered consciousness may be related to differences in the temporal distortions.

CONCLUSIONS

To synthesize our studies of temporal distortions during marihuana intoxication, we should like to point out that the increased concentration on the present, reported in this paper, has been found to covary significantly with a confusion of past, present, and future and the emergence of a sense of timelessness. The different types of temporal distortions induced by marihuana are, therefore, interrelated processes. These related changes in time sense may be summarized as follows: Under the influence of marihuana, when a subject becomes less able to integrate past, present, and future, his awareness becomes more concentrated on present events; these instances, in turn, are experienced as prolonged or timeless when they appear isolated from the continual progression of time—that is, when the present events no longer seem to be transitions from the past to the future.

REFERENCES

1. Tart C.T.: Marihuana intoxication: Common experiences. *Nature* 226:701–704, 1970.
2. Clark L.D., Hughes R., Nakashima E.N.: Behavioral effects of marihuana. *Arch Gen Psychiat* 23:193–198, 1970.

3. Melges F.T., Tinklenberg J.R., Hollister L.E., et al.: Marihuana and temporal disintegration. *Science* 168:1118–1120, 1970.

4. Melges F.T. Tinklenberg J.R., Hollister L.E., et al.: Temporal disintegration and depersonalization during marihuana intoxication. *Arch Gen Psychiat* 23:204–210, 1970.

5. Song C.H., Kanter S.L., Hollister L.E.: Extraction and gas chromatographic quantification of tetrahydrocannabinol from marihuana. *Res Comm Chem Path Pharm* 1:375–382, 1970.

6. Mechoulam R.: Marihuana chemistry. *Science* 168:1159-1166, 1970.

7. Cohen J.: *Psychological Time in Health and Disease.* Springfield, Ill., C. C. Thomas Publisher, 1967, pp 27–39.

8. Nowlis V.: Research with the mood adjective check list, in Tomkins S., Isard C. (eds): *Affect, Cognition, and Personality.* New York, Springer Publishing, 1965, pp 352–389.

9. Wallace M., Rabin Al: Temporal experience. *Psychol Bull* 57:213–236, 1960.

10. Melges F.T., Bowlby: J.: Types of hopelessness in psycho-pathological process. *Arch Gen Psychiat* 20:690–699, 1969.

11. Tinklenberg, J.R., Melges F.T., Hollister L.E., et al.: Marihuana and immediate memory. *Nature* 226:1171–1172, 1970.

12. Caldwell D.F., Myers S.A., Domino E.F., et al.: Auditory and visual threshold effects of marihuana in man. *Percept Motor Skills* 29:755–759, 1969.

13. Tart C.T. (ed): *Altered States of Consciousness: A Book of Readings.* New York, John Wiley & Sons Inc., 1969.

14. Kenna J.C., Sedman G.: The subjective experience of time during lysergic acid diethylamide (LSD-25) intoxication. *Psychopharmacologia* 5: 280–288, 1964.

15. Huxley A.: *The Doors of Perception.* New York, Harper & Row Publishers Inc., 1963, p 21.

This study was supported in part by grants MH-03030 and KI-MH-29163 from the Public Health Service and by Stanford University grant 2HSZ-558.
Dr. H. Kraemer, C. Owen, J. Ettenborough, and S. Kanter assisted in this project.

Part 6

Marihuana and Memory

Considerable attention has been directed at the effects of marihuana on human memory. The anecdotal literature is replete with instances in which subjects report having to pause in the middle of a sentence because they have forgotten what they have just said. Preliminary studies of the effects of marihuana on speech patterns have in fact been conducted by Weil and Zinberg,[1] who confirm that marihuana does indeed have such an effect. In summarizing their results, these investigators observe that "this speech difficulty has two principal manifestations: simple forgetting of what one is going to say next and a strong tendency to go off on irrelevant tangents because the line of thought is lost." Weil and Zinberg also hypothesize that the reason marihuana has this effect is that it disrupts immediate rather than long-term memory.

The terminology surrounding the construct of memory is sometimes confusing, but basically the memory process can be thought of as involving the following steps. First, information must be acquired. In other words, there must be a stimulus input. This input then goes to a short-term store which is sometimes also referred to as immediate memory. From here, some of the input passes into a long-term storage, sometimes called permanent memory. The reason that all of the input does not go into permanent memory is that the neural traces corresponding to this information tend to decay with time. Therefore, only some of the traces will be fresh enough to be passed into long-term memory. In order to increase the probability that a piece of information does enter permanent memory, it is thus necessary to keep it in the immediate memory until it is encoded. This can be accomplished if that material is "rehearsed," i.e., the individual must repeat it over and over again to himself. A practical example is that of trying to retain a new telephone number in one's memory. To do this, the individual often says the number over and over again until it is dialed. Then it is promptly forgotten. However, if one has to make the same call a number of times, then the mere repetition of the numbers on each occasion helps to transfer it into permanent memory.

To recall information from permanent memory, a process called "retrieval" must occur. This process is analogous to a search through desk files. However, the search through the "files" of the brain is usually accomplished with incredible speed, so fast is it normally, that it almost seems automatic. However, sometimes there is an impediment to the search and it may take several minutes or even days before a fact is remembered. In the case of retrieval from permanent memory, the more cues there are to aid in the search, the easier it is to remember. In the case of retrieval from immediate memory, however, information can only be retrieved if it has not decayed at the time of the search.

To return now to the problem at hand—the effects of marihuana on memory—the following series of articles presents experimental evidence that the point in the memory process that is most affected by marihuana is the initial stage, that is, the one involving short-term or immediate memory. The first two articles in this chapter involve verification that marihuana does in fact affect memory and that this impediment can be demonstrated in the laboratory. In the next two studies, Abel presents evidence that permanent memory is not significantly affected by marihuana whereas acquisitional processes involving immediate memory do appear to be affected. This conclusion has been tendered by other investigators who have been working on the same problem but with a different methodology.[2] The last article constitutes a direct examination of the influence of marihuana on immediate memory and in general, the results tend to support the hypothesis. Given an equal chance to drop out of the short-term or immediate store, there is a greater loss following marihuana than without.

REFERENCES

1. A. T. Weil, and N. E. Zinberg, "Acute effects of marihuana on speech." *Nature,* 1969, *222,* 434–437.

2. F. T. Melges, J. R. Tinklenberg, L. E. Hollister, and H. K. Gillespie, "Marihuana and the temporal span of awareness," *Archiv. of Gen. Psychiat.,* 1971, *24,* 564–567; J. R. Tinklenberg, F. T. Melges, et al., "Marihuana and immediate memory." *Nature,* 1970, *226,* 1171-1172.

13

Marijuana and Memory

Ernest L. Abel

The effects of marijuana are not consistent from subject to subject.[1] Any discussion of its effect on human memory[2,3] must therefore consider whether valid generalizations can be drawn from the subjects who have been examined. One way of minimizing individual differences is to use subjects as their own controls, as is done in the present study which investigates the effects of marihuana on the recall of narrative material.

The subjects were eight men and women aged from 22 to 37. All but one were college students, and all had used marijuana several times before the experiment. Each was tested singly in two sessions separated by more than a month. In the first session, half of them were given marijuana and half acted as controls; in the second session, the roles were reversed. Those receiving the drug were given two marijuana cigarettes the tetrahydrocannabinol content of which had not been ascertained. After smoking both, each subject was allowed to relax or read. Five minutes later the experimenter asked the subject whether he felt "high." All subjects answered affirmatively.

The experimenter, who remained in the same room throughout the

Reprinted with permission of the publisher (Macmillan Journals), from *Nature*, 1970, *227*, 1151–1152.

test, then gave the subject a copy of Bartlett's *War of the Ghosts*,[4] and told him to read it through twice, at his own speed. When the subject had finished, the story was removed. Fifteen minutes later the experimenter gave the subject a pen and paper and asked him to recall as much of the story as he could accurately remember, using the same words and phrases if possible. When the subject had finished, the session was over. The control subjects were put through the same test without taking marijuana.

The protocols were subjected to King's method of analysis[5] which involves determining:

(1) The total number of words in each subject's version of the story.
(2) The number of "content words" with the exclusion of all articles, prepositions, conjunctions, and so on. Content words must have appeared in the original story, but can be misspelt or out of sequence.
(3) The number of two word sequences in the recalls which had appeared in the original.
(4) The number of correctly recalled four word sequences.
(5) The number of "idea units," appearing in the recalls, as defined by a division of the original protocol into such units.

Because this task required a certain amount of arbitrary judgment, the estimation was made by three arbiters who did not know the subjects or the conditions of the experiment. Their three scores were averaged to give the idea score for each recall. Table 1 shows the results of the analysis.

TABLE 1
COMPARISON OF RECALL MATERIAL UNDER MARIHUANA (M)
AND IN CONTROL CONDITIONS (C)

Subject	Total words		Identical content words		Two word sequences		Four word sequences		No. of idea units	
	C	M	C	M	C	M	C	M	C	M
S_1	227	214	66	66	45	30	9	5	52	42
S_2	267	256	67	59	39	49	10	11	53	55
S_3	234	155	61	27	41	17	9	1	50	28
S_4	55	45	15	12	11	1	2	0	12	5
S_5	170	159	42	30	31	17	6	4	34	26
S_6	265	221	73	47	51	36	7	10	50	32
S_7	215	197	63	51	39	34	9	6	40	40
S_8	177	204	68	53	32	44	6	12	47	40
Total	1,610	1,451	455	345	289	228	58	49	338	268
Average	201·3	181·4	56·9	43·1	36·1	28·5	7·3	6·1	42·3	33·5
	$t = 1·84$		$t = 3·69$		$t = 2·72$		$t = 0·91$		$t = 3·10$	
	n.s.		$P < 0·005$		$P < 0·025$		n.s.		$P < 0·01$	

Seven of the eight subjects wrote less under marihuana than in the control condition. On the binomial test for one-sample cases[6] this effect is significant at the 0·035 level. The difference between the total scores for two conditions, however, was not significant. When only the content words are considered, not only do the subjects perform worse under the influence of marihuana (P=0·035), but the number of recalled content words is also significantly less in this condition (P<0·005). The means were 56·9 and 43·1 for control and marijuana conditions respectively. The difference was evaluated by the t test for correlated means[7].

With the two-word sequences, only six subjects did worse under marijuana than in the control condition. This effect was not significant. When the total number of two-word sequences in the two conditions is considered, however, the difference between the two means (36·1 and 28·5 for control and marijuana conditions respectively) is significant at above the 0·025 level.

The final index was the number of idea units in the recalls. Once again, subjects under marijuana tended to do worse but the trend was not significant. The means for the marijuana and the control conditions were 42·3 and 33·5 respectively (P<0·01), indicating that when there was an effect, it was significant.

The result of being "high" in this experiment was that subjects were not as capable of reproducing material which they had recently read. Not only were subjects worse at recalling exact words, they were also worse at recalling the ideas of the story they had just read. It is also noteworthy that the degree of impairment is significant. One can thus expect more than minor differences in behaviour as a result of smoking marijuana. The nature and direction of these differences await further study. But although individuals did do worse under marijuana, they were still able to read, remember and write when they needed to.

One difficulty with this type of research is in determining the locus of the effect on memory; the methodology made it impossible to know whether the same amount of information entered the memory faculties before the subjects were asked to recall the material. If this were so, then the effects of marijuana would not be on memory but on the input of information before it can enter the memory. On the other hand, the material may enter the memory stores equally well in control and in "high" conditions, and the difficulty may be with retrieval, as Weil and Zinberg suggest[3]. This problem could be answered by having subjects read the same material under marijuana and then asking some to recall it under marijuana while others recall in control conditions.

REFERENCES

1. McGlothlin, W. H., *The Marihuana Papers* (Signet, New York, 1968.).

2. Mayor's Committee on Marihuana, *The Marihuana Problem in the City of New York* (1944).

3. Weil, A. T., and Zinberg, N. E., *Nature,* 222, 434 (1969).

4. Bartlett, F. C., *Remembering* (Cambridge University Press, 1932).

5. King, D. J., *J. Gen. Psychol.*, 75, 39 (1966).

6. Siegel, S., *Nonparametric Statistics* (McGraw-Hill, New York, 1956).

7. Hays, W. L., *Statistics for Psychologists* (Holt, Rinehart and Winston, New York, 1963).

I thank Miss C. Edwards, Miss M. Coombs and Mr K. Stang for acting as arbiters. This study was conducted while I was a postdoctoral fellow at the University of California at Berkeley.

14

Effects of Marijuana on Recall of Narrative Material and Stroop Colour-Word Performance

Loren Miller
W. G. Drew, and Glenn F. Kiplinger

Two recent articles[1,2] report that marijuana interferes with the recall of narrative material learned in either a drug or no drug state and recalled in the drug state, but the evaluation of the results is hampered by (1) the lack of specification of the Δ^9-THC content of the marihuana cigarettes and (2) an absence of placebo controls. We have set out to test the effects of marijuana on narrative recall and Stroop colour-word performance and to remedy these defects of experimental design. The Stroop test was selected because performance has been shown to be impaired by depressants such as amobarbital[3] and because marijuana has barbiturate-like effects[4].

Twelve paid volunteer students over 21 yrs old served as subjects. All of them smoked cigarettes and several had some previous experience with marijuana, but neither chronic marijuana users nor users of potent hallucinogens were included. Subjects were randomly divided into two equal groups and were allowed to smoke either a marijuana

Reprinted with permission of the authors and publisher (Macmillan Journals) from *Nature*, 1972, *237*, 172–173.

Loren Miller and W.G. Drew are affiliated with the Department of Psychiatry, Laboratories of Behavioral Neurophysiology, University of Kentucky Medical Center, Lexington, Kentucky. Glenn F. Kiplinger is affiliated with the Lilly Laboratory for Clinical Research and Department of Toxicology, Indiana University School of Medicine, Indianapolis, Indiana.

cigarette (500 mg) calibrated to deliver a dose of Δ^9-THC equivalent to 25 μg/ kg or a marijuana placebo cigarette, consisting of cannabinoid exhausted marijuana[8]. An observer was present to ensure that the cigarettes were smoked properly. Each subject smoked to a preset butt length within a 10-min period. All testing was performed in a double-blind fashion.

Thirty minutes after smoking began, an examiner read the Babcock Story and the subject was then asked to tell the examiner all he could remember about the story. Four degrees of increasing distortion[5] were noted together with two other recall errors. The four types of distortion were:

(1) type A (weight of 1) which involved substitution of words with similar meanings or the use of vague terms;

(2) type B (weight of 2) which consisted of a more radical type A distortion including the introduction of new elements;

(3) type C (weight of 3) which involved the introduction of new material having an emotional tone which had no specific source in the original story;

(4) type D (weight of 4) which involved the inclusion of arbitrarily unrelated material having a strong emotional tone which radically altered the story;

(5) out-of-place memories which were recorded when some segment of the story was recalled out of its correct sequence and separated from its original place by a complete thought;

(6) fragmentary memories were scored when a phrase or part of a phrase was remembered, but its relation to the story was lost.

After recall, Stroop colour-word performance was evaluated. Subjects were asked to view a screen on which a sequence of 100 words, 10 horizontal rows of 10 words each, were printed on a black background. Each of these words was printed in a colour which was unlike the word itself. Subjects were first required to read the words, and then to say the colour each word was printed in. Both the number of errors and the time to completion on each part of the test were the dependent variables.

The results of the Babcock-recall test are presented in Table 1. Differences between the marijuana and placebo groups on each of the distortions and memory units were evaluated by t tests. Marijuana-treated subjects made significantly more type C and D distortions and out-of-place distortions. There were no significant differences on type *A* and *B* distortions and fragmentary memories. The controls also recalled significantly more specific memory units as reflected in the unit score differences.

TABLE 1
EFFECTS OF MARIJUANA ON RECALL OF NARRATIVE MATERIAL

| | Distortions | | | | | | |
Treatment	*A*	*B*	*C*	*D*	Out of place	Frag-mentary	Memory units
Marijuana	3.17	2.33	3.00	8.00	3.00	2.00	7.50
Placebo	3.16	2.00	0.50	1.33	0.66	4.67	12.00
	NS	NS	$P < 0.025$	$P < 0.025$	$P < 0.05$	NS	$P < 0.025$

Stroop test performance did not vary as a function of marijuana treatment. Although the time to read the words was significantly shorter than the time to read colours, there were no significant differences between the marijuana and placebo groups. Error scores also were not different.

Performance on Babcock Story recall in the present study generally supports Abel's findings. The memory deficits seen here, however, not only involved an inability to remember specific material, but also involved the introduction of material not originally included in the narrative. The intrusion of irrelevant associations in the recall of narrative material has previously been noted by Clark[6]. Whether memory distortion is due to faulty acquisition or an impaired ability to retrieve information cannot be answered from this study. Performance on the Stroop colour-word test was unaffected by marijuana. It is possible that higher doses of THC in the cigarettes might produce both depressant and psychotomimetic effects which would affect Stroop test performance. According to Callaway, depressants and psychoto-mimetic drugs broaden the attention span resulting in an increase in responsiveness to environmental stimulation[7]. The subjects' ability to filter out irrelevant stimuli would be thus impaired. Whether or not marijuana can produce this effect can only be answered by increasing the dosage of Δ^9-THC delivered in the cigarette smoke.

REFERENCES

1. Abel, E. L., *Nature,* 227, 1151 (1970).
2. ———, *Nature,* 231, 260 (1971).
3. Callaway, E., *J. Ment. Sci.,* 105, 382 (1959).
4. Masur, J., Marty, R. M. W., and Carlini, E. A., *Psychophar-macologia,* 19, 388 (1971).

5. Rapaport, D., Gill, M. M., and Schafer, R., *Diagnostic Psychological Testing* (International University Press, New York, 1968).

6. Clark, L. D., Hughes, R., and Nakashima, F. N., *Arch. Gen. Psychiat.*, 23, 193 (1970).

7. Callaway, E., and Dembro, D., *Amer. Med. Assoc. Arch. Neurol. Psychiat.*, 79, 74 (1958).

8. Manno, J., Kiplinger, G. F., Bennett, I. F., Hayes, S., and Forney, R. B., *Clin. Pharmacol. Therap.*, 11, 808 (1970).

This study was supported by a grant from the US Public Health Service.

15

Retrieval of Information after Use of Marihuana

Ernest L. Abel

There is anecdotal and experimental evidence that human memory is adversely affected by smoking marihuana[1,2] but it remains to be determined where in the memory system this impairment occurs. In particular, does marihuana interfere with the encoding or registration of information in the memory or with the retrieval of information once it has been stored? This study is a preliminary investigation of the effects of marihuana on the retrieval aspect of memory.

Adult men and women between 21 and 30 were invited to take part in an experiment dealing with memory. Volunteers were asked whether they had previously used marihuana and only those admitting to such usage were then asked whether they wished to participate in one of the conditions of the experiment, that was to be given marihuana. Those not admitting usage were never given this option.

The experiment[3,4] involved the reading, to individual subjects, of fifteen lists of ten words each. Immediately after each ten-word list, the subject was required to recall, in any order, as many of the words as he could remember; this tested immediate free recall (IFR). They were allowed 1 min for this, after which the experimenter began to read the next list.

Reprinted with the permission of the publisher (Macmillan Journals) from *Nature*, 1971, *231*, 58.

After recall of the last list, experimental subjects smoked one marihuana cigarette (with an undetermined tetrahydrocannabinol content) for about 5 min. During the remainder of the interval before retesting, subjects were free to relax, read, or eat food that had been provided for them. Controls were treated exactly alike except that they were given no marihuana. Twenty-five minutes after the last list had been read to them, subjects were given 5 min. to write out as many of the words in the previous lists as they could remember; this tested delayed free recall (DFR). The subject was then given a list of three hundred words containing the one hundred and fifty "old" words interspersed with the same number of "new" words, and asked to encircle all words which he felt had been on the lists previously read to him. After completing this task, the Jackson personality research form (BB)[5] was administered to each subject to determine whether there were any differences between groups in their responses to the "achievement motivation" statements as a result of smoking marihuana. Jackson[5] has defined achievement motivation as a willingness "to put forth effort to attain excellence." The purpose of this questionnaire was to find out whether subjects in the marihuana group were less motivated to do well on the recall and recognition tasks. As a result, any differences obtained would be attributable not so much to impairment of retrieval processes, but rather to the fact that subjects in the marihuana group are not willing to put forth the effort needed to perform well on the memory tasks.

Of the twenty-four volunteers, ten subjects per group were matched as closely as possible on the basis of their performance in the IFR test. A Mann–Whitney analysis[6] indicated that the matching had resulted in no significant differences between groups on this initial, pretreatment task. These mean scores, along with those from the DFR, recognition, and motivation tasks, are presented in Table 1.

TABLE 1
Effects of Marihuana on Free Recall, Recognition and Achievement Motivation

Condition	Hits	False alarms	d'	β	IFR	DFR	Achievements
Control	63.5	8.7	1.068	2.560	100.6	13.9	11.1
Marihuana	77.7	38.9	0.667	1.209	91.9	15.2	10.4
	$U = 31$	$U = 15$	$U = 21$	$U = 13$	$U = 28$	$U = 36$	$U = 41$
	n.s.	$P < 0.01$	$P < 0.03$	$P < 0.01$	n.s.	n.s.	n.s.

The Mann–Whitney test indicated that the groups also did not differ on the DFR task or on the number of "old" words correctly recognized as being "old" (that is, the number of "hits"). Subjects given marihuana, however, reported significantly more "new" items as being "old" ("false alarms") than did controls (U=15, $P<0.01$). If the principles of signal detection theory[7] are applied to the recognition task, it is possible to examine the ratio of "hits" to "false" alarms" on the basis of the subject's true sensitivity (d') independent of any motivational factors or response biases which might have affected his discrimination between items, and it is also possible to determine how stringent a criterion (β) the subject uses in making his decision.

Analysis of these two indices indicates that not only does marihuana impair sensitivity or acuity in this type of discrimination task, it also tends to lower significantly the criterion on which he bases his decisions (Table 1). On the other hand, the scores from the Jackson[5] achievement motivation scales did not differ significantly for the two groups, which suggests that although marihuana lowers the subject's criterion, he, or she, still wishes to do as well on the experimental tasks as the control subject who has not been given marihuana.

The nonsignificant results of the DFR test suggest that marihuana does not interfere with the retrieval of information already stored in the memory. This then suggests that any impairment in memory caused by marihuana occurs because information fails to become encoded in the memory stores and therefore is not available for retrieval. We are examining this possibility at present.

To refer to the recognition task, however, it is clear that marihuana renders the individual less sensitive in discrimination problems involving a delayed response task. The "hit" and "false alarm" rates indicate that the marihuana and control groups were separated only by the number of "new" items each was willing to accept as "old." In other words, subjects under the influence of marihuana were as capable of picking out "old" items from the lists as the controls, but were less inclined to reject "new" items. This increased willingness to accept, or decreased tendency to reject, is similarly reflected in the lower criterion scores of subjects under the influence of marihuana.

REFERENCES

1. Abel, E. L., *Nature,* 227, 1151 (1970).
2. Tart, C. T., *Nature,* 226, 701 (1970).
3. Cohen, R. L., *J. Verbal Learning and Verbal Behavior* (in the press).
4. Craik, F. I. M., *J. Verbal Learning and Verbal Behavior,* 9, 143 (1970).

5. Jackson, D. N., *Personality Research Form* (Research Psychologists Press, Goshen, New York, 1966).

6. Siegel, S., *Nonparametric Statistics* (McGraw-Hill, New York, 1956).

7. Green, D. M., and Swets, J. A., *Signal Detection Theory and Psychophysics* (Wiley, New York, 1966).

16

Marihuana and Memory: Acquisition or Retrieval?

Ernest L. Abel

Marihuana has been shown to have deleterious effects on human memory.[1] The actual process by which this occurs, however, has not as yet been determined. For instance, marihuana may interfere with either acquisition of information, or storage of acquired information, or retrieval of stored material, or any combination of these processes. An earlier study[2] failed to detect any effect of marihuana on retrieval, thereby suggesting that acquisition or storage processes were being affected. The following studies were designed to investigate this possibility.

The first of the present studies constitutes a replication and extension of work by Abel[2] wherein marihuana was found to have no significant effect on the retrieval of information already present in memory. Forty-nine adult males and females served as either marihuana, placebo, or control subjects. Assignment of subjects was similar to that previously described[2], the only provision being that subjects that had not used marihuana previously were placed in either the control or the placebo condition. Subjects that were familiar with the effects of marijuana were allocated to any of the three test conditions.

Reprinted with the permission of the publisher from *Science*, 1971, *173*, 1038–1040. Copyright 1971 by the American Association for the Advancement of Science.

The design of the study was similar to that used by Cohen[3]. Eighteen ten-item lists of words were read aloud at a rate of approximately 1.5 seconds per word. One minute was allowed for spoken free recall of a list immediately after its presentation. After completion of the initial free recall of the last list, the subject was presented with a list containing 60 words, 30 of which had appeared on the first three lists of the prior test, along with 30 new items, or "lures." The subject was asked to circle all those he thought were on the prior lists, and for each item circled he was to indicate how confident he felt about the accuracy of response, using a 5-point scale similar to that used by Murdock[4]. This task lasted approximately 8 to 10 minutes, and will be referred to as the immediate recognition test.

Upon completing the task, subjects in the marihuana group were allowed to smoke one marihuana cigarette, the tetrahydrocannabinol content of which had not been determined. Subjects in the placebo group were given a cigarette containing ordinary tobacco, but were told that it had been dipped in tetrahydrocannabinol, the active ingredient in marihuana, and that as a result it would "taste and smell like tobacco, but the psychological effect will be like that of smoking marihuana." The smoking period lasted approximately 5 to 10 minutes. Control subjects were left undisturbed during this period.

Immediately after the smoking period, the experimenter made a pretense of testing "concept formation" and administered the Block Design Test and the Picture Arrangement Test—two subjects of the Wechsler-Bellevue Intelligence Test[5]. These tests were conducted for purposes of occupying the subjects with some distracting task in the time period between the end of the initial free recall test and the start of the next phase of the study. Twenty-five minutes after the initial free recall test, subjects in the marihuana and placebo conditions were given a 10-point rating scale and were asked to rate how "high" they felt at that moment (1, not high at all; 3, slightly high; 5, moderately high; 8, very high; 10, extremely high). The subjects were then given 5 minutes to write out as many words as they could remember from the prior lists (this task being delayed free recall). After this, a second recognition task was administered (delayed recognition). The test lists in this second recognition test contained 300 items, 150 items from the last 15 lists and 150 lures, none of which had been used in the first recognition test.

Only marihuana subjects who rated themselves at 5 or more were included in the analysis of the data. The marihuana subjects were then matched by inspection with an equal number of subjects in the control and placebo groups on the basis of their scores on the initial free recall test (N = 13 for each group). The words used in the initial free recall and recognition tests were selected from the lists in Thorndike and Lorge[6]. One-third were high-frequency words (A and AA), one-third were of low frequency (five or fewer occurrences per million), and the remaining third were of moderate frequency (20 to 30 per million). All words in a list were of the same word frequency.

The results are presented in Table 1. An analysis of variance[7] indicated that the differences between the three groups on the initial free recall test were not significant. The measures for the recognition test are taken from signal detection theory[8]. Briefly, "hits" refer to the number of items correctly identified as being on the lists previously read. "False alarms" refer to the number of lure items incorrectly identified as being on the lists. The index, d', is a measure of the subject's ability to discriminate between the correct and the incorrect items. It is based on the notion that the memory trace of a list item is similar to a signal which must be differentiated from background noise. This measure is assumed to be independent of any motivational bias. This latter factor is represented by β, which is an index of how cautious the subject is in making his decision.

TABLE 1
MARIHUANA EFFECTS ON RETRIEVAL MECHANISMS
Table 1. Effects of marihuana on retrieval mechanisms in free recall and recognition (mean number of words per subject).

Item	Treatments		
	Control	Placebo	Marihuana
Initial free recall	106.5	100.8	106.1
Immediate recognition			
Hits	6.1	6.1	5.9
False alarms	2.0	2.5	2.0
d'	1.8	1.6	1.5
β	2.0	2.2	1.8
Delayed free recall	11.9	9.9	8.0
Delayed recognition			
Hits	67.5	59.2	59.4
False alarms	19.5	16.2	26.8*
d'	1.2	1.2	0.8*
β	2.4	3.0	1.8*

* $P < .05$.

The differences between groups were not significant for any of these measures in the immediate recognition task. Although not presented in Table 1, words of high frequency were correctly recalled and recognized significantly more often than words of lower frequency, but this factor did not interact with any of the treatment factors.

There were also no significant differences between the groups in the delayed free recall task, although there was a slight trend in the direction of poorer recall under the marihuana condition. The analysis of the data, however, indicates that marihuana does not significantly interfere with the retrieval of information already present in the memory. On the other hand, recognition processes were significantly influenced by marihuana. While the number of items correctly identified was the same for all groups, subjects who had smoked marihuana were prone to accept more incorrect items as well. This latter difference is reflected in their lower sensitivity (d') and criterion (β) indices. These findings are similar to those previously reported[2] and indicate that under the influence of marihuana there is (i) a decrease in the ability of an individual to discriminate between items that were on a prior learning list and those that were not, and (ii) a tendency for individuals to be less cautious in reporting signals that may or may not have been presented in a prior learning list.

Having eliminated the possibility that retrieval processes are influenced by marihuana, I designed the following experiment to study the effects of marihuana on acquisition and storage.

The subjects were ten adult males and females, all of whom were familiar with the effects of marihuana. Each subject was tested twice. In the first session, one-half the subjects served as controls; the other half smoked marihuana prior to being tested. Approximately 1 week later, the roles were reversed, so that those that had been controls before were now given marihuana, and vice versa.

The procedure used by Caldwell et al.[9] was followed in allowing subjects to smoke as much marijuana as they wished in order to attain their own subjective "high." The experiment began 5 minutes after a subject had finished smoking the marihuana. As in the previous study, subjects were asked to rate how "high" they felt; all subjects rated themselves at either 7 or more on the 10-point scale. The test material consisted of ten lists of 12 words each. Two different sets of 10 word lists were employed so that subjects were not tested twice with the same material. The words were all of moderate frequency, and the rate of presentation was the same as that used in the first study. After the last list had been tested, subjects were given 5 minutes to write down as many of the words as they could recall from the test lists just presented.

All ten subjects remembered fewer words in the marihuana

condition in initial free recall ($P < .001$, binomial test). The mean total words recalled per subject were 66.7 and 50.9 for the control and the marihuana conditions, respectively. This is a difference of 13.17 percentage points based on the total 120 words. In the delayed free recall test, eight subjects out of ten did worse in the marihuana condition, one subject did better, and for the remaining subject there were no differences between conditions in total words recalled. If this latter subject is eliminated from the analysis, this result is also highly significant by the binomial test ($P < .02$). The mean numbers of words recalled per subject in delayed free recognition were 16.7 and 11.4 for control and marihuana conditions, respectively. This represents a difference of 4.42 percent.

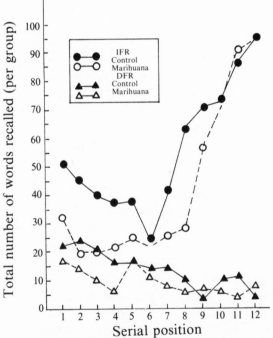

Fig. 1. Free recall as a function of serial position; *IFR,* initial free recall; *DFR,* delayed free recall.

These results demonstrate that marihuana interferes with learning processes. The nature of the effect on memory is depicted in Fig. 1, which shows the number of words correctly recalled for each serial position in the list. These data can be readily interpreted in terms of the model of human memory described by Shiffrin and Atkinson[10].

Applying this model to the initial free recall curves in Fig. 1, items in serial positions 10 to 12 may be assumed to be recalled from the sensory register component of memory. This is the store which receives information from the sense organs, and from which information is subject to rapid decay. Inspection of the curves for the marihuana and control conditions indicates that there are virtually no differences in this part of the curve, indicating that subjects are receiving information equally well in each condition. Items in serial positions 6 to 9 represent information recalled from the short-term store, which temporarily holds information that has entered it from the sensory register. Forgetting from the short-term store occurs via spontaneous decay. To prevent such decay, the subject must rehearse the information he wishes to retain so that it remains in the short-term store long enough to be transferred to the long-term store, which holds information permanently.

It can be seen from Fig. 1 that according to the model just described, there are more items recalled from both the short-term store (items 6 to 9) and the long-term store (items 1 to 5) for subjects in the control condition than in the marihuana condition. This means that information is probably being rehearsed to a greater extent in the control condition and, as a result, more information is entering the long-term store. The fact that more information enters the long-term store under control conditions is confirmed by the greater number of items that are recalled in delayed free recall in the control condition as compared with the marihuana condition.

Finally, for items to be rehearsed, subjects must fix their attention on retaining information after it has been presented. Upon being interviewed after the experiment, many of the subjects stated that after smoking marihuana they were simply unable to concentrate on the task long enough for them to perform to their best ability. This inability to concentrate is thus the most likely reason memory is adversely affected by marihuana. In not being able to concentrate, subjects cannot rehearse. As a result, information cannot be transferred to permanent memory.

REFERENCES AND NOTES

1. E. Abel, *Nature,* 227, 1152 (1970).
2. ———. *ibid.,* in press.
3. R. L., Cohen. *J. Verb. Learn. Verb. Behav.* 9, 672 (1970).

4. B. B. Murdock. *J. Exp. Psychol.* 70, 443 (1965).

5. D. Wechsler, *The Measurement of Adult Intelligence* (Williams, New York, 1939).

6. E. L. Thorndike and I. Lorge, *The Teacher's Handbook of 30,000 Words* (Columbia Univ. Press, New York, 1944).

7. A. L. Edwards, *Experimental Design in Psychological Research* (Holt, Rinehart & Winston, New York, 1965).

8. W. P. Banks, *Psychol. Bull.* 74, 81 (1970).

9. D. F. Caldwell, S. A. Myers, E. F. Domino, P. E. Merriam, *Percept. Mot. Skills* 29, 755 (1969).

10. R. M. Shiffrin and R. C. Atkinson, *Psychol. Rev.* 76, 179 (1969).

I thank R. L. Cohen for his helpful criticisms in the wording of this report.

17

Marijuana, Memory, and Perception

Rhea L. Dornbush
Max Fink, and Alfred M. Freedman

Previous experimental studies of the effects of marijuana on perceptual and cognitive functions have demonstrated minimal performance decrements, particularly with "low" doses.[1-3] Indeed, the most recent study[4] concludes that marijuana effects a very slight decrease in highest cortical functions. Where adverse effects have been obtained, they have been related to higher dose, task, and degree of experience with the drug[2,3,5].

In the present experiment, tests of short-term memory, reaction time, and time estimation were employed. While the latter two have been studied previously, no experiment has compared the differential effects of marijuana on performance in both the visual and auditory modalities, as was done in the present situation. In addition, heart rate and blood sugar were measured. (The latter has been used in the past as an index of hunger[3].) Finally, the relation of cortical activity, as reflected by electroencephalogram (EEG), to behavioral change was studied.

Reprinted with permission of the authors and publisher from the *American Journal of Psychiatry,* Vol. 128, 1971, pp. 194–197. Copyright 1971, the American Psychiatric Association.

Rhea L. Dornbush, Ph.D., is Assistant Professor, Max Fink, M.D., is Professor, and Alfred M. Freedman, M.D., is Professor and Chairman with the Department of Psychiatry, New York Medical College, New York, New York.

METHOD

Subjects. Ten first-year medical students served as paid subjects. Their mean age was 22 years, six months (standard deviation = six months). The subjects were selected from a larger sample on the basis of an interview and EEG and had similar histories of marijuana use. Each subject participated in six sessions: two placebo, two "high" dose sessions, and two "low" dose sessions, the order of which was randomized.

Procedure. Each subject was brought to the EEG laboratory and made comfortable on a couch in a supine position. Electrodes were applied for EEG recording and the subject was given appropriate instructions. The protocol used is shown in table 1. Double-blind procedures were employed, and minimal subject-experimenter interaction occurred.

TABLE 1
PROTOCOL FOR THE EXPERIMENT

Procedure	APPROXIMATE TIME Hours	Minutes
Blood Sample	0	00
EEG and heart rate	0	10
Smoking	0	25
EEG and heart rate	0	47
Task 1	0	52
EEG and heart rate	1	08
Task 2	1	13
EEG and heart rate	1	29
Task 3	1	34
EEG and heart rate	1	50
Blood sample	1	55

Marijuana. The marijuana, supplied by the National Institute of Mental Health, had a 1.5 percent delta-9-tetrahydrocannabinol (THC) content. Two doses were used as follows:

	low	high
Marijuana	500 mg.	1500 mg.
THC content	7.5 mg.	22.5 mg.

Marijuana doses were divided equally into two hand-rolled cigarettes, each consisting of 1 gm. of material as follows:

	low	high	placebo
Marijuana	250 mg.	750 mg.	-0-
Oregano	750 mg.	250 mg.	1000 mg.
	1000 mg.	1000 mg.	1000 mg.

Oregano was used as filler material and as placebo because it is similar to marijuana in appearance, odòr, and taste.

Each subject smoked the first cigarette at his own rate but was paced as to the length of draw and maintenance of the inhalation. There were no significant differences in number of puffs per cigarette for each subject or mean smoking time among sessions.

Tasks. The three tasks were presented in prearranged random order. For short-term memory, the subject was presented with a consonant trigram, e.g., DKF, and required to recall that trigram either immediately or after filled retention intervals of 0, 6, 12, or 18 seconds. One list of 16 trigrams was used at each session, four trigrams at each retention interval. Trigrams were presented on a preprogrammed auditory tape.

Simple reaction time in both the visual and auditory modalities was measured by requiring the subject to respond as rapidly as possible to either a single auditory stimulus or a single visual stimulus. There were 24 auditory and 24 visual trials counterbalanced for practice and fatigue effects; the preparatory interval was varied.

For time estimation, the method of reproduction in which the subject has to reproduce the duration of a prior stimulus was used. As in reaction time, time estimation was measured in both the visual and auditory modalities by the presentation of either a single visual or a single auditory stimulus. Three stimulus durations were employed: one second, two seconds, and five seconds. There were 24 auditory and 24 visual trials, and each stimulus duration occurred eight times (randomly) in each modality.

The EEG was recorded from the right occipital-vertex derivation, using a Grass polygraph. The magnetic tape records were analyzed by period analysis, using an IBM 1800 digital computer, 320 samples per second in 20-second epochs.

RESULTS

Short-term memory. Data from low-dose conditions did not differ from placebo; the greatest interference with memory was seen in the high-dose conditions and the effect was greater with longer delays in reporting the trigrams. The data were analyzed by a three-way analysis of variance, which indicated that the effects of sessions ($F_{5.45} = 3.89$), retention intervals ($F_{3.27} = 41.20$), and the interaction between sessions

FIGURE 1
Effects of Marijuana on Short-Term Memory

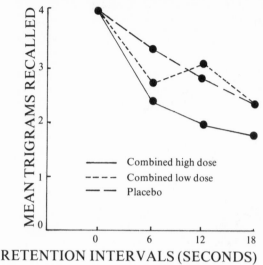

RETENTION INTERVALS (SECONDS)

and retention intervals ($F_{15.135} = 2.01$) were significant beyond the .05 level (figure 1).

Reaction time. As with short-term memory, low-dose marijuana did not affect auditory or visual reaction time, but reaction time in both modalities was longer ($F_{5.39} = 4.08$; $p < .05$) with higher doses (figure 2). Auditory reaction time was shorter than visual ($F_{1.8} = 16.28$; $p < .01$), but this finding is not specific to marijuana.

Moment-to-moment fluctuation in reaction time did occur but with equal frequency in each group, including placebo.

Time estimation. Estimation of time was unaffected by either dose of marijuana; typically, however, smokers report that the perception of time is changed under the influence of marijuana. That such was not the case here may be related to the method of measurement used—that of reproduction; this method has been found not to be sensitive to changes in time estimation[6].

Blood sugar. Blood sugar levels were not significantly affected by marijuana; however, they did increase significantly over time ($F_{1.9} = 8.19$; $p < .05$). When questioned at the end of each session, one-half of the subjects indicated increased hunger, the remaining subjects indicated no increase. As blood sugar was measured once before smoking and once at the end of the experiment, it is possible that changes

FIGURE 2
Effects of Marijuana on Reaction Time

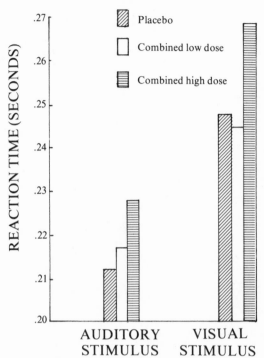

may have occurred between these measurements that were unobserved.

Heart rate. This measure was clearly altered by marijuana. Heart rate was measured (simultaneously with EEG) before smoking, immediately after smoking, and 20 minutes, 40 minutes, and 60 minutes after smoking. In the placebo condition, heart rate decreased consistently from presmoking levels. Heart rate under the high-dose conditions increased immediately after smoking and then gradually decreased, reaching presmoking levels approximately 40 minutes after smoking (figure 3). Heart rate after low doses also increased immediately after smoking and then decreased, reaching presmoking levels within 20 minutes; it then followed the course of placebo.

An analysis of variance indicated a drug effect on heart rate ($F_{4.36} = 11.19$; $p < .001$) reflecting differences between low and high dose, and between high-dose and placebo conditions. There was also a significant difference in heart rate depending on the time it was measured ($F_{4.36} = 35.07$; $p < .001$). In this instance, heart rate was different at each point

FIGURE 3
Effects of Marijuana on Heart Rate

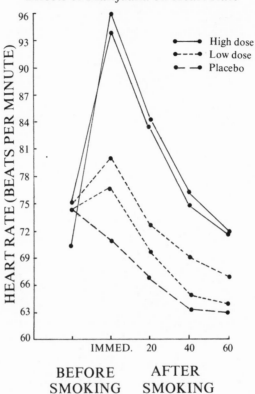

BEFORE   AFTER
SMOKING   SMOKING

from every other point except for presmoking versus 20 minutes after smoking, and 40 minutes after smoking versus 60 minutes after smoking. The interaction of drug and time of heart rate measurement was also significant ($F_{16.140} = 12.16$; $p < .001$), representing changes in heart rate in both high and low conditions immediately after smoking.

EEG. The EEG results are presented in summary here and more fully elsewhere.[7] The EEG effects were rapid in onset and changed at the time of the first postsmoking record (immediately after smoking). The principal changes were an increase in percent time alpha (8–13.5 Hz), and decreases in percent time theta (4–7.5 Hz) and beta (18.5–24.5 Hz) activities. Using regression analysis, the differences between high dose and both low dose and placebo effects are seen principally in the differences in intercepts.

DISCUSSION

These data support and extend the reports by Rodin and associates[4] and Weil and Zinberg[3]. On the tasks that were adversely affected by marijuana (short-term memory and reaction time), behavioral changes were observed only at the high dose. At the low dose, performance was indistinguishable from placebo. It is interesting to note, however, that even though overt behavior is unaffected by low doses of marijuana, heart rate, EEG, and possibly other physiological measures not observed in this experiment are altered with low doses.

It is difficult to extend the definition of "high" and "low" from the laboratory to the social situations in which subjects smoke marijuana. However, even knowing the *amount* of marijuana consumed in social situations is not adequate, as its chemical constituents, and therefore its potency, may vary from a similar amount of marijuana used on another occasion. In fact, even in the laboratory there is a need to determine and carefully monitor the content of active constituents in marijuana and its extracts throughout any given study. Ongoing analyses in our laboratory and the report by Rodin and associates[4] indicate that the potency of marijuana, measured by its constituents such as THC, deteriorates rapidly. The content of delta-9-THC is used as the standard for defining potency of cannabis preparations. This approximation may be invalid since constituents other than delta-9-THC may be the "active" principal constituent, and indeed some recent studies have been focused on other derivatives[8].

The direct relationship between dose and effect with cannabis suggests that this compound follows established principles of clinical pharmacology; studies that fail to identify the type of material, dose and amount of chemical constituents, and assay methods and standards ought to be ignored.

REFERENCES AND NOTES

1. Clark LD, Nakashima EN: Experimental studies of marihuana. *Amer J Psychiat* 125:379–384, 1968
2. Melges FT, Tinklenberg JP, Hollister LE, et al: Marihuana and temporal disintegration. *Science* 168:1118–1120, 1970
3. Weil AT, Zinberg NE, Nelsen JM: Clinical and psychological effects of marihuana in man. *Science* 162:1234–1242, 1968
4. Rodin EA, Domino EF, Porzak JP: The marijuana-induced "social high." *JAMA* 213:1300–1302, 1970

5. Hollister LE: Marijuana in man: three years later. *Science* 172:21–29, 1971

6. Carlson VR, Feinberg I: Individual variations in time and judgment and the concept of an internal clock. *J Exp Psychol* 77:631–640, 1968

7. Volavka J, Dornbush R, Feldstein S, et al: Marijuana, EEG, and behavior. *Ann NY Acad Sci* (in press)

8. Christensen HD, Freudenthan RI, Gidley JT, et al: Activity of Δ^8- and Δ^9-tetrahydrocannabinol and related compounds in the mouse. *Science* 172: 165–167, 1971

Read at the 124th annual meeting of the American Psychiatric Association, Washington, D.C., May 3–7, 1971.

This work was supported in part by Public Health Service grants MH-13358 and MH-18172 from the National Institute of Mental Health and by a contract from the New York State Narcotic Addiction Control Commission.

Part 7

Effects of Marihuana on Psychomotor Skills

In a recent study that has received a great deal of publicity, Crancer and his coworkers reported that marihuana had very little effect on simulated driving skills. Since performance on such simulated tasks has previously been shown to correlate with actual driving records, these results were accepted by some as evidence that marihuana does not affect true driving skills, although Crancer and his coworkers were much more cautious in their conclusions. Another of the controversial aspects of this study involved the attempt to compare the effects produced by marihuana with those of alcohol. The reason for the criticism was that only single doses of these drugs were used and no attempt was made to equate the drugs on the basis of dosage.

A similar study of the effects of marihuana on simulated driving skills has been reported by Rafaelsen and his associates.[1] These investigators, in contrast to the Crancer group, found that "socially relevant" amounts of marihuana, taken orally, had the effect of increasing "brake time."

One factor that should be taken into consideration in investigations of this sort, however, involves comparisons of the effects on naive and chronic users of marihuana. For example, the La Guardia commission[2] found that cannabis had much less of an effect on choice reaction time and hand steadiness in chronic users compared to drug-naive subjects. Similarly, Weil, Zinberg, and Nelson[3] observed dose-dependent decreases in the performance of drug-naive subjects on a "Pursuit Rotor Test" (which involves attention and muscular coordination) but could find no effect on this task in experienced users, even with high doses. Similar results have also been noted by Clark, Hughes, and Nakashima,[4] and Manno et al.[5]

These experiments involving simple motor skills suggest that marihuana may in fact not have any major effects on more complicated skills for chronic users of marihuana, provided, of course, that the amount of marihuana is not greater than that usually taken. However, these studies are still only in the preliminary stage of research and it will be quite some time before the effects of marihuana on driving skills are fully known.

REFERENCES AND NOTES

1. O. J. Rafaelsen, P. Bech, J. Christiansen, H. Christrup, I. Nybor, and L. Rafaelsen, "Cannabis and Alcohol: Effect on Simulated Car Driving," *Science,* 1973, *173,* 920–923

2. Mayor's Committee on Marihuana. *The Marihuana Problem in the City of New York*. Lancaster, Penn.: J. Cattell Press, 1944.

3. A. T. Weil, N. E. Zinberg, and J. M. Nelson, "Clinical and Psychological Effects of Marihuana in Man," *Science,* 1968, *162,* 1234–1242.

4. L. D. Clark, R. Hughes, and E. N. Nakashima, "Behavioral effects of marihuana." *Archiv. Gen. Psychiat.,* 1970, *23,* 193–198.

18

Comparison of the Effects of Marihuana and Alcohol on Simulated Driving Performance

Alfred Crancer, Jr.
James M. Dille, Jack C. Delay
Jean E. Wallace, and Martin D. Haykin

We have determined the effect of a "normal social marihuana high" on simulated driving performance among experienced marihuana smokers. We compared the degree of driving impairment due to smoking marihuana to the effect on driving of a recognized standard—that is, legally defined intoxication at the presumptive limit of 0.10 percent alcohol concentration in the blood. This study focused attention on the effect of smoking marihuana rather than on the effect of ingesting Δ^9-tetrahydrocannabinol (Δ^9-THC), the principal active component.

Weil et al.[1] have studied the clinical and psychological effects of smoking marihuana on both experienced and inexperienced subjects. They suggest, as do others[2], that experienced smokers when "high" show no significant impairment as judged by performance on selected tests; they also establish the existence of physiological changes that are useful in determining whether a subject smoking marihuana is "high." A review of the relation of alcohol to fatal accidents[3] showed that

---

Reprinted with the permission of the authors and publisher from *Science*, 1969, *164*, 851–854.
Copyright 1969 by the American Association for the Advancement of Science.
Alfred Crancer, Jr., Jack C. Delay, and Jean E. Wallace are all affiliated with the Division of Research, Department of Motor Vehicles, Olympia, Washington. James M. Dille is associated with the Department of Pharmacology and Martin D. Haykin with the Department of Psychiatry at the University of Washington, Seattle, Washington.

nearly half of the drivers fatally injured in an accident had an alcohol concentration in the blood of 0.05 percent or more.

Crancer[4] found a driving simulator test to be a valid indicator for distinguishing driving performance; this result was based on a 5-year driving record. Further studies[5] indicated that a behind-the-wheel road test is not significantly correlated to driving performance. We therefore chose the simulator test, which presents a programmed series of emergency situations that are impractical and dangerous in actual road tests.

Subjects were required to be (i) experienced marihuana smokers who had been smoking marihuana at least twice a month for the past 6 months, (ii) licensed as a motor vehicle operator, (iii) engaged in a generally accepted educational or vocational pursuit, and (iv) familiar with the effects of alcohol. The subjects were given (i) a physical examination to exclude persons currently in poor health or under medication, and (ii) a written personality inventory (Minnesota Multiphasic Personality Inventory) to exclude persons showing a combination of psychological stress and inflexible defense patterns. Seven of the subjects were females and 29 were males (mean age, 22.9).

We compared the effects of a marihuana "high," alcohol intoxication, and no treatment on simulated driving performance over a 4 1/2-hour period. We used a Latin-square analysis of variance design[6] to account for the effects of treatments, subjects, days, and the order in which the treatments were given. To measure the time response effects of each treatment, simulator scores were obtained at three constant points in the course of each experimental period. A sample of 36 subjects was determined to be sufficient in size to meet the demands of this experimental design.

Three treatments were given to each subject. In treatment M (normal social marihuana "high"), the experimental subject stated that he experienced the physical and psychological effects of smoking marihuana in a social environment comparable to his previous experiences. This subjective evaluation of "high" was confirmed by requiring a minimum consumption of marihuana established with a separate test group, and by identifying an increase in pulse rate[1].

In treatment M, the subjects smoked two marihuana[7] cigarettes of approximately equal weight and totaling 1.7 g. They completed smoking in about 30 minutes and were given their first simulator test 30 minutes later.

Some confirmation that the amount of marihuana smoked was

sufficient to produce a "high" is found in Weil's[1] study. His subjects smoked about 0.5 g of marihuana of 0.9 percent Δ^9-THC.

In treatment A, subjects consumed two drinks containing equal amounts of 95 percent alcohol mixed in orange or tomato juice. Dosage was regulated according to subject's weight with the intended result of a 0.10 blood alcohol concentration as determined by a Breathalyzer reading[8]. Thus, a subject weighing 120 pounds received 84 ml of 95 percent laboratory alcohol equally divided between two drinks. This was equivalent to about 6 ounces of 86 proof liquor. The dosage was increased 14 ml or 1/2 ounce for each additional 15 pounds of body weight. A Breathalyzer reading was obtained for each subject about 1 hour after drinking began; most subjects completed drinking in 30 minutes.

Treatment C consisted of waiting in the lounge with no treatment for the same period of time required for treatments M and A. The experimental subject stated that his physiological and psychological condition was normal. Subjects were requested to refrain from all drug or alcohol use during the time they were participating in the experiment.

A driver-training simulator was specially modified to obtain data on the effect of the treatments. The car unit was a console mockup of a recent model containing all the control and instrument equipment relevant to the driving task. The car unit faced a 6- by 18-foot screen upon which the test film was projected. The test film gave the subject a driver's eye view of the road as it led him through normal and emergency driving situations on freeways and urban and suburban streets. From the logic unit, located to the rear of the driver, the examiner started the automated test, observed the subject driving, and recorded the final scores.

A series of checks was placed on the 23-minute driving film which monitored driver reactions to a programmed series of driving stimuli. The test variables monitored were: accelerator (164 checks), brake (106 checks), turn signals (59 checks), steering (53 checks), and speedometer (23 checks). There was a total of 405 checks, allowing driver scores to range from zero to 405 errors per test. Errors were accumulated as follows.

1) Speedometer errors: Speedometer readings outside the range of 15 to 35 mile/hour for city portion of film and 45 to 65 mile/hour for freeways. The speed of the filmed presentation is

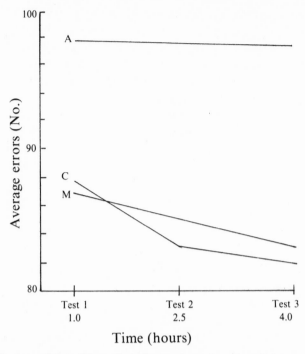

Fig. 1. Display of the effect of each treatment on simulator error scores over a 4-hour period. Alcohol (A), marihuana (M), and control (C).

not under the control of the driver. Therefore, speedometer errors are not an indication of speeding errors, but of the amount of time spent monitoring the speedometer.

2) Steering errors: Steering wheel in other than the appropriate position.

3) Brake errors: Not braking when the appropriate response is to brake, or braking at an inappropriate time.

4) Accelerator errors: Acceleration when the appropriate response is to decelerate, or deceleration when it is appropriate to accelerate.

5) Signal errors: Use of turn signal at an inappropriate time or position.

6) Total errors: An accumulation of the total number of errors on the five test variables.

Two rooms were used for the experiment. The lounge, designed to provide a familiar and comfortable environment for the subjects, was approximately 12 feet square and contained six casual chairs, a refrigerator, a desk, and several small movable tables. The room was lighted by a red lava lamp and one indirect red light, and contemporary rock music was played. Snacks, soft drinks, ashtrays, wastebaskets, and a supply of cigarettes were readily available. Subjects remained in this room except during simulator tests.

The driving simulator was located in a larger room about 50 feet from the lounge. The simulator room was approximately 20 by 30 feet and was kept in almost total darkness.

Each subject took three preliminary tests on the driving simulator to familiarize himself with the equipment and to minimize the effect of learning through practice during the experiment. Subjects whose error scores varied by more than 10 percent between the second and third tests were given subsequent tests until the stability criterion was met.

The experiment was conducted over a 6-week period. Six subjects were tested each week. On day 1, six subjects took a final test on the driving simulator to assure recent familiarity with the equipment. A "normal" pulse rate was recorded, and each was given two marihuana cigarettes of approximately 0.9 g each. Subjects smoked the marihuana in the lounge to become acquainted with the surroundings and other test subjects, and with the potency of the marihuana. A second pulse reading was recorded for each subject when he reported that he was "high" in order to obtain an indication of the expected rate increase during the experiment proper. They remained in the lounge for approximately 4 hours after they had started smoking.

Three of the subjects were scheduled for testing in the early evening on days 2, 4, and 6; the remaining three subjects for days 3, 5, and 7. A single treatment was given each evening. Within a given week, all subjects received treatments in the same order. Treatment order was changed from week to week to meet the requirements of a Latin-square design. Procedure for each evening was identical except for the specific treatment.

Subject 1 arrived at the laboratory and took the simulator warm-up test. Treatment A, M, or C was begun at zero hour and finished about 1/2 hour later. One hour after treatment began, subject 1 took simulator test 1, returning to the lounge when he was finished. He took simulator test two 2 1/2 hours after treatment began, and test three 4 hours after treatment began. Pulse or Breathalyzer readings, depending on the treatment, were taken immediately before each simulator test.

Subject 2 followed the same schedule, beginning 1/2 hour after subject 1. Time used in testing one subject each evening was 4 1/2 hours, with a total elapsed time of 5 1/2 hours to test three subjects.

The three simulator tests taken after each treatment establish a time response effect for the treatment. For each treatment the total error scores for each time period were subjected to an analysis of variance. Table 1 presents the analysis of variance for period 1 scores; results comparable to these were obtained for scores in periods 2 and 3.

The simulated driving scores for subjects experiencing a normal social marihuana "high" and the same subjects under control conditions are not significantly different (Table 1). However, there are significantly more errors ($P < .01$) for intoxicated than for control subjects (differences of 15.4 percent). This finding is consistent with the mean error scores of the three treatments: control, 84.46 errors; marihuana, 84.49 errors; and alcohol, 97.44 errors.

The time response curves for "high" and control treatments are comparable (Fig. 1). In contrast, the curve for alcohol shows more total errors ($P < .01$). These higher error scores for alcohol persist across all three time periods with little evidence of the improvement shown under the other two treatments.

TABLE 1
DRIVING SIMULATOR ERROR ANALYSIS

Analysis of variance of total driving simulator error scores for three treatments: marihuana (M), control (C), and alcohol (A).

Source of variation	Sum of squares	Degrees of freedom	Mean square	Mean square ratios
Treatments	2,595.1	2	1,297.5	6.7*
M versus C	(11.7)	(1)	11.7	0.1
A versus M and C	(2,583.4)	(1)	2,583.4	13.3**
Days	738.5	2	369.3	1.9
Subjects	40,872.5	24	1,703.0	9.7**
Squares	13,708.5	11	1,247.2	6.4**
Pooled error	13,253.8	68	194.9	
Total	71,168.4	107		

$*P < .05.$ $**P < .01.$

A separate Latin-square analysis of variance was completed for each test variable to supplement the analysis of total errors (Table 2). In comparison of intoxicated and control subjects, significant differences ($P < .05$) were found for accelerator errors in periods 1 and 2, for signal errors in periods 1, 2, and 3, for braking errors in periods 2 and 3, and for speedometer errors in period 1. In the comparison of marihuana smokers and controls, a significant difference ($P < .05$) was found for speedometer errors in period 1. In all of these cases, the number of errors for the drug treatments exceeded the errors for the control treatment.

TABLE 2
DRIVING SIMULATOR ERROR LATIN-SQUARE ANALYSIS

Significant treatment differences from Latin-square analysis of variance *(P* < .05). Accelerator, signal, and total errors are significantly correlated with driving performance for normal drivers. No correlation was found for brake, speedometer, and steering errors; A > C, M > C indicate that error scores for alcohol (A) or marihuana (M) treatment are greater than control (C).

Simulator test	Test variable errors					
	Accelerator	Signal	Total	Brake	Speedometer	Steering
Period 1	A > C	A > C	A > C	None	A > C M > C	None
Period 2	A > C	A > C	A > C	A > C	None	None
Period 3	None	A > C	A > C	A > C	None	None

Other sources of variation are Latin squares, subjects, and days. In all of the analyses, the effect of subjects and Latin squares (representing groups of subjects) were significant (*P*<.05). In contrast, the effect of days was not significant, thus indicating that no significant amount of learning was associated with repeated exposure to the test material.

For normal drivers, Crancer[4] found a significant correlation (*P* < .05) between the three simulator test variables (signals, accelerator, and total errors) and driving performance. An increase in error scores was associated with an increase in number of accidents and violations on a driving record. In the same study, error scores for brake, speedometer, and steering were not correlated with driving performance.

It may not be valid to assume the same relationship for persons under the influence of alcohol or marihuana. However, we feel that, because the simulator task is a less complex but related task, deterioration in simulator performance implies deterioraton in actual driving performance. We are less willing to assume that nondeterioration in simulator performance implies nondeterioration in actual driving. We therefore conclude that finding significantly more accelerator, signal, and total errors by intoxicated subjects implies a deterioration in actual driving performance.

Relating speedometer errors to actual driving performance is highly speculative because Crancer[4] found no correlation for normal drivers. This may be due in part to the fact that the speed of the filmed presentation is not under the control of the driver. However, speedometer errors are related to the amount of time spent monitoring the speedometer. This increase of speedometer errors by intoxicated or "high" subjects probably indicates that the subjects spent less time monitoring the speedometer than under control conditions.

This study could not determine if the drugs would alter the speed at which subjects normally drive. However, comments by marihuana users may be pertinent. They often report alteration of time and space perceptions, leading to a different sense of speed which generally results in driving more slowly.

Weil et al.[1] emphasize the importance and influence of both subject bias (set) and the experimental environment (setting). For this study, the environmental setting was conducive to good performance under all treatments.

Traditional methods for controlling potential subject bias by using placebos to disguise the form or effect of the marihuana treatment were not applicable. This is confirmed by Weil et al.[1]; they showed that inexperienced subjects correctly appraised the presence or absence of a placebo in 21 of 27 trials.

The nature of selection probably resulted in subjects who preferred marihuana to alcohol and, therefore, had a set to perform better with marihuana. The main safeguard against bias was that subjects were not told how well they did on any of their driving tests, nor were they acquainted with the specific methods used to determine errors. Thus, it would have been very difficult intentionally and effectively to manipulate error scores on a given test or sequence of tests.

A further check on subject bias was made by comparing error scores on the warm-up tests given before each treatment. We found no significant difference in the mean error scores preceding the treatments of marihuana, alcohol, and control. This suggests that subjects were not "set" to perform better or worse on the day of a particular treatment.

In addition, an inspection of chance variation of individual error scores for treatment M shows about half the subjects doing worse and half better than under control conditions. This variability in direction is consistent with findings reviewed earlier, and we feel reasonably certain that a bias in favor of marihuana did not influence the results of this experiment.

A cursory investigation of dose response was made by retesting four subjects after they had smoked approximately three times the amount of marihuana used in the main experiment. None of the subjects showed a significant change in performance.

Four additional subjects who had never smoked marihuana before were pretested to obtain control scores, then given marihuana to smoke until they were subjectively "high" with an associated increase in pulse rate. All subjects smoked at least the minimum quantity established for the experiment. All subjects showed either no change or negligible improvement in their scores. These results suggest that impairment in simulated driving performance is not a function of increased marihuana dosage or inexperience with the drug.

A significant difference ($P < .01$) was found between pulse rates before and after the marihuana treatment. Similar results were reported[1] for both experienced and inexperienced marihuana subjects. We found no significant difference in pulse rates before and after drinking.

Thus, when subjects experienced a social marihuana "high," they accumulated significantly more speedometer errors on the simulator than under control conditions, but there were no significant differences in accelerator, brake, signal, steering, and total errors. The same subjects intoxicated from alcohol accumulated significantly more accelerator, brake, signal, speedometer, and total errors than under control conditions, but there was no significant difference in steering errors. Furthermore, impairment in simulated driving performance apparently is not a function of increased marihuana dosage or inexperience with the drug.

REFERENCES AND NOTES

1. A. T. Weil, N. E. Zinberg, J. M. Nelsen, *Science* 162, 1234 (1968).
2. Mayor's Committee on Marihuana, *The Marihuana Problem in the City of New York* (1944).
3. W. J. Haddon and V. A. Braddess, *J. Amer. Med. Ass.* 169, No. 14, 127 (1959); J. R. McCarroll and W. J. Haddon, *J. Chronic Dis.* 15, 811 (1962); J. H. W. Birrell, *Med. J. Aust.* 2, 949 (1965); R. A. Neilson, *Alcohol Involvement in Fatal Motor Vehicle Accidents in Twenty-Seven California Counties in 1964* (California Traffic Safety Foundation, San Francisco, 1965).
4. A. Crancer, *Predicting Driving Performance with a Driver Simulator Test* (Washington Department of Motor Vehicles, Olympia, 1968).
5. J. E. Wallace and A. Crancer, *Licensing Examinations and Their Relation to Subsequent Driving Record* (Washington Department of Motor Vehicles, Olympia, 1968).

6. A. E. Edwards, *Experimental Design in Psychological Research* (Holt, Rinehart & Winston, New York, 1968), pp. 173–174.

7. The marihuana was an assayed batch (1.312 percent Δ^9-THC) from NIH through the cooperation of Dr. J. A. Scigliano.

8. L. A. Greenberg, *Quart. J. Studies Alcohol,* 29, 252 (1968).

Part 8

Physiological Effects

The two most commonly reported physiological effects resulting from the use of cannabis are a reddening of the eyes and an increase in heart pulse rate. The effect on the eyes has been attributed to a swelling of the minor conjunctival blood vessels in this area. The increase in pulse rate has been extensively documented and has been shown to be dose-dependent. The more Δ^9-THC given to the subject, the greater the pulse rate. This dose response effect is described in the first article by Johnson and Domino. The next paper by Renault and his coworkers corroborates this dose-response relationship and describes one of the ways in which inhalation patterns can be brought under laboratory control so that equal amounts of the drug can be administered to each subject in a manner that resembles the typical way of using marihuana outside the laboratory.

The paper by Renault and his associates is also interesting in that these investigators did not discern any differences between inexperienced and experienced users of marihuana with respect to the increase in heart rate produced by marihuana. The second point of interest in their study is the large intersubject variability in responsiveness to this drug; while all subjects manifest the same kind of change in pulse rate, the extent of this change differs in each subject.

The third paper by Galanter, Wyatt and their associates is also worth noting because of the fact that these investigators were able to demonstrate time differences in the onset of heart rate changes and psychological changes. Although the effects of Δ^9-THC on pulse rate reach a peak around fifteen minutes after administration of the drug, subjective experiences do not reach their peak until one hour after drug-taking. The demonstration that these subjective experiences follow the physiological changes may also have important implications for the panic reactions which cannabis produces in individuals who have not previously used the drug. Not knowing exactly what to expect, these naive users may become alarmed by autonomic changes such as the increased heart rate which they have previously encountered—primarily in fight-flight situations.

19

Some Cardiovascular Effects of Marihuana Smoking in Normal Volunteers

Stephen Johnson and Edward F. Domino

Many observers[6, 7, 10] have noted a significant dose-related increase in pulse rate in subjects smoking marihuana. While studying the effects of marihuana on the electroencephalogram (EEG) and on tests of perception and cognitive function, we observed premature ventricular contractions in 2 healthy subjects. A search of previous publications on marihuana revealed little detail about its cardiovascular effects. In view of the large number of marihuana smokers of all ages and the increasing interest in possible therapeutic uses of marihuana, we thought it important to investigate more thoroughly its cardiovascular actions.

MATERIALS AND METHODS

This study was performed in two parts. In 1969, 10 subjects took part in a low-dose (0.5 percent Δ-9-tetrahydrocannabinol [THC]) marihuana study and then in a single-blind placebo (0 percent Δ-9-THC)

Reprinted with permission of the authors and publisher from *Clinical Pharmacology and Therapeutics*, *12:* 762—768, 1971; copyrighted by the C. V. Mosby Company, St. Louis, Mo.

Stephen Johnson, M.D., is a resident in neurology at the Montreal Neurological Hospital, Montreal, Quebec. Edward F. Domino, M.S., M.D., is affiliated with the Lafayette Clinic, Detroit, Michigan, and with the Department of Pharmacology of the University of Michigan Medical School, Ann Arbor, Michigan.

study. In early 1971, 15 different subjects took part in a high-dose (2.9 percent Δ-9-THC) marihuana study. All subjects were men between the ages of 21 and 33. All had smoked marihuana previously, but only 4 of 10 in the low-dose study and 2 of 15 in the high-dose study were daily users. One of the subjects in the high-dose study was able to tolerate a large dose (30 mg. Δ-THC) with little change in his outward behavior or conversation. The other 14 subjects reported they were "as high or higher than ever before" during the high-dose marihuana study.

The subjects received thorough medical histories, reviews of systems, and psychiatric and physical examinations. None had scores outside the normal range on the Minnesota Multiphasic Personality Inventory (MMPI). None had a history of heart disease or hypertension, nor did they have elevated blood pressure readings, irregularities of pulse, cardiac murmurs, abnormal electrocardiograms (ECG), or other evidence of cardiovascular disease on physical examination.

Marihuana was obtained from the National Institute of Mental Health. The first batch was shown by independent analysis[1] to contain 0.5 percent Δ-9-tetrahydrocannabinol. Subsequently, it was found to contain 0.2 percent Δ-9-THC.[2] It was used for the low-dose studies and arbitrarily assumed to contain 0.5 percent during most of the study. A second batch of marihuana for the high-dose study contained 2.9 percent Δ-9-THC.[3] All marihuana was administered as 300 mg. cigarettes which were smoked to the shortest possible butt. Butts were weighed to determine the approximate dose smoked. In the low-dose study, subjects smoked from 2 to 5 cigarettes. In the high-dose study, subjects were instructed to smoke until they were as high as they had ever been on marihuana and felt they could not smoke any more. This required from 1 to 4 cigarettes. Subjects were told to inhale deeply and to let none of the smoke appear in the exhaled air. No corrections were made for pyrolysis, exhaled smoke, and cigarette smoke burned but not inhaled.

Electrocardiograms of the 3 standard limb leads and the six chest leads were obtained in the supine position before and within 1/2 hour after finishing the marihuana in 8 subjects. In 2 of the subjects ECG's were also obtained after single-blind administration of placebo extract marihuana on which the subjects felt subjectively high and also after exercise.

[1]Dr. Monroe E. Wall, Director, Research Triangle Institute, Research Triangle Park, N. C.
[2]Dr. Robert B. Forney, Professor of Pharmacology and Toxicology, Indiana University Medical Center, Indianapolis, Ind.
[3]Per information from Dr. Scigliano, National Institute of Mental Health.

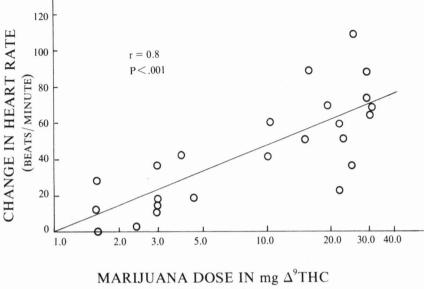

MARIJUANA DOSE IN mg Δ^9THC

(LOG SCALE)

Fig. 1. Dose-effect relationship of marihuana smoking on heart rate. Adult male volunteers were given various amounts of marihuana of varying Δ-9-THC content. The maximal increase in heart rate above control is given on the y axis and the total amount of Δ-9-THC in the cigarettes on the x axis. Each point represents an individual subject. The coefficient of correlation is 0.8 for which $p < 0.001$.

Blood pressure was measured at least three times before smoking marihuana to obtain a stable baseline. It was recorded three times again within 1/2 hour after smoking. Diastolic pressure was recorded at the muffling of the Korotkow's sound. The difference in means of the blood pressures before and after marihuana is reported as the change in blood pressure.

Pulse rate was recorded from a continuous polygraph record in those subjects who did not have complete ECG's. The change in pulse rate is the difference between a baseline rate and the highest rate obtained within one hour of smoking marihuana.

RESULTS

Our experiments show that the increase in heart rate after smoking marihuana is dose-related (Fig. 1). The coefficient of correlation between $\log_{10}$ dose and the increase in heart rate is 0.8 for which p

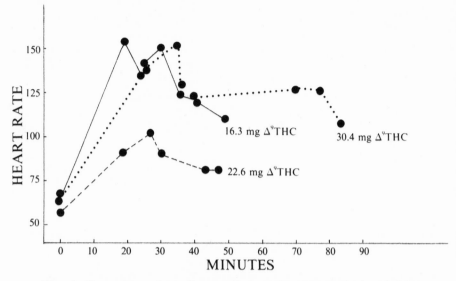

Fig. 2. Duration of marihuana-induced tachycardia in 3 different subjects. Subjects smoked varying amounts of 2.9 per cent Δ-9-THC containing marihuana. Note the more prolonged heart rate increases occurred with the larger doses.

< 0.001. One subject, a daily user of marihuana, seemed to be extremely tolerant of the psychic effects. However, his heart rate increased from 55 to 120 after a 30 mg. dose. The marihuana-induced tachycardia persists at least 90 minutes (Fig. 2). The maximum heart rate was usually reached within 30 minutes after smoking the marihuana.

The systolic blood pressure was significantly elevated in subjects receiving more than 10 mg. of marihuana (p < 0.01 on the Wilcoxin sign test for differences in related samples). The rise in systolic blood pressure appeared to be dose-related, although the coefficient of correlation was only 0.3 and and the p value < 0.10. The diastolic blood pressure was also significantly elevated after marihuana smoking (p < 0.02 on the Wilcoxin test). For the diastolic pressure data, the coefficient of correlation of the $\log_{10}$ dose response curve was only 0.3. Systolic and diastolic blood pressure data are shown in Fig. 3.

The data from the single-blind placebo extract experiments showed no significant changes in heart rate or blood pressure.

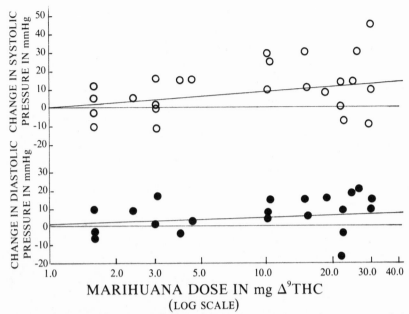

MARIHUANA DOSE IN mg Δ⁹THC
(LOG SCALE)

Fig. 3. Dose-effect relationship of marihuana smoking on arterial blood pressure. The upper graph illustrates the change in systolic and the lower graph the change in diastolic blood pressure. Each point represents a given subject as in Fig. 1. Note the trend for a slight increase in blood pressure which was greater for systolic than diastolic. See text for discussion of the significance of these slight changes.

Fig. 4 shows selected portions of Leads I, II, and V₅ of the ECG tracings, the baseline, placebo, post-15.3 mg. Δ-9-THC, and post-exercise results. Smoking marihuana tended to flatten T waves, especially in the chest leads, in many subjects, but T wave flattening was not a constant finding. T wave changes induced by exercise are more prominent than those induced by the marihuana smoking. Two of 15 subjects in the high-dose study developed premature ventricular contractions (PVC's). The PVC's occurred less than 1 per 25 beats after marihuana smoking but did not appear in control ECG rhythm strips of 1 to 2 minutes in length or on control polygraph recordings. Two of the PVC's from one of the subjects are shown in Fig. 5. Besides the PVC's in 2 subjects and the tachycardia and frequent T wave flattening in others, no ECG changes were noted.

LEAD I   LEAD II   LEAD V₅

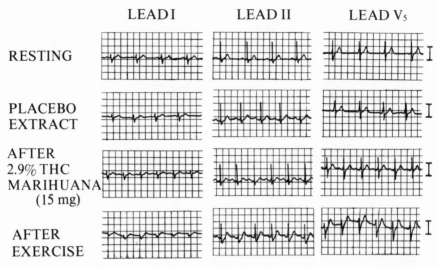

RESTING

PLACEBO
EXTRACT

AFTER
2.9% THC
MARIHUANA
(15 mg)

AFTER
EXERCISE

Fig. 4. ECG changes following extracted and active marihuana compared to control and exercise. A portion of each lead tracing is as
shown. On different days the same subject was given 15.8 mg. of active
2.9 per cent Δ^9-THC and extracted marihuana cigarettes as well as the
exercise of running up a flight of stairs. Note the tachycardia after
marihuana smoking compared with the tachycardia of exercise. T
wave changes are less marked.

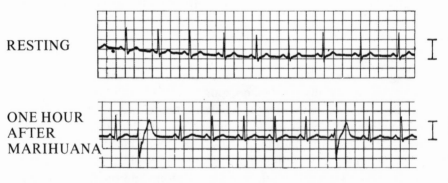

RESTING

ONE HOUR
AFTER
MARIHUANA

Fig. 5 Premature ventricular contractions after marihuana smoking.
During the control sessions (10 min. tracing) the subject never showed
PVC's but did after taking 18.9 mg. of 2.9 per cent Δ^9-THC marihuana
cigarettes. This particular record was taken one hour after smoking but
the PVC's were seen on a polygraph record shortly after smoking as
well.

DISCUSSION

Marihuana causes a significant increase in heart rate[6, 7, 10] Isbell and associates[4] and Hollister and associates[3] have shown that Δ-9-THC produces most of the psychic effects of marihuana and also the tachycardia. A recent report by Manno and associates[6] shows that the increased heart rate after marihuana is dose-related. Our study also indicates a significant dose-response relationship between the Δ-9-THC dose and the increased heart rate. The coefficient of correlation of 0.8 indicates that about 65 percent of the variance in heart rate is associated with the dose of Δ-9-THC in these experiments. Variability in heart rate response to a given dose could result from a number of factors. Calculation of the marihuana dosage on a milligram per kilogram basis did not reduce the variation in the data and therefore are not included as a separate table.

As indicated in the Material and Methods section, the effects of pyrolysis,[4] the efficiency of absorption of smoke by the lungs, and escape of smoke from the burning cigarette were not calculated into the dose. The dose indicated in the figures is the maximum possible dose each subject could have smoked. However, we believe that the actual dose absorbed is proportional to the total dose—that is, that losses of Δ-9-THC were similar for all subjects in the study.

A third possible explanation for variability of response at a given dose is that some subjects were tolerant to marihuana.[10] However, the one subject able to smoke 30 mg. of Δ-9-THC without feeling as high as he had ever been did have an increase of 65 beats per minute even though he seemed able to talk and reason as well as before he smoked. Hence, tolerance does not seem to develop as easily to the cardiovascular actions of marihuana as to its psychic effects. This is being pursued in another study separating subjects into tolerant and non-tolerant groups.

Anxiety-producing and sedative effects of marihuana do change the magnitude of the tachycardia. This mood induced by the dose of marihuana may account for most of the variability in heart rate for a given dose. One subject, who became panicky after a 25 mg. dose of Δ-9-THC, had a heart rate increase of 108. Another who became somnolent after 25 mg. had a heart rate increase of only 36.

Other investigators[3, 4, 10] have noted variable blood pressure changes after marihuana smoking. With low doses of Δ-9-THC, we noted no significant changes in blood pressure.[9] At doses above 10 mg. we noted significant increases in both systolic and diastolic blood pressures. Whether the changes in blood pressure are dose-related is difficult to say. The coefficients of correlation of blood pressure and log dose are low. The changes in blood pressure correlated better with tachycardia than with dose of Δ-9-THC: for increase in heart rate versus increase in systolic pressure, r = 0.381, p < 0.07.

Concerning changes in the electrocardiograms, we observed premature ventricular contractions in 2 of 15 subjects receiving 10 mg. or more of marihuana. The subjects themselves were unaware of them. Flattening of T waves was observed, especially in the chest leads, but this was neither a constant nor a specific finding. That ECG changes are minor after marihuana agrees with the conclusions of the La Guardia Study[7] and the study by Hollister and associates.[3] The latter reported uniformly negative ECG's in patients who received large oral doses of Δ-9-THC or pyrahexyl. This difference might indicate that the effects were related to smoking rather than to a pharmacological effect of THC.

The mechanism of the cannabis tachycardia remains unclear. The PVC's we observed may implicate catecholamine release. However, dry mouth, suggesting an atropine-like effect, and conjunctival injection, suggesting a vasodilatory action, are also present. We attempted to produce a cannabis tachycardia in an unanesthetized dog paralyzed with decamethonium. After intravenous doses of Δ-9-THC from 0.32 to 3.2 mg. per kilogram we observed electroencephalographic slowing and also hypotension and bradycardia. Species differences in the cardiovascular effects and the augmentation of the tachycardia by anxiety and its reduction by sedation, suggest that the cannabis tachycardia is mediated through the central nervous system.

Although no deaths have been reported from marihuana intoxication alone,[5] the tachycardia, hypertension, and PVC's it can produce indicate that marihuana should be used with caution by people with heart disease. Like nicotine and caffeine, marihuana may be a cause of PVC's in susceptible individuals. This was a relatively rare finding and may be due to smoking rather than to pure Δ-9-THC. The two susceptible subjects merely had a "before" control tracing which did not show PVC's but did "after." Further studies are clearly indicated, for marihuana smoke contains many other chemical substances. The clinical significance of our finding is probably no greater than that for susceptible subjects now smoking tobacco and drinking caffeine-containing beverages.[2]

REFERENCES

1. Caldwell, D., Myers, S., Domino, E., and Merriam, P. E.: Auditory and visual threshold effects of marihuana in man: *Addendum, Percept. Mot. Skills* 29:922, 1969.

2. Goodman, L. S., and Gilman, A., editors: The pharmacological basis of therapeutics, ed. 4, New York, 1970, The Macmillan Company, p. 1794.

3. Hollister, L. E., Richards, R. K., and Gillespie, H. K.: Comparison of tetrahydrocannabinol and synhexyl in man, CLIN. PHARMACOL. THER. 9: 783–791, 1968.

4. Isbell, H., Gorodetzky, D., Jasinski, D., Claussen, V., Spulale, F., and Korte, F.: Effects of (-) Δ^9 trans-tetrahydrocannabinol in man, *Psychopharmacologia* 1:184–188, 1967.

5. Jaffe, J.: Drug addiction and drug abuse, *in* Goodman, L. S., and Gilman, A., editors: The pharmacological basis of therapeutics, New York, 1970, The Macmillan Company.

6. Manno, J. E., Kiplinger, G. F., Haine, S. E., Bennett, I. F., and Forney, R. B.: Comparative effects of smoking marihuana or placebo on human motor and mental performance, CLIN. PHARMACOL. THER. 11:808–815, 1970.

7. Mayor's Committee on Marihuana: The marihuana problem in the City of New York, Lancaster, Pa., 1944, Jacques Cattell Press.

8. Pillard, R. C.: Marijuana, *N. Engl. J. Med.* 283:294–303, 1970.

9. Rodin, E., Domino, E., and Porzak, J.: The marijuana induced social high—Neurological and electroencephalographic concomitants, *J. A. M. A.* 213:1300–1302, 1970.

10. Williams, E. G., Himmelsbach, C. K., Wikler, A., Ruble, D. C., and Lloyd, Jr., B. J.: Studies on marijuana and pyrahexyl compound, *Public Health Rep.* 61:1059–1083, 1946.

Supported in part by United States Public Health Service Grant MH-11846.

20

Marihuana: Standardized Smoke Administration and Dose Effect Curves on Heart Rate in Humans

Pierre F. Renault, Charles R. Schuster
Richard Heinrich, and Daniel X. Freeman

Marihuana research in humans has been difficult to evaluate because of conflicting results[1]. A major problem complicating the comparability and replicability of studies has been the lack of a standard way of administering doses of marihuana[2,3]. Smoking marihuana cigarettes introduces at least two major sources of error: first, considerable and indeterminable amounts of smoke are lost to the air, and second, there is no way of determining the actual amount of smoke inhaled by the subject. Giving marihuana orally carries no assurance that the same substances pharmacologically active in smoke are being administered[2].

In an effort to overcome these problems, we have developed a system to deliver a measured quantity of smoke to a subject. Using change in heart rate as the measured effect, we investigated various dosages of marihuana to determine the efficiency of this delivery system.

Ten subjects were used, four inexperienced with marihuana, and six experienced smokers. An experienced smoker is defined as one who is currently engaged in smoking marihuana at least once a week. Three of

Reprinted with permission of the authors and publisher from *Science*, 1971, *174*, 589–591. Copyright 1971 by the American Association for the Advancement of Science.

Pierre F. Renault, Charles R. Schuster, Richard Heinrich and Daniel X. Freeman are affiliated with the Department of Psychiatry, University of Chicago, Chicago, Illinois.

the inexperienced subjects had never had any contact with marihuana before, and one had smoked marihuana three times 6 months before. All subjects were experienced tobacco smokers.

The subjects were all males. Nine were between 24 and 30 years of age, and one inexperienced smoker was 45. They were all judged to be in good health on the basis of routine medical history, physical examination, complete blood count, urinalysis, chest x-ray, and psychiatric examination.

All subjects were advised of the nature of the experiment and that both marihuana and placebo would be administered to them. They were also advised of the dangers of marihuana before they signed forms consenting to be subjects[4].

The marihuana and placebo were obtained from the National Institute of Mental Health. The marihuana was assayed to contain 1.5 percent Δ-9-tetrahydrocannabinol. Placebo had been commercially prepared by multiple extractions with alcohol to remove most of the Δ-9-tetrahydrocannabinol. Dosages of marihuana administered were the smoke from the total combustion of 62.5 mg, 125 mg, 250 mg and 435 mg of marihuana. The doses of placebo were equivalent to those of marihuana, but since all produced similar reactions, they were combined for purposes of our analysis.

The basic apparatus consists of a 12-liter spirometer and a machined aluminum crucible or pipe attached to the tubing so that as the inside bell of the spirometer is raised, air is drawn through the crucible into the spirometer. When marihuana, suitably chopped for burning, is placed in the crucible and ignited while air is being drawn through it, all of the smoke produced is drawn into the apparatus. Since the spirometer collapses to only half its size, the smoke is diluted by one-half with air. Once combustion is complete, the aluminum crucible is quickly disconnected, and the subject, with respiratory mask in place, is connected to the spirometer and inhales the smoke from it. Essentially, this is a closed, partially collapsible system which contains a fixed amount of smoke, and from which no smoke is lost into the atmosphere. The subject receives the same amount of smoke each time he empties the spirometer. The dose can easily be changed by varying the amount of marihuana burned, resulting in different concentrations of the smoke. Placebo can be administered in the same fashion, insuring the possibility of a double blind for any given dose.

Other variables in administering smoke are the duration of inhalation and the interval between inhalations. These variables were brought under stimulus control by instructing the subject to breathe according to a series of four lights. (i) A "ready" light signals the approaching cycle for 5 seconds. (ii) An "inhale" light comes on for 5 seconds, during which the subject inhales continuously. (iii) This is followed by the "hold" light, during which the subject holds the smoke in his lungs. This has a 15-second duration, and, during the breath-holding, the technician turns a valve closing the spirometer connection and opening the respiratory pathway to the atmosphere. (iv) Thus, when the "exhale" light comes on, the subject empties his lungs into the atmosphere and breathes room air as he wishes for 35 seconds, after which the "ready" light signals the start of a new cycle. This closed system and the instructional control insures greater reliability in the dosage of marihuana than can be achieved with conventional smoking.

Since the system collapses to only one-half its size, the amount of inhaled smoke can be only one-half of the amount of marihuana combusted. For example, after the smoke from 500 mg of marihuana is drawn into the 12-liter spirometer, the subject can remove only 6 liters, or the equivalent of the smoke from 250 mg. A 250-mg smoke equivalent remains in the residual 6 liters. We have found that the spirometer can be rapidly refilled with room air and the subject can then take in an additional 6 liters, or one-half of the residual, or the equivalent of 125 mg of marihuana. In these two installments, a total dose of 375 mg can be thus administered. We have repeated this process still once more for a total dose of approximately 435 mg.

Most subjects can take in the 6 liters in three inhalations, or 3 minutes (1 minute for each cycle). This means a total of 9 minutes to administer the maximal 435-mg dose.

Subjects reported to the laboratory for 3 hours at weekly intervals. For each experiment, subjects had electrodes placed on their chests, and these were connected by cable to an E & M Physiograph in another room where the electrocardiogram and respiratory and tachygraphic tracings were recorded. An experimenter could monitor the subjects by closed-circuit television to note movements or other artifacts on the record. During the first 30 minutes of each session, baseline heart rate, electrocardiogram, and respiratory tracings were collected. A stable 10-minute segment of this baseline was used to calculate the percentage change in heart rate produced by the marihuana or placebo administered during that session.

Figure 1 shows the percentage change in heart rate as a function of marihuana dosage graphed separately for naive and experienced subjects. Over the dose range tested, heart rate can be observed to

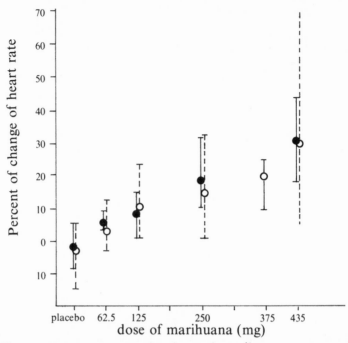

Fig. 1. Heart rate response to placebo and marihuana, expressed as percent of change from the baseline heart rate. Open circles and dotted lines, mean and range, respectively, of heart rate changes of experienced subjects. Solid circles and solid lines, mean and range of heart rate changes of inexperienced subjects.

increase linearly as a function of dosage of marihuana. This is most evident when mean values are compared. As indicated on the graph, the measured effect is the change of rate compared to baseline values. This is expressed as a percentage change to compensate for the week-to-week variations in baseline. Each point on the graph was arrived at by taking the average of the minute-to-minute heart rate between 10 and 20 minutes after the beginning of administration of marihuana. The difference between this average and that of the same 10-minute segment of baseline was then divided by the average of that same 10-minute segment of baseline to obtain the final percentage change graphed in the figure. The period from 10 to 20 minutes after the beginning of administration of drug was selected for heart rate measurement because marihuana was found to have a definite and sustained effect on heart rate during that time segment.

No differences were found between inexperienced and experienced smokers in relation to heart rate increases produced by marihuana. Placebo produced no heart rate increase.

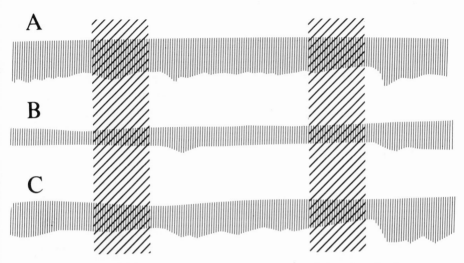

Fig. 2. Effect of marihuana on Valsalva maneuver. Cross-hatched areas are the period of inspiration and breath-holding. Cycle length is 1 minute. *A* is a baseline tracing. *B* was taken 10 minutes after administration of marihuana smoke was begun. *C* was taken 50 minutes later.

The variance between subjects in their responsiveness to marihuana was remarkably great and this accounts for the wide range at each dose as seen in Fig. 1. However, individual subjects showed linear increases in heart rate as a function of marihuana dosage and little variability in their response to a given dose of marihuana from one session to another.

In studying the interbeat interval, we observed a consistent effect of marihuana on cardiac rhythm. The most direct effect is the suppression of the normal sinus arrythmia. Since this nonspecific response is mediated by the vagus, it suggests that marihuana may have its effects on heart rate by altering normal autonomic tone. The diminution of sinus arrythmia was not attributable to changes in respiration.

In order to further study the effects of marihuana on autonomic tone, several subjects were asked to perform Valsalva maneuvers every 60 seconds during baseline and after various doses of marihuana. In short, marihuana suppressed the cardiac slowing during the Valsalva maneuver. This response was completely obliterated during peak effects at very high doses. Figure 2 shows a series of tachygraphic recordings at the baseline and after the beginning of inhalation of the smoke from 435 mg of marihuana. The vertical shaded areas indicate the period of breath-holding. Tracing A is baseline and it shows the typical cardiac slowing and gradual return. There is the additional slowing or "overshoot" for a few beats with exhalation, and this is followed by normal sinus arrythmia. Tracing B is a peak effect of 150 beats per minute at its height (90 at its lowest point). This was taken 10 minutes after administration of marihuana began. Clearly there is no response during Valsalva maneuvers; however, pulse slowing after exhalation does persist. Tracing C was taken 50 minutes after the dose and has an average pulse rate of about 100 beats per minute. The response during Valsalva maneuvers is still blocked, but the slowing of the pulse after exhalation is markedly enhanced. This is prolonged and at times appears to be followed by sinus arrythmia.

The maximum heart rates obtained in response to large doses of marihuana were in the range of 140 to 160 beats per minute. These rates correspond to heart rates seen in the absence of vagal tone and further suggest that marihuana alters heart rate by altering autonomic tone.

In conclusion, we have been able to use a spirometer to deliver reliable quantities of marihuana and placebo smoke to human subjects. The reliability of this procedure is attested to by the production of linear dose-effect curves and the replicability of dose effects in the same subject from one session to another. Using this system of administration of marihuana smoke, we observed no differences between experienced and inexperienced smokers in responsiveness to heart rate increases produced by marihuana.

REFERENCES AND NOTES

1. S. Gershon, *Behav. Neuropsychiatry* 1, 9 (1970).

2. A. T. Weil, N. E. Zinberg, J. M. Nelson, *Science* 162, 1234 (1968).

3. J. E. Manno, G. F. Kiplinger, S. H. Haine, I. F. Bennett, R. B. Forney, *Clin. Pharmacol. Ther.* 11, 808 (1970).

4. A. T. Weil, *N. Engl. J. Med.* 282, 997 (1970).

5. Presented at the meeting of the National Research Council Committee on Problems of Drug Dependence, Toronto, 1971. Supported in part by a grant from the State of Illinois Drug Abuse Rehabilitation Program.

21

Marijuana Intoxication: Interaction Between Physiologic Effects and Subjective Experience

Marc Galanter, Richard J. Wyatt
Louis Lemberger, Herbert Weingartner
Tom B. Vaughan, and Walton T. Roth

Numerous studies have been carried out to assess the effects of marijuana[1]. In many of these studies, natural marijuana or its putative active component, Δ^9-tetrahydrocannabinol (Δ^9-THC), was administered by smoking. Correlations of the concentration of Δ^9THC in plasma with psychological and physiologic effects after administration by smoking were not, however, made.

We report here on a comparison between a 10-mg dose of synthetic Δ^9THC and placebo marijuana material, both administered to 12 subjects by smoking. The subjective description of effects was qualitatively similar but quantitatively different for the two states. The magnitude of the syndrome as described subjectively by individuals receiving active Δ^9THC correlated very highly with their respective pulse increments.

In order to assess the time course of these variables, we administered to three of the subjects the same dose of Δ^9THC, a portion of which was in the form of [^{14}C]Δ^9THC. These subjects were then studied for 24

Reprinted with permission of the authors and publisher from *Science*, 1972, *176*, 934–936, where it appeared as "Effects on Humans of Δ^9-Tetrahydrocannabinol Administered by Smoking." Copyright 1972 by the American Association for the Advancement of Science.

Marc Galanter, Richard J. Wyatt, Louis Lemberger, Herbert Weingartner, Tom B. Vaughan, and Walton T. Roth are all affiliated with the Laboratory of Clinical Psychopharmacology, National Institute of Mental Health, St. Elizabeth's Hospital, Washington, D.C.

hours. The time course of the pulse rate was highly correlated with the time course of the concentrations of Δ^9THC in plasma. Subjective symptoms, however, appeared later and dissipated more slowly. The setting of the study produced a strong effect on the subjective experience.

The 12 male subjects ranged in age from 21 to 26 years. All had smoked marijuana at least 50 to 75 times; seven had smoked it at least 500 times, and had taken lysergic acid diethylamide (LSD) on one or more occasions. All were free of significant psychiatric or medical illness.

In the initial part of the experiment, each of the 12 subjects smoked a different one of the following on each of the 3 days: (i) placebo marijuana material alone, (ii) placebo material injected with 10 mg of synthetic Δ^9THC, or (iii) natural marijuana assayed to contain 10 mg of Δ^9THC[2]. The order of administration was balanced over the 12 subjects.

All subjects were instructed not to smoke marijuana or to drink alcohol for the 24 hours preceding each experimental day, and not to ingest any other drug for 48 hours preceding that day. Urine samples were analyzed for alkaloids, barbiturates, and amphetamines. These assays were negative in the urine for all subjects.

To assure a consistent pattern of inhalation, only regular cigarette smokers were accepted as subjects. A standard smoking technique was practiced and applied: The subjects inhaled for a period of 2 to 4 seconds, maintained each inhalation for 15 seconds, then exhaled, and waited for 5 seconds. They repeated this procedure until the cigarettes were finished; the time elapsed was 10 minutes. All data are reported in terms of time elapsed from the onset of smoking.

The following observations were made during each session. Radial pulse was measured 30 minutes before smoking; this figure was then subtracted from the pulse rate measured 25 minutes after the onset of smoking to give the pulse increment. Comparative subjective "high" was a single assessment in which subjects rated how "high" they felt during the 90 minutes after the onset of smoking. A scale of 0 to 10 was used in which 0 meant "not high at all" and 10 was the "highest" the subject had ever felt smoking marijuana on any previous occasion. This rating, therefore, reflected the subjects' previous marijuana experiences, as well as the experience of the specific session.

A symptom checklist, a list of 62 subjective symptoms, was given to the subjects after 90 minutes. It was prepared from a questionnaire on subjective drug effects developed by Waskow et al.[3] for the study of psychoactive drugs. We included items that were found by Waskow *et al.* to differ significantly between 20 mg of orally ingested Δ^9THC and placebo, as well as additional items from the questionnaire, which were relevant to this study[4]. Each item was graded by the subject from 0 ("not felt at all") to 3 ("felt very much more than usual").

All data were examined by a mixed nested analysis of variance (ANOVA) comparing results for the effects of placebo, Δ^9THC, and marihuana conditions. The Tukey test was then applied for individual mean differences between conditions. Results of both tests were significant, as follows: For the comparative subjective "high" (ANOVA, $F = 30.64$; d.f. $= 2,22$; $P < .01$), the mean scores were 2.08 for placebo and 5.25 for Δ^9THC ($P < .01$). The mean pulse increment over baseline (ANOVA, $F = 21.54$; d.f. $= 2,22$; $P < .01$) was 7.3 for placebo and 43.5 for Δ^9THC ($P < .01$). On the symptom checklist (ANOVA, $F = 10.03$; d.f. $= 2,22$; $P < .01$) scores were 18.0 for placebo and 31.6 for Δ^9THC ($P < .01$).

The subjects' total scores for individual symptoms on the symptom checklist correlated well (Pearson product-moment $r = .94$, $P < .01$) with their subjective "high" rating scores. Similarly, the symptom checklist scores correlated well (Pearson product-moment $r = .70$, $P < .01$) with the magnitude of their respective pulse increments.

Three of the 12 subjects were subsequently studied during 24 hours after they smoked labeled synthetic Δ^9THC. We were thus able to compare the time course of the other variables with that of Δ^9THC concentration in plasma. A total dose of 10 mg of synthetic Δ^9THC, 0.5 mg (10 μc) of which was in the form [^{14}C]Δ^9THC, was injected into two cigarettes prepared from the placebo marijuana material. Blood samples were drawn at the intervals indicated in Fig. 1, and all urine voided was collected. The amount of unchanged Δ^9THC in plasma was determined by extraction at pH 7.4 with four volumes of heptane containing 1.5 percent isoamyl alcohol and was assayed for radioactivity by liquid scintillation spectrometry[5]. Urine was assayed for Δ^9THC and its metabolites by measuring the total radioactivity of the samples.

During the 24 hours after administration of the [^{14}C]Δ^9THC, at the intervals indicated in Fig. 1, baseline and interval radial pulse measurements were made, a symptom checklist was administered, and each subject was asked for a standardized "high" rating. They were now told to grade the "highest" they had felt during all of the smoking sessions as 10 and to grade not feeling "high" at all as 0. If they felt more "high" than they had in the initial part of the study, they were to extrapolate up from this 10-point scale.

Different time courses were found for the variables studied. Both the

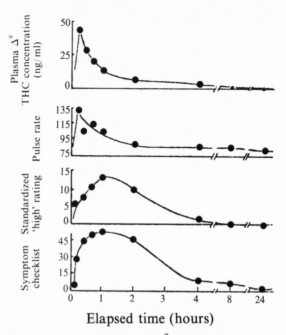

Elapsed time (hours)

Fig. 1. The time course of plasma Δ^9THC concentration, pulse, and subjective experience in three subjects were studied over the course of 24 hours after they had smoked 10 mg of synthetic Δ^9THC injected into placebo cigarettes. Measurements were taken at zero time, 15 minutes elapsed time (that is, 5 minutes after completion of smoking), 25, 40 minutes, and at 1, 2, 4, 8, and 24 hours.

plasma concentration of Δ^9THC and the pulse increment peaked at 15 minutes, and then rapidly declined (Fig. 1). The subjective experience, however, reached a peak at 1 hour, and declined more slowly. These two different time courses were reflected in product-moment correlations examined over the 24-hour period. Plasma concentration of Δ^9THC showed a significant product-moment correlation with pulse increment ($r=.95$, $P<.01$), but neither of these correlated significantly with the subjective measures. This suggests that the Δ^9THC concentration is more closely related to changes in pulse than to changes in subjective ratings.

The three subjects absorbed different quantities of Δ^9THC. This variation was apparent in peak Δ^9THC concentrations in the plasma for the three subjects, namely, 67, 37, and 21 ng/ml. An estimate of the portion of Δ^9THC absorbed from the original cigarettes was made from the portion of total tracer present in the 24-hour urine samples.

Lemberger *et al.*[6] reported that when Δ^9THC was administered intravenously to chronic users, 20 percent of it was excreted in the first day's urine. If the same portion of Δ^9THC and its metabolites administered by smoking is excreted in the 24-hour urine, then our subjects absorbed 41, 20, and 15 percent, respectively, of the quantity of Δ^9THC in the original cigarettes.

Manno *et al.*[7], using a mechanical smoking device, assayed the portion of cannabinols in the smoke of marijuana cigarettes, and found that approximately 50 percent of the Δ^9THC in the cigarettes was delivered unchanged in the smoke. This figure is comparable to that of 41 percent absorbed by one of our three subjects, but the other two absorbed less than half that amount. This is an indication of the marked variability of Δ^9THC absorbed when marijuana is administered by smoking, even under standardized conditions.

The subjective experience was responsive to both placebo and change in setting. Although the 12 subjects rated themselves as less "high" on placebo, there was good correlation of symptoms experienced under the influence of placebo and Δ^9THC (rank-order r=.544, P<.01). The smokers appeared to be conditioned to a particular subjective syndrome triggered by the stimulus of smoking marijuana-like material. This may in part explain the greater sensitivity to marijuana reported by experienced smokers. The 12 most frequently checked symptoms while the subjects were under the influence of Δ^9THC were: mouth drier, feels high, throat drier, hungrier, dreamier, feels more like paying close attention to things, skin tingling, memory seems worse, movements slower, head heavier, sees images when eyes are closed.

When three of the subjects were subsequently studied on the same dose in a more austere setting and subjected to venipuncture, the variability in the subjective experience was apparent. Two of the subjects vomited while at the peak of their subjective "high," whereas neither had done so on that dose when it was administered under more congenial circumstances earlier in the study. As one of the two reported on the day of blood drawing, "I just freaked out when I saw that needle." He checked off "very much more than usual" for the symptoms, "have you felt less in control of your body"; "felt less in control of your feelings"; and "had a weird feeling." He had checked "not at all" on the previous occasion.

REFERENCES

1. L. E. Hollister [*Science* 172, 21 (1970)] reviews these studies and

discusses some of the problems implicit in administration of marijuana by smoking.

2. The materials were obtained from the Psychotomimetic Agents Advisory Committee, National Institute of Mental Health. They were assayed by gas-liquid chromatography by TRW-Hazleton Laboratories both before and after the study, as follows: natural marijuana, 1.6 percent Δ^9THC, less than 0.05 percent Δ^8THC, 0.1 percent each of cannibinol and cannabidiol; placebo marijuana material (produced from marijuana plant material by four extractions in 95 percent alcohol), 0.05 percent Δ^9THC, 0.05 percent Δ^8THC, 0.01 percent each of cannabinol and cannabidiol; synthetic Δ^9THC, 92 percent Δ^9THC, 6 percent Δ^8THC, and 1 percent each of cannabinol and cannabidiol. Purity of the [^{14}C]Δ^9THC was shown to be greater than 98 percent.

3. E. E. Waskow, J. E. Olsson, C. Salzman, M. M. Katz, *Arch. Gen. Psychiat.* 22, 97 (1970).

4. A copy of the abbreviated questionnaire is available on request.

5. L. Lemberger, S. D. Silbertstein, J. Axelrod, I. J. Kopin, *Science* 170, 1320 (1970).

6. L. Lemberger, N. R. Tamarkin, J. Axelrod, *ibid.* 173, 72 (1971).

7. J. E. Manno, G. F. Kiplinger, S. E. Haine, I. F. Bennett, R. B. Forney, *Clin. Pharmacol. Ther.* 11, 808 (1970).

Part 9

Adverse Psychological Effects

Adverse psychological effects refer to those side-effects attendant upon drug-taking that are undesirable from the point of view of the subject. The main psychological characteristic of such effects is that they are unpleasant. One might alternatively define adverse psychological effects from the point of view of society. In that case, the point of contention would involve some definition of general good and then the adverse effect could be stated in terms of behavior that deviated from the norm. For the sake of discussion, we will skirt this problem and deal with it in terms that lie nebulously between these two positions.

The kinds of psychological reactions that fall into the adverse category are anxiety, panic, depression, long-term personality changes, psychoses, and so forth. Although cannabis has been associated with the onset of such symptoms in the Far and Middle East, all such reports are suspect. In the words of the 1971 United States *Marihuana and Health report,*

> In evaluating the significance of overseas studies of the relationship of cannabis use to mental deterioration, it is important to recognize the comparatively low level of attention that can be paid to psychiatric illness and to the fate of the mentally ill in countries where life for the bulk of the population is one of marginal survival

and there are more pressing public health problems. Here crippling chronic illnesses long since eliminated in the West are still endemic, and mental hospitals and trained psychiatrists do not rank high on the list of national health priorities. Yet some of the most widely quoted studies in the literature on marihuana and psychosis have originated from poorly staffed and maintained psychiatric hospitals operating with a minimum of professionally trained psychologists.

A cautionary statement similar in tone was made by the Indian Hemp Drug Commission as far back as 1893: "It may seem extraordinary that statistics based on such absolutely untrustworthy material should have been submitted year after year in the asylum reports. It is extraordinary and cannot be fully justified."

Nevertheless, these reports are still echoing in the present-day controversy surrounding discussion of the effects of cannabis use among North Americans. Moreover, the increasing number of clinical reports presently appearing in the West indicates that the question will not be settled for some time to come. In this chapter, some of these clinical reports and their attendant problems will be examined.

One of the first studies of the problem in North America was reported by Bromberg (1934). Although he described "psychotic reactions" among a number of cannabis users, it was not possible to determine any cause-and-effect relationships and in a somewhat later study (Bromberg, 1939), he was unable to detect evidence of psychoses among 67 users of marihuana whom he had an opportunity to study.

In 1944, the La Guardia committee reported that of the 77 subjects it studied, nine developed what was regarded as a psychotic state, the main features of which were delirium and feelings of anxiety. Six of these nine subjects were judged to be cases of acute intoxication. Of the other three subjects, one was an epileptic whose psychosis was thought to be related to his disease. The other two were thought to be suffering from "prison psychosis" at the time of the study and so the role of marihuana in precipitating their condition was difficult to assess.

Recently, however, there have been an increasing number of reports in which marihuana has once again been implicated in the precipitation of psychotic behavior. In general, however, the individuals so affected appear to be those who have "disturbed" personalities prior to their taking marihuana, or they are individuals taking marihuana (in rather high doses) for the first time.

With respect to the first group, Keeler interviewed a number of individuals who reported adverse reactions following the taking of marihuana and from those interviews he concluded that, "perhaps all investigators would agree that marihuana cannot produce functional psychopathology but can only precipitate it in individuals so predisposed." A similar conclusion is voiced by Halikas and his associates: "It is concluded that at least some regular marihuana users come from a population at high risk for psychiatric problems, and that these difficulties almost always precede use of marihuana."

However, adverse reactions sometimes occur in individuals who are "psychologically well-balanced." In such cases, however, more often than not, the situation is one in which the individual is experiencing the effects of marihuana (usually potent) for the first time. For example, in their study of marihuana-induced psychosis occurring among U.S. soldiers stationed in Vietnam, Talbot and Teague reported that "in all instances, this [psychotic episode] was the patient's first admitted exposure to marihuana and in each case marked physical symptoms appeared soon after the subjects began to smoke."

Some of the symptoms they describe have already been noted, e.g., heaviness in the limbs, impaired coordination, irritation of the eyes and throat, feelings of nausea, a rushing of ideas, confusion of thought, etc. Given that the potency of the marihuana used in Vietnam is likely much greater than that used in the United States, and that the naive user of marihuana may not be prepared for these uncontrollable physiological changes, it is not difficult to imagine the panic that may be experienced at the sudden and unexpected onset of these sensations. Moreover, the added stresses attendant upon being stationed in Vietnam are also likely to contribute to what might be labelled as a predisposing factor. Finally, it should also be kept in mind that the marihuana being used in Vietnam may have contained other materials such as opium or heroin which may also have contributed to these functional disorders. Consequently, the evidence linking marihuana and incipient psychosis must be evaluated with a great deal of caution before any final statement can be made regarding its involvement in the etiology of psychopathology.

The fourth article in this section, by Tennant and Groesbeck, examines some of these questions in a much larger population of subjects than were examined in the previous two papers. Their conclusions support the opinion that cannabis can induce psychosis in predisposed individuals but cast some doubt on the opinion that cannabis itself will produce this condition in normally healthy individuals. However, used in conjunction with other psychoactive drugs, cannabis may produce undue adverse effects and this may possibly account for Talbot and Teague's findings as noted above.

The next two articles by Abel, however, demonstrate that subjects under the influence of marihuana do experience subjective changes in anxiety and in exhibitionism. In addition, they indicate the importance of experimental design in conducting research of this nature.

A certain "amotivational syndrome" has also recently been described among chronic North American users of marihuana by McGlothlin and West (1968). The characteristics of this syndrome are changes in personality and behavior and consist of apathy, reduced drive and ambition, low frustration tolerance, unwillingness to carry out long-term goals, and so forth. Although no experimental verification of this phenomenon has been documented for human subjects, Masur and her associates have recently reported one of the most intriguing animal studies involving marihuana and behavior which bears on this point. Briefly, Masur taught water-deprived rats to bar-press for water reward. When the rats were subsequently placed into the apparatus in pairs, one of the animals would be observed to be doing nearly all of the bar-pressing for the two, while the other would do nearly all of the drinking owing to the fact that it stood near the water delivery system and got to the water before the worker rat. After the worker rat is given Δ^9-THC, however, there is an inversion of this labor pattern. The drugged animal begins to work much less and remains in the area of the water deliverer while the previously non-working rat takes over the duty of bar-pressing.

22

Adverse Reaction to Marihuana

Martin H. Keeler

Eleven individuals who reported adverse reactions associated with the use of marihuana were interviewed. Their difficulties included one report of panic and fear, one report of depersonalization, one report of gross confusion and disorientation, two reports of depression, and four reports of paranoid phenomena during the drug reaction. The individual who reported confusion during the reaction also experienced recurrence of confusion and hallucinations intermittently afterwards. One of the individuals who experienced depression during the reaction had similar experiences thereafter.

Two other individuals reported major changes in behavior and style of life after the use of marihuana. Four others were interviewed who had become schizophrenic subsequent to the combined use of marihuana, lysergic-acid-diethylamide, and amphetamine. All 17 of these individuals were of superior intelligence and all were, or had been, university students. None was a delinquent in the usual sense; none had ever been arrested. All but two came from middle-class backgrounds; two came from upper lower-class families.

More detailed presentation of the clinical data will be preceded by

Reprinted with permission of the author and publisher from the *American Journal of Psychiatry*, 1967, *124*, 674–677. Copyright 1967 by the American Psychiatric Association.

Martin H. Keeler, M.D., is Associate Professor of Psychiatry, University of North Carolina School of Medicine, Chapel Hill, North Carolina.

description of the marihuana reaction and followed by presentation of other reports of adverse reaction and consideration of the problems involved in the evaluation of such data.

DESCRIPTION OF THE MARIHUANA REACTION

Knowledge of usual reaction is required to interpret reports of unusual drug reaction. Bouquet[4] summarized the effects of marihuana in terms that are consistent with the statements made by marihuana users interviewed in the clinic from which this study derives. Euphoria, a feeling of well-being, increase of self-confidence, and decreased self-criticism occur.

The user feels that he is unusually aware of the function of his limbs and that he could perform feats of physical agility or grace but that he is too tranquil to do so. The power to focus concentration is lost or relinquished. Associations are rapid and disorganized. Concepts of time and space are altered. Illusions, visual and auditory hallucinations, and sensitivity to sound occur.

Allentuck[1] described the effects of the administration of marihuana to 78 subjects. He stated that euphoria and difficulties in concentration and sustaining attention were frequent. Excitement, anxiety, and/or dysphoric reactions occurred in some subjects.

Physiologic responses to marihuana include tachycardia, mydriasis, and suffusion of the conjunctiva. Subjective sensations often include feelings of tightness, heaviness or pressure in the head, dryness of the mouth, and a "floating sensation."

CASE REPORTS

Case 1. A 21-year-old man stated that after smoking more than his usual amount he became disoriented to time and place, could not think, and had difficulty in controlling his limbs. For some weeks thereafter he intermittently experienced hallucinations resembling those he had had during the reaction. These sensations were accompanied by a degree of anxiety approaching panic.

Case 2. A 19-year-old woman stated that during a marihuana reaction she had become intensely anxious and apprehensive without any idea of what she was afraid of. She said that she had been agitated and in a state of panic.

Case 3. A 20-year-old woman stated that while smoking marihuana she would become convinced that she did not exist in a spatial sense.

She would think that she was merged with the universe or, alternatively, a point in space without dimensions. Such ideation, accompanied by anxiety, would persist for some hours after the use of the drug.

Case 4. A 19-year-old man reported that during a marihuana reaction he became convinced that his internal organs were rotting and that he would die. This was related to a conviction that he had done evil things.

Case 5. A 23-year-old woman stated that during the marihuana reaction and for some hours afterwards she would have the "horrors." She described this as a feeling that indescribably evil things would happen to her because of the kind of person she was.

Case 6. A 20-year-old woman reported that during a marihuana reaction she became convinced that her friends had informed the police that there would be a marihuana party so that they might raid the house and catch her using the drug.

Case 7. A 22-year-old man stated that during the drug reaction he would become convinced that his taking the drug was part of some gigantic plot but that he did not know what the plot was.

Case 8. A 20-year-old man stated that during the marihuana reaction he would become preoccupied with whether his friends thought he was a homosexual. There was no reality testing of this conviction during the drug reaction.

Case 9. A 23-year-old man stated that during the marihuana reaction he would become preoccupied with the possibility of a police raid and would interpret every noise he heard as caused by approaching police.

Case 10. A 20-year-old man stated that after taking marihuana he recognized that his previous goals, including what he called conventional ambition, conformity, and fear, were not as important as the need to express himself and achieve independent identity. His interest and achievement in academic areas deteriorated and his dress became nonconventional.

Case 11. A 22-year old woman stated that after taking marihuana she recognized that her graduate school work did not permit adequate self-expression. She did not drop out of school and her intelligence was such that she continued to do passable work. She stated that her academic work had once been a source of pleasure but that she now recognized that she had been "brainwashed" by the system.

Four individuals who demonstrated sufficient thinking disorders and inappropriate affect to justify the diagnosis of schizophrenia were interviewed, and they admitted to the almost daily use of amphetamine and marihuana and the regular use of LSD.

OTHER REPORTS OF ADVERSE REACTION

Allentuck[1] administered the equivalent of between 30 and 330 mg. of tetrahydrocannabinol orally to 72 subjects. Six subjects had acute brain syndromes during the reaction. Three others became psychotic within the next few weeks. It was Allentuck's opinion that these latter psychoses would have occurred even if the drug had not been administered.

Ames[2] administered between .24 and .46 gm. of a cannabis extract orally to each of ten subjects. One subject experienced intense anxiety and five subjects exhibited some degree of delusional thinking.

De Farias[6] observed nine subjects smoking 2.82 gm. and seven of the same subjects smoking 1.56 gm. of cannabis. Delirium and confusion with apprehension of impending death occurred in one subject.

Chopra and associates[5] implicated marihuana in the difficulties of 600 patients admitted to mental hospitals in India. They classified these reactions as acute mania, chronic mania, and dementia. Hallucinations, a dare-devil attitude with unresistible impulses to do willful damage, and amnesia for the attack upon remission characterized acute mania. The patients with chronic mania were cheerful, boastful, and had a sense of well-being. Data such as these have been questioned by many on several accounts. Such a large proportion of the population involved uses cannabis that a high proportion of hospitalized patients would give such a history even if the drug were harmless. The criteria whereby psychoses caused by marihuana differ from other psychoses are not explicit.

Benabud[3] reported evidences of acute or subacute cannabis effect in 49 percent of the 1,252 patients admitted to a Moroccan mental hospital in 1956. He considered certain types of excitation, impulsivity, oneiric, and visual hallucinatory states to be cannabis-induced. One or more of these phenomena were present in such disorders or were superimposed on other psychopathological conditions.

Benabud defined six percent of the admissions in the year studied as "cannabis-mobilized psychoses." This is defined as a psychosis of a functional type precipitated by cannabis intoxication. He defined 11 percent of the admissions in the year studied as "cannabis-aggravated psychoses." This is defined as a preexistent psychotic condition made worse by the use of cannabis.

Benabud's report, like that of Chopra and associates, has been subjected to some criticism. So many people in the area use cannabis that many hospital patients would have done so by chance alone. Many difficulties ascribed to cannabis could have resulted from other causes.

The reports of Allentuck,[1] Ames,[2] and De Farias,[6] previously noted, do not have the weakness of the Chopra and associates and the Benabud reports. Specific psychotic syndromes were observed to occur during the marihuana reaction.

DISCUSSION

There is good reason for controversy as to the prevalence of adverse reaction to marihuana. For proper evaluation of adverse drug effect, information is required as to number of untoward reactions, the size of the population using the drug, dosage, and the nature of the population using the drug. As will be discussed below, none of this information is available for marihuana.

In the case of marihuana a definition of adverse reaction is also required. The evaluation of adverse reaction is, in addition, dependent on the interpretation of such a statement as, "Marihuana in itself does not produce functional psychopathology but may precipitate such in individuals who are so predisposed."

There is no accurate or reasonably accurate way of determining how many acute difficulties occur during or immediately after marihuana use. Most of these reactions do not come to medical attention. There are great differences in the potency of different preparations. The populations from which the reports of adverse reactions in this study are derived might be defined as university nonconformist. These individuals are of superior intelligence, more than average education, and not delinquent in the usual sense. It is not justified to assume that adverse reactions would be the same in this group, a delinquent group in a large city of the United States, and the urban poor of Morocco.

There is some difficulty in the evaluation of changes in style of life subsequent to marihuana use. Many individuals so change direction without drug use; many begin to use drugs only after they have so changed direction. No one has the right to define a change in style of life and goals of life as psychopathology. Nevertheless, when this occurs immediately after drug use it may be permissible to consider such a change to be an adverse drug reaction.

Perhaps all investigators would agree that marihuana cannot produce functional psychopathology but can only precipitate it in individuals so predisposed. Many would interpret this as an exoneration of the drug. Others would hold that the occurrence of psychopathology in an individual at a given time requires many factors and that more people have predisposition to mental illness than develop it. In this sense marihuana usage might precipitate trouble that would not have otherwise occurred or would have otherwise occurred at a later time.

It is the author's opinion that the literature does indicate that marihuana, depending on dose and subject, can precipitate acute brain syndromes, panic, and delusional thinking during the reaction. The use of the drug can initiate changes in style of life. It is left to others to decide whether this constitutes psychopathology.

It is the clinical impression of the author that this dissolution of ordinary adaptive and defensive psychological structure that occurs during the marihuana reaction is potentially dangerous for individuals with a predisposition to schizophrenia.

The evaluation of the harm a drug does requires some consideration of its benefits. Users of marihuana state that it is a source of positive pleasure, that it enhances creativity, that it provides insight, and that it enriches their lives. These are hardly minor claims. All but two of the 11 individuals reporting adverse reactions considered the benefits to far outweigh the unfortunate aspects and planned to continue use of the drug.

REFERENCES

1. Allentuck, S.: "Medical Aspects," in *The Marihuana Problem in the City of New York* (Mayor's Committee on Marihuana). Lancaster, Pa.: Jacques Cattell Press, 1944.

2. Ames, F.: A Clinical and Metabolic Study of Acute Intoxication with Cannabis Sativa and Its Role in the Model Psychoses, *J. Ment. Sci.* 104:972–999, 1958.

3. Benabud, A.: Psychopathological Aspects of the Cannabis Situation in Morocco: Statistical Data for 1956, *Bulletin on Narcotics* 9:1–16, 1957.

4. Bouquet, J. R.: Cannabis, *Bulletin on Narcotics* 3:22–45, 1951.

5. Chopra, R. N., Chopra, G. S., and Chopra, I. C.: Cannabis Sativa in Relation to Mental Diseases and Crime in India, *Indian J. Med. Res.* 30:155–171, 1942.

6. De Farias, C.: Use of Maconha (Cannabis Sativa L.) in Brazil, *Bulletin on Narcotics* 7:5–19, 1955.

Read at the 123rd annual meeting of the American Psychiatric Association, Detroit, Mich., May 8–12, 1967.

23

Marihuana Use and Psychiatric Illness

James A. Halikas
Donald W. Goodwin, and Samuel B. Guze

Marihuana use has been linked to antisocial behavior and mental illness.[1] Early reports have been discounted because of methodologic flaws or other inadequacies.[2] Psychiatric disorders in 38 young adults were recently reported by Kolansky and Moore, who concluded that the illnesses were caused by marihuana use.[3] Their work has been faulted on multiple grounds.[4]

This study was designed to determine the incidence and type of psychiatric problems found among regular marihuana users, compare these to nondrug-using controls, and study the temporal relationship of psychiatric problems and marihuana use.

METHOD

A total of 100 regular marihuana users and 50 nonuser friends were interviewed by a psychiatrist between July 1969 and March 1970.

Criteria for admission to the study were minimal. Subjects had to be at least 18 years of age and white. They had to be self-defined as *regular*

Reprinted with permission of the authors and publisher from the *Archives of General Psychiatry*, 1972, *27*, 162–165. Copyright 1972 by the American Medical Association.

James A. Halikas, M.D., Donald W. Goodwin, M.D., and Samuel B. Guze, M.D., are all affiliated with the Department of Psychiatry, Washington School of Medicine, St. Louis, Missouri.

marihuana users and to have used marihuana on at least 50 occasions during at least six months. This was designed to obtain a sample that viewed themselves not as experimentors or casual, social users, but as regular, committed users; to assure, also, that these self-defined users had had extensive experiences in its use; and to assure a sufficient time period of use to have made changes in their lifestyle, develop patterns of use, and have had a period of risk during which psychiatric, social or legal consequences might have occurred. The controls, also at least 18 years old and white, could not have used marihuana, if at all, more than a few times.

Subjects were obtained through word-of-mouth chains of referrals. Three "source" people known to have access to different groups of drug users in the community were asked to "spread the word," explain the outlines of the study, and encourage participation. Financial remuneration or personal participation with these three individuals was not involved. Each volunteer was paid $10. Subjects were assured of anonymity and no identifying data were obtained. After the interview, subjects were requested to tell their friends, both users and nonusers, about the study. Up to nine "generations" of referrals were obtained in an arborization effect.

The primary focus of the interview was a systematic psychiatric evaluation. In addition, childhood experiences, parental habits and rearing practices, educational background and experiences, chronologic development and social landmarks, medical history, family history, personal drug use including alcohol and tobacco, were explored by open-ended and structured questioning. Extensive information was also obtained from the users concerning their marihuana use and its consequences.

The interviews were marked by rapid rapport, good cooperation, and candid exploration. The users' interviews lasted from two to four hours; the controls' from one to two hours. All were performed by the same person (J. H.).

Agreement on diagnostic criteria was achieved before the study was begun. Where questions arose concerning diagnosis, that subject's interview was independently reviewed by the other two authors, and then agreement among the three was reached.

Diagnoses were based on standard criteria consisting of specific psychiatric symptoms and life-patterns. For example, to receive a diagnosis of primary affective disorder, depressed type, a subject had to report an episode of low mood characterized by feeling depressed, sad, despondent, blue, etc, plus five of the following eight symptoms for a "definite" diagnosis or four of the eight symptoms for a "probable" diagnosis:

(1) unplanned change in appetite and weight,
(2) sleep difficulty, including hypersomnia,
(3) loss of energy,
(4) agitation, irritability, internal restlessness, or retardation,
(5) change in libido, loss of interest, or withdrawal,
(6) alteration in thinking, memory, or ability to concentrate,
(7) suicidal ideas or explicit death wishes,
(8) self-depreciatory ruminations.

This cluster of symptoms must have lasted at least two weeks; symptoms could not be explainable on the basis of any medical problem, social activity, or side effect of any drug use; and subjects must have been free of any preexisting psychiatric illness.

The criteria outlined by Robins[5] were used for sociopathy. As used here, antisocial behavior in at least five life areas was required, with onset prior to age 15: being a "problem" child to parents, truancy, fighting during school years, school problems requiring parental and principal's involvement, overnight runaway prior to age 16, school suspensions or expulsions, police trouble as a juvenile, stealing as a child, pathological lying, fighting after the age of 18, police trouble as an adult, incarceration, wanderlust, job firings, military service difficulties and marital problems where applicable.

Criteria for other diagnoses are enumerated elsewhere.[6-8] Feighner et al. have recently summarized these criteria.[9] No separate diagnoses of drug dependency (DSM-II, 304.0-304.9) were made. Direct consequences of drug abuse were not considered as contributing to diagnostic criteria, eg, an arrest on drug charges did not contribute towards a diagnosis of sociopathy.

RESULTS

Sample—Subjects in both groups were, in general, well-educated and articulate, although of diverse backgrounds and interests. Demographic information is summarized in Table 1. The model subject could be thought of as being a young male of upper middle-class background who grew up in the suburbs, attended public schools, and was now in college. Compared to the nonusers, the users were slightly younger, somewhat more likely to have come from homes of no religion (10% to

TABLE 1
DEMOGRAPHIC DATA

	No.	Sex		Age Range	Average Age	Religion of Upbringing				Marital Status	
		M	F			Catholic	Protestant	Jewish	None	Single	Married
Users	100	61	39	18-31	22	30	29	31	10	90	10
Nonusers	50	26	24	18-33	23	12	17	20	1	32	18

	Home Background			Educational Level			Parents' Occupation (ODD Scales*) Mean Index	Predominant Schooling Through High School	
	Urban	Suburban	Rural or Small Town	High School or Less	Some College	Graduate Level Education		Public	Private or Parochial
Users	32	54	14	9	62	29	53	75	25
Nonusers	11	34	5	0	29	21	57	39	11

*More than 50% of both groups' parents' occupations rank higher than 60 on the Otis Dudley Duncan Socioeconomic Index, in contrast to the national average of 36.[10]

2%), and more likely to be unmarried (90% vs 64%). Among the users, the average duration of marihuana use was slightly more than two years. The average frequency of their marihuana use in the year prior to interview was, for more than two-thirds, at least once per week, including 12% who used it five or more times per week; 24 were using marihuana one to four times per month; and for seven there had been a decrease from previous regular use to less than once per month. Other aspects of their marihuana use have been described previously.[11, 12] Although the controls were self-selected as "nonusers," about half had tried marihuana, averaging seven trials each, including two who had used marihuana more than 20 times.

Psychiatric Illness—There was a strikingly high lifetime incidence of psychopathology in *both* groups. Approximately *half* of both the regular marihuana users and the control group fulfilled criteria for a "definite" or "probable" psychiatric diagnosis (Table 2).

TABLE 2
INCIDENCE OF PSYCHIATRIC ILLNESSES IN MARIHUANA
USERS AND NONMARIHUANA-USING FRIENDS

Diagnosis	% Users, No. = 100	% Nonusers, No. = 50	Significance
Probable affective disorder	21	18	
Definite affective disorder	8	16	
Total affective disorder	29	34	NS
Probable sociopathy	6	0	
Definite sociopathy	6	0	
Total sociopathy	12	0	< .05
Primary homosexuality	5	4	NS
Other sexual deviance	3	0	NS
Hysteria	0	4	NS
Anxiety neurosis	0	2	NS
Alcoholism	3	0	NS
Schizo-affective disorder	1	0	NS
Schizophrenia	0	0	NS
Undiagnosed psychiatric illness	8	10	NS
Total percentage of each group who received a psychiatric diagnosis*	52	46	NS

*More than one diagnosis was given to eight of the users and four of the nonusers.

About one-third of each group received a diagnosis of primary affective disorder. A significant difference was noted with respect to the incidence of sociopathy: among users, 12% received a diagnosis of definite or probable sociopathy, compared to *none* of the controls. Anxiety neurosis and hysteria were found more frequently among the nonusers, and homosexuality or other sexual deviance was more common among the users, but these differences were not significant. No schizophrenics were found in either group.

Another *quarter* of each group reported past psychiatric manifestations, which, however, did not fulfill the diagnostic criteria (Table 3). For both users and nonusers, a past depressive period was the most frequently reported problem; it was seen more often in the control group. Three other types of difficulty—antisocial activity, multiple homosexual experiences, problems from drinking—all occurred substantially more frequently among the marihuana users, but only the difference in antisocial behavior was significant.

No significant differences in incidence or types of pathology were found between the nonusers who had experience with marihuana and the nonusers who had never tried it.

TABLE 3
INCIDENCE OF NONDIAGNOSTIC PAST
PSYCHIATRICALLY SIGNIFICANT BEHAVIOR

Behavior Type	% Users, No. = 100	% Nonusers, No. = 50	Significance
Past depressive episode*	26	36	NS
Past antisocial behavior**	12	0	< .05
More than two homosexual experiences***	15	6	NS
Problem from alcohol****	18	8	NS
Total percentage of subjects included here but not in Table 2	21	28	

*At least some psychological and vegetative symptoms of depression were noted, but relatively few and short-lived.
**At least involving, on separate occasions, school authorities, parents, and legal authorities.
***Postpubertal homosexual genital contacts made by choice on more than two different occasions.
****The occurrence of at least one of the following symptoms: multiple blackouts, a bender, morning shakes, morning drinking; or problems in one of the following life areas caused by alcohol: school, job, legal, health, or family.

Psychiatric Treatment—Information was obtained from all subjects concerning psychiatric treatment. Five of the 100 marihuana users had been psychiatrically hospitalized a total of 13 times. Six of the 50 controls had had a total of 17 psychiatric hospitalizations. Fifty percent of the users and 40% of their nonuser friends had at some time seen a psychiatrist, psychologist, or other professional counselor. Psychotherapy was the most frequent type of treatment received by both groups, with psychotropic drugs less commonly used. One from each group had received electroconvulsive therapy. Psychiatrists available through an agency, whether school health service, public clinic, or state hospital facility, were as often utilized as psychiatrists in private practice. Other counselors were usually seen through an available agency.

Onset of Problem—With each subject, careful attention was paid to dating the onset of psychiatric symptoms and characterizing the time course of the process. It was therefore possible, for the user group, to determine whether the psychiatrically significant episode occurred or began before or after the first use of marihuana. This relationship is demonstrated in Table 4.

TABLE 4
FIRST ONSET OR OCCURRENCE OF PSYCHIATRICALLY
SIGNIFICANT BEHAVIOR, RELATIVE TO FIRST MARIHUANA
USE AMONG REGULAR USERS (No. = 100)

	Total No. in Whom It Occurred	Before First Marihuana Use	After First Marihuana Use
A. Diagnosable illness			
Affective disorder	29	18	11
Sociopathy	12	12	0
Homosexuality or deviance	8	8	0
Other diagnoses	12	12	0
B. Psychiatrically significant past behavior			
Depressive episode	26	13	13
Antisocial behavior	12	10	2
More than two homo-sexual experiences*	15	12	3
Problem from alcohol†	18	14	4
Onset of psychiatrically significant problem or behavior (global estimate)‡	73	57	16
C. Past socially or psychiatrically significant experience			
Received professional help	50	26	24
Psychiatric hospitalization	5	2	3
Suicide attempt	9	4	5
Any police trouble	29	21	8
Nondrug arrest	14	10	4
Any homosexual experience*	26	19	7
Any period of heavy drinking†	31	21	10
First smoked tobacco	70	59	11
First drank alcohol	97	84	13
First sexual intercourse§	81	66	15

*Excludes subjects with homosexuality diagnosis (five).
†Excludes subjects with alcoholism diagnosis (three).
‡Based on inclusion in category A or B (73 subjects).
§Asked of 87 subjects.

Except for one fourth of the affective disorders, *every* diagnosed psychiatric illness began *before* first marihuana use. Further, all forms of psychiatrically significant experiences occurred before the first use of marihuana in the great majority of instances.

The chronology of additional landmarks is recorded in category C of Table 4. Included in this list are socially acceptable as well as marginal limit-testing activities, in addition to experiences of psychiatric importance. Use of alcohol and tobacco usually preceded marihuana. Sexual intercourse nearly always antedated marihuana experience. "Acting out" behavior in marginal areas—police trouble, arrests, homosexual experience, heavy drinking—when they occurred, more often preceded marihuana experience than followed it. Utilization of professional help was equally likely to have preceded as followed marihuana use. This was also true for suicide attempts and psychiatric hospitalizations.

COMMENT

An ideal research design would involve collecting and studying a random sample of *all* regular marihuana users and a sample of *all* their nonusing friends, and a group of matched controls taken from the general population. Such a design would also include "blind" interviews, controlling for biases inherent in the interviewing psychiatrist's knowledge of each subject's drug use category. At present, however, practical problems prevent collecting such truly representative samples from a wide variety of socially unaccepted subgroups in our society. Thus, volunteer samples are studied.

Volunteers in any study may differ from the behavioral group from which they are drawn. In a marihuana study, additional considerations further bias sampling. Concern for anonymity, fear of legal consequences, desire to proselytize, relative attraction of financial remuneration, apprehension concerning an interview with a psychiatrist—all may affect the process of volunteering for such a study.

In this study, no analysis of the universe from which these volunteers came was possible because of the word-of-mouth referral system. Also, because of the design, no second control group from the general population could be studied for comparisons. Generalizations from our data therefore must be considered provisional.

The findings, nevertheless, are interesting. Both groups—the regular users and their friends—had a high incidence of psychopathology. One disorder, sociopathy, was found to distinguish the two groups: it was significantly more frequent among the users. The control group of nonuser friends demonstrated the self-selecting process of friendship. More importantly, the high incidence of psychopathology among the controls indicated that at least some regular marihuana users come from a population at *high risk* for psychiatric problems. And, as importantly, these psychiatric difficulties almost always precede use of marihuana.

That one group uses marihuana and the other does not may be a reflection of the significantly higher incidence of "acting out" behavior found in the user group. Regular marihuana use, therefore, may be a symptom of preexisting significant psychopathology.

REFERENCES

1. Benabud A: Psycho-pathological aspects of the cannabis situation in Morocco: Statistical data for 1956. *Bull Narcotics* 9:1-16, 1957.

2. Kaplan J: *Marijuana: The New Prohibition.* New York, World Publishing Co, 1970, pp 88-198.

3. Kolansky H, Moore WT: Effects of marihuana on adolescents and young adults. *JAMA* 216:486-492, 1971.

4. Benson VM: Marihuana "study" critique. *JAMA* 217:1391, 1971.

5. Robins E: Antisocial and dyssocial personality disorders, in Freedman AM, Kaplan HL (eds): *Comprehensive Textbook of Psychiatry.* Baltimore, Williams & Wilkins Co, 1967.

6. Perley MJ, Guze SB: Hysteria: The stability and usefulness of clinical criteria. *New Eng J Med* 266:421-426, 1962.

7. Guze SB, Goodwin DW, Crane BJ: Criminality and psychiatric disorders, *Arch Gen Psychiat* 20:583-591, 1969.

8. Saghir MT, Robins E: Male and female homosexuality: Natural history. *Compr Psychiat* 12:503-510, 1971.

9. Feighner JP, Robins E, Guze SB, et al: Diagnostic criteria for use in psychiatric research. *Arch Gen Psychiat* 26:57-63, 1971.

10. Blau PM, Duncan OD: *The American Occupational Structure.* New York, John Wiley & Sons Inc, 1967, p 136.

11. Halikas JA, Goodwin DW, Guze SB: Marihuana effects: a survey of regular users. *JAMA* 217:692-694, 1971.

12. Halikas JA, Goodwin DW, Guze SB: Pattern of marihuana use: A survey of 100 regular users. *Compr Psychiat* 13:161-163, 1972.

This study was supported in part by Public Health Service grants MH 13002, MH 09247, MH 05804, MH 47325, and MH 07081.

24

Marihuana Psychosis: Acute Toxic Psychosis Associated with the Use of Cannabis Derivatives

John A. Talbott and James W. Teague

In light of the intensive contact of man with *Cannabis* it is surprising to find the literature so lacking in regard to adverse reactions to *smoking* marihuana. Ames[1] and Allentuck[2] reported psychiatric symptoms following ingestion of marihuana concentrate, and Keeler interviewed persons who had previously had adverse reactions to smoking marihuana,[3] but, to our knowledge, the only report describing individuals studied while experiencing adverse reactions to smoking marihuana is that of Bromberg in 1934.[4]

Knowledge concerning the effects of *Cannabis* derivatives is controversial if not confusing. *Cannabis* derivatives have been used for medicinal purposes since the third century BC. Shen Nung, the Emperor of China, 2737 BC, extolled *Cannabis* derivatives as healthful and as psychic liberators. During the 19th century more than 100 medical reports were published in the United States recommending the

Reprinted with the permission of the authors and publisher from the *Journal of the American Medical Association*, 1969, *210,* 299–302. Copyright 1969 by the American Medical Association.
John A. Talbott, M.D., is affiliated with the Division of Community Psychiatry, St. Luke's Hospital Center, New York, New York. James W. Teague, M.D., is affiliated with the Department of Social Community Psychiatry, UCLA Neuropsychiatric Institute, Los Angeles, California. The data presented in this communication were gathered when the authors, then US Army medical officers, were assigned in South Vietnam to the 935th Medical Detachment (KO) from May 1967 to February 1968.

use of *Cannabis* derivatives.[5] Although by 1950 worldwide usage was estimated in excess of 200 million persons, only recently have medical investigators begun to study the effects of smoking marihuana.[6]

Individuals are affected by *Cannabis* derivatives on a continuum ranging from a benign intoxicating "high" to a frank schizophrenic-like psychosis. Smoking marihuana for most persons is a pleasant, nonthreatening, and ego-syntonic experience. The degree of intoxication, pleasure, and mystical experience is variable and depends on the individual's personality, the existing emotional set before and in regard to the experience, and the amount of marihuana smoked or swallowed.

Adverse reactions to marihuana are also varied, but the experiences are generally unpleasant, threatening, and ego-dystonic. Symptoms include anxiety, fear, tachycardia, dyspnea, crying, depression, suspicion, dissociation, depersonalization, disorientation, confusion, paranoid ideation, delusions, and auditory hallucinations. Most adverse reactions are treated by the individual's peers in much the same manner as belligerent drunkenness is handled—with time, patience, and sobering up. However, when symptoms persist, or the individual or his peers become frightened of the behavior, medical care may be sought.

Physicians in Vietnam have been impressed by the severity and frequency of adverse reactions to smoking *Cannabis* derivatives.[7-11] Several of the psychiatrists on active duty in Vietnam had previous experience with adverse reactions to marihuana in large metropolitan hospitals in the United States and questioned whether there was a difference between the reactions in Vietnam and the United States. During the early part of 1967 we saw several cases of perplexing psychotic reactions which cleared in one to four days, and a few which lasted a week or longer.

In order to study adverse reactions to marihuana, all patients whose diagnosis was acute toxic psychosis associated with the smoking of *Cannabis* derivatives were examined independently by two psychiatrists and their course followed closely. This report will present 12 cases with which we had personal contact. Three cases will be presented in detail and the others will be summarized in the Table and their common characteristics discussed.

METHODOLOGY

The case material was collected during our tour of duty as psychiatrists with the US Army in Vietnam from 1967 to 1968. All military personnel requiring psychiatric hospitalization from the III and IV Corps areas were seen as well as many persons handled through the judicial system and all stockade prisoners. This allowed clinical access to psychiatric cases requiring intensive psychiatric hospitalization from a population of more than 350,000 as well as judicial cases from a population of more than 500,000. In all cases involving the question of *Cannabis* derivatives as a causal factor, the opinion of a second psychiatrist was sought. In six cases it was possible to secure collaborative information regarding the smoking of *Cannabis* derivatives by the patients.

Since the possession of *Cannabis* is illegal, it is quite possible that we saw only those cases demanding professional intervention. Patients with less severe symptoms were probably handled in the community by nonprofessionals. The environment of a war zone makes the symptomatology potentially more dangerous, eg, walking into a mine field, or having a loaded weapon readily available, etc. Similarly, the same environment may have an effect on the nature of the symptoms.

REPORT OF CASES

Case 1—A 26-year-old, single, white man, second lieutenant registered nurse, with no history of psychiatric difficulties was hospitalized after smoking his first cigarette containing *Cannabis* derivatives. Immediately after smoking, he became aware of a burning, choking sensation in his throat and following this, he went to a civilian bar. Shortly thereafter he felt apprehensive, anxious, and suspicious. The symptoms rapidly increased in intensity and the subject became fearful that the "nationals" in the bar meant him harm. He fled in terror and returned to the bachelor officers' quarters. Shortly thereafter, one of us was called to see him.

When examined the patient was anxious and disoriented as to time, but not as to place and person. Anxiety, as well as the fear of being harmed by nationals, seemed to intensify and decrease in wavelike fashion. The fear of being harmed at its intensified peak we believed to be delusional. He was unable to identify the nature of the harm he feared. Affect was judged to be appropriate but labile. Thinking was rapid and disjointed, as if he were unable to follow a line of thought and as if he were experiencing a wide variety of thoughts (in rapid fashion) dissimilar in nature except for a common apprehensive quality. Proverbs were handled adequately, but with poor concentration and he quickly returned to his fears of being harmed. He did not acknowledge loosening of associations. Judgment and insight were impaired, and any evaluation of intelligence was precluded by his general condition. There were no hallucinations.

Abnormal physical findings included the following: a generalized impairment of coordination, as demonstrated by heel-to-toe walking and finger-to-nose testing; there was a positive Romberg sign; there was some injection of the conjunctivae; reflexes were generally and symmetrically hyperactive; and vital signs reflected a psychomotor agitation or excitement.

The patient was hospitalized and treated with phenothiazines and sedatives. He was also seen in brief psychotherapy. The patient was able to be discharged to his quarters in 36 hours and was returned to duty in 48 hours. No recurrence of symptoms was noted in the next three months.

Further work-up revealed no other evidence of psychiatric difficulties sufficient to diagnose a preexisting psychiatric condition. The patient was not seen by another psychiatrist. A second cigarette containing *Cannabis* derivatives was in his possession and was examined. The patient's condition was diagnosed as acute toxic psychosis.

*Case 2—*A 19-year-old, single, white soldier, private first class, was referred for examination by another psychiatrist. He was alleged to have shot and killed an individual while on guard duty.

Sworn statements and a formal judicial investigation revealed that while on guard duty the victim shared a "marihuana cigarette" with the subject, the subject's first. The victim was described as a joker whose humor was sometimes "a little sick and cruel." Shortly after having the cigarette the victim began to pick on some nearby Vietnamese children. He reportedly told them that he was "Ho Chi Minh" and fired his weapon near them. Although the subject questioned if he was Ho Chi Minh, when the victim showed him the name on his shirt, the subject became terrified and fired his rifle. He then left his guard post and entered the base camp in a confused fashion, saying that he had killed Ho Chi Minh. Upon saying this he displayed a T-shirt with that name written on it and urged those around him to accompany him to see the body. On the way, he spoke in a disjointed and confused fashion. Upon arrival at the guard post, actually an observation tower, the bare-chested body of a Negro soldier, with several gunshot wounds on the left anterior portion of the chest, was found. Due to the subject's confused state and his bizarre story, he was taken to the division psychiatrist.

Upon examination the patient was confused and apprehensive, but quite proud, in a patriotic manner, of having killed Ho Chi Minh. When confronted with the fact that the individual killed was an American Negro soldier, the subject held up the bloody, bullet-torn T-shirt, with Ho Chi Minh written across the chest, and stated rather emphatically that he had shot Ho Chi Minh, not an American soldier. He stated that the victim had told him that he was Ho Chi Minh, that the victim was disguised and had infiltrated American lines, and had proved his identity by showing his name written on the shirt. The subject then believed him, became scared, shot him, and took the T-shirt back to camp to prove that he had indeed shot and killed Ho Chi Minh. The psychiatrist's opinion was that the subject was delusional and suffering from an acute toxic psychosis; one of us (J. W. T.) concurred at a later examination.

Further examination revealed no evidence of hallucinations nor any other indication of a thought disorder. The subject was concerned and became increasingly anxious with any mention of the victim being an American soldier. He was apprehensive and unable to understand why no one believed him. He was puzzled at being seen by a psychiatrist rather than being treated as a hero for having killed Ho Chi Minh.

Following a short period of hospitalization, the subject's condition changed and he evidenced grief and depression about the preceding events.

Contact with this individual continued over the next several months without any further signs of psychotic thinking or behavior. It should be noted that the subject also stated that upon first smoking the cigarette containing *Cannabis* derivatives he experienced a burning-like irritation and an urge to cough. In addition to this he noted some mild sensations of choking and transient tingling in his extremities.

Case 3—A 24-year-old single Negro, private first class, was admitted to the hospital on transfer from another hospital. He had smoked a pipeful of "strange tasting tobacco" two days previously and had felt light-headed and "funny." He subsequently had feelings of depersonalization and derealization, and thought his mind was split into two parts—good and evil. He expressed the morbid preoccupation that he was dead, admitted to unusual illusions or hallucinations (clouds pulling him in, bright lights coming out of the clouds toward him), and expressed frightening fears that he would kill someone or be killed by someone. He was disoriented, confused, and forgetful. He was treated with chlorpromazine (Thorazine) hydrochloride with some improvement, and after two days was transferred to the psychiatric facility. On admission the patient was apprehensive, worried, and preoccupied with fears, sensations, and impulses. His restlessness, tremulousness, agitation, and rapid speech alternated with staring, mutism, and inability to complete his thoughts. He continued to express the belief that his mind was split, but denied hallucinations, delusions, or other unusual sensations. He seemed adequately oriented, and denied any prior exposure to marihuana. The patient's history included the absence of a father in the family when he was growing up, aggressive outbursts in late adolescence, excessive drinking, and difficulty in being able to keep a job.

The patient was given chlordiazepoxide hydrochloride (Librium) and his anxiety abated rapidly. He was active in group therapy and presented no problems in ward management. He was discharged with no residual symptoms seven days after he had smoked marihuana.

VIETNAMESE MARIHUANA

To place the following findings in proper perspective several factors should first be mentioned. Marihuana is cheap and readily available in Vietnam, disguised in regular American cigarette packs. This is so well done that it is virtually impossible to tell the difference without either removing the filling from the cigarettes or smoking them.

Vietnamese marihuana is reported by the Army Chemical Laboratory in Japan to be about twice as potent (content of resins) as that normally sold or found in the United States. Because the resins are produced by the plant as a protective agent against the harmful effects of the sun,[12] it is easy for anyone familiar with the climatic conditions of Vietnam to understand the plants' increased resin production. South Vietnam lies between the eighth and the 17th parallels, and thus has a much more tropical climate than the United States ($24°$-$49°$) or Mexico ($15°$-$33°$), where the most potent marihuana sold in the United States is grown. The resins are concentrated in the tops and seed pods of the female plant. In Vietnam the plant is so abundant that most preparations make use of only the female tops and seed pods.

In addition, approximately 50% of the *Cannabis* contraband seized in Vietnam contains opiates. Therefore, the quality of the *Cannabis* derivatives used there is likely to produce a much stronger effect on the consumer.

The smoking of Cannabis derivatives is not uncommon in Vietnam.

TABLE 1
SUMMARY OF CASES*

Case No.	Age	First Exposure to Marihuana	Physical Symptoms	Impaired Cognitive Functioning	Mental Symptoms	Delusions	Premorbid Personality	Treatment	Duration of Symptoms
1	26	+	+	+	Paranoid anxious	+	—	Chlorpromazine hydrochloride 50 mg 4 times daily	36 hr
2	19	+	+	+	Paranoid	+	—	—	3 days
3	24	+	+	+	Paranoid anxious	+	Aggressive	Chlordiazepoxide as necessary and chlorpromazine hydrochloride 50 mg 4 times daily	7 days
4	21	+	+	+	Paranoid	+	Psychopathic	Chlorpromazine hydrochloride 25 mg 4 times daily	2 days
5	20	+	+	+	Paranoid	+	—	Chlorpromazine hydrochloride 50 mg 4 times daily	2-3 days
6	22	+	+	+	Anxious	—	—	—	1 day
7	21	+	+	+	Anxious	—	—	—	2 days
8	21	+	+	+	Paranoid	+	—	—	3 days
9	22	+	+	+	Suicidal paranoid	+	—	—	11 days
10	22	+	+	+	Anxious paranoid	+	—	Chlorpromazine hydrochloride 25 mg 4 times daily	2 days
11	19	+	+	+	Anxious paranoid	+	—	Chlorpromazine hydrochloride 25 mg 4 times daily	3 days
12	19	+	+	+	Paranoid	+	—	—	2 days

*+ indicated positive; —, negative.

Several surveys indicated that more than 30% (30%-65%) of the soldiers used *Cannabis* derivatives at least once during their tour of duty in Vietnam.[10, 11] Our experience confirms this estimate.

FINDINGS

The findings in the 12 cases of acute toxic psychosis associated with *Cannabis* intoxication are presented in the Table. In all instances, this was the patient's first admitted exposure to marihuana and in each case marked physical symptoms appeared soon after the subjects began to smoke. Symptoms included burning and irritation of the respiratory tract accompanied by an urge to cough; impaired coordination and difficulty with fine movements; odd, irregular, and vague aching of the large muscles of the extremities (especially the legs); and irritation of the conjunctivae.

Impaired cognitive functioning was also present in each soldier. This included impairment of orientation to either time or place; severe impairment of memory, most particularly of recent memory; impairment of intellectual functioning manifested by confusion, short attention span, and difficulty concentrating; impaired thinking with tangential and disjointed qualities, and impaired judgment.

The 12 exhibited lability of affect and marked anxiety and fearfulness. Ten showed paranoid symptoms including suspiciousness, referentiality, and delusions or hallucinations. Expressed fear of overt homosexual assault on the patient was frequently a factor in bringing the soldier to the medical facility.

Two patients had significant psychiatric histories and diagnosis of personality disorder could be made. The remainder had a negative history and no evidence of preexisting personality disorder.

None of the cases presented any serious difficulty during hospitalization. In all cases the patient was able to return to duty within a week. Informal follow-up disclosed no further difficulties. All except the soldier involved in the shooting incident successfully completed their tour of duty in Vietnam. Initially the first patients hospitalized were treated with moderate doses of phenothiazines and soporifics. In addition they received individual as well as group therapy. It soon became apparent that the phenothiazines were doing more for the therapist and the ward personnel than for the patients. Following this realization no drugs were used.

COMMENT

The material presented above is similar to the cases originally described by Bromberg in 1934,[4] the only difference being our emphasis on the "organic" signs present and the short duration of the psychotic state. Reports and personal communications from Vietnam indicate that similar cases continue to be seen, and at about the same rate, ie, one to two per month.[8] This raises several questions. (1) Is this a valid clinical syndrome, and if so, is the involvement of *Cannabis* derivatives essential, or is it merely an added stress? (2) If this is a valid clinical syndrome, why has it not been reported in the past 30 years? (3) Are there factors present in Vietnam which predispose the occurrence of this condition there, but not in the United States?

It would seem that this is a valid clinical syndrome having a central core, consistent signs, and characteristic symptoms. The condition immediately followed inhalation of the smoke of a cigarette containing *Cannabis* derivatives and the symptoms rapidly intensified. In each case this was the first experience with *Cannabis* derivatives. The signs and symptoms had a definite toxic, organic quality and the condition seemed to be self-limiting. Recovery was complete and the symptoms did not recur. More than one psychiatrist made the diagnosis of psychosis in 11 of the 12 cases. In no instance was a similar case seen which did not involve the use of *Cannabis* derivatives.

Since the incidence of combat reactions in Vietnam is low in comparison with other wars, and since the visible incidence of marihuana psychosis seems so high, some observers have postulated that we are encountering the same syndrome, except that it is precipitated by marihuana, not combat. This study is unable to confirm or deny this postulate. However, these cases differ from most combat reactions reported.

We believe that *Cannabis* is directly and essentially involved in the development of the syndrome. Environmental stresses may potentiate, exaggerate, or otherwise affect the symptoms. The same environment may also have caused nonprofessionals to handle those persons less severely affected by smoking *Cannabis* derivatives, leaving only those severely affected with toxic psychosis to be seen in medical facilities.

While many of the environmental factors of Vietnam are not present in the United States, it is quite likely that the syndrome described above does occur here. Most cases are probably handled within the community by nonprofessionals, and only a few persons are seen by physicians. Those persons who seek a physician's care may not volunteer or admit to *Cannabis* usage because it is illegal. As the symptoms clear in a relatively short period of time, the physician may be satisfied and look no further into the cause. Even if the patient does admit to using *Cannabis*, will the physician accept this as a possible etiology?

One of us (J. W. T.) recently heard of such a case. A young woman was admitted to a university psychiatric hospital in a psychotic state with a history of having smoked *Cannabis* derivatives for the first time. Her symptoms were quite similar to those we observed, and she was discharged after several days. The physician in charge had no knowledge of the possibility of *Cannabis* producing the psychosis, and the etiology of her transient psychotic state was not determined.

Cannabis derivatives, as a causal or precipitating agent, should be considered whenever a young person presents with an acute toxic psychosis with paranoid features. Since possession of the drug is illegal, accurate histories may not be obtainable, but the physician must be alert to the possibility of marihuana psychosis in cases resembling acute schizophrenic reaction, acute paranoid psychosis, or acute toxic-metabolic psychosis.

REFERENCES

1. Ames, F.: A Clinical and Metabolic Study of Acute Intoxication with *Cannabis sativa* and Its Role in the Model Psychosis, *J Ment Sci* 104:972–999, 1958.

2. Allentuck, S.: "Medical Aspects" in *The Marijuana Problem in the City of New York*, 1941, reprinted in Solomon, D. (ed.): *The Marijuana Papers*, New York: Bobbs-Merrill, Company, Inc., 1966, pp 269–284.

3. Keeler, M.D.: Adverse Reactions to Marijuana, *Amer J Psychiat* 124:674–677, 1967.

4. Bromberg, W.: Marijuana Intoxication, *Amer J Psychiat* 91:303–330, 1934.

5. Maurer, D. W., and Vogel, V. H.: *Narcotics and Narcotics Addiction*, Springfield, Ill: Charles C. Thomas, Publisher, 1962.

6. Weil, A. T.; Zinberg, N. E.; and Nelsen, J. M.: Clinical and Psychological Effects of Marijuana in Man, *Science* 162:1234–1242 (Dec 13) 1968.

7. Talbott, J. A.: Pot Reactions, *USA RV Med Bull* 40–7:40–41 (Jan-Feb) 1968.

8. Fidaleo, R. A.: Marijuana: Social and Clinical Observations, *USARV Med Bull* 40–8:58–59 (March-April) 1968.

9. Heiman, E. M.: Marijuana Precipitated Psychoses in Patients Evacuated to CONUS, *USARV Med Bull* 40–9:75–77 (May-June) 1968.

10. Postel, W. B.: Marijuana Use in Vietnam, *USARV Med Bull* 40–11:56–59 (Sept-Oct) 1968.

11. Casper, E.; Janecek, J.; and Martinelli, H.: Marijuana in Vietnam, *USARV Med Bull* 40–11:60–72 (Sept-Oct) 1968.

12. Walton, R. P.: *Marijuana: America's New Drug Problem,* New York: J. B. Lippincott, Co., 1938, p. 42.

Generic and Trade Names of Drugs. Chlorpromazine hydrochloride—*Thorazine Hydrochloride*. Chlordiazepoxide hydrochloride—*Librium*.

25

Psychiatric Effects of Hashish

Forest S. Tennant, Jr., and C. Jess Groesbeck

Adverse psychiatric effects reported to result from smoking products of *Cannabis sativa* are panic reactions,[1-2] toxic psychosis,[3-5] flashback phenomena,[6] prolonged psychosis analogous to schizophrenic reactions,[7-10] and the "amotivational" syndrome.[11-13] The latter manifestation occurs with long-term cannabis usage and is characterized by apathy, withdrawal, poor judgment, and failure to achieve. Other symptoms ascribed to long-term cannabis use include paranoia, memory loss, and delusions.[14, 15]

During the three-year period between September 1968 and September 1971, we had the opportunity to observe and study an accessible, defined population of approximately 36,000 American soldiers stationed in West Germany in the area served by the US Army Hospital in Wurzburg, West Germany. Hashish, a potent product of *Cannabis sativa,* is the only form of cannabis normally available in West Germany. Large questionnaire surveys of 5,300 subjects were

Reprinted with permission of the authors and publisher from the *Archives of General Psychiatry,* 1972, 27, 133—136. Copyright 1972 by the American Medical Association.

MAJ Forest S. Tennant, Jr., MC, USA, and MAJ C. Jess Groesbeck, MC, USA, prepared this article while at the Special Action Office for Drug Abuse, HQ, USAREUR & Seventh Army, Heidelberg, West Germany. Dr. Tennant is currently at the Department of Preventive & Social Medicine, UCLA School of Public Health, Los Angeles, California.

conducted in the fall of 1970 and 1971. They revealed that approximately 46% of the American soldier population in West Germany have smoked hashish on at least one occasion and 16% smoke it over three times per week.[16] Our personal experience with hashish consumers involves direct medical and psychiatric consultation with 720 users. It is the purpose of this paper to describe the psychiatric manifestations associated with hashish use in this large group. An accessible, defined American population created an opportunity to assess the prevalency and prospectively observe adverse effects of a potent cannabis product.

BACKGROUND INFORMATION

Hashish in West Germany is available from ubiquitous illegal sources at a price of approximately $1 to $1.50 per gram. In the United States, illicit hashish sells for $5 to $10 per gram depending on locale. The alleged source of hashish in Europe is the Middle East and Mediterranean areas. Until recently hashish use in the United States has been relatively uncommon compared to marihuana, but its use is increasing according to our drug-abuse patients. Hashish, although occasionally ingested and rarely injected, is usually smoked in a standard pipe and often mixed with tobacco. Approximately 1,000 confiscated hashish samples are analyzed monthly at the US Army Crime Laboratory in Frankfurt, West Germany, utilizing microscopic, Duquenois, and chromatographic techniques.[17, 18] Only 3% of the hashish samples are found to be contaminated—usually with cocaine, opiates, spices, shoe polish, or feces. Hashish available in West Germany contains 5% to 10% tetrahydrocannabinol (THC) while the marihuana marketed in the United States usually contains less than 1% THC.[13, 19]

PATIENT SELECTION

All 720 patients were either self-referred or referred by their commander to one of us for one or more psychiatric and/or medical symptoms (Table 1). Medical complaints were usually of a respiratory nature.[20] Of these patients, 392 were experimental or occasional hashish users limiting their consumption to a maximum of 10 to 12 gm monthly. A total of 110 patients severely abused hashish by smoking 50 to 600 gm per month for periods ranging from 3 to 18 months. Eighteen patients presented with a short-term panic reaction of toxic psychosis following a single, high dose of hashish. Three persistent schizophrenic reactions occurred in moderate hashish smokers. A total of 85

TABLE 1
CLASSIFICATION OF 720 HASHISH USERS

No.	Dose per mo, gm	Frequency Use	Reason for Medical Consultation
392	0-12	1-3 times per week	Respiratory ailment or drug information
18	0-25	Experimental or occasional	Acute panic reaction or toxic psychosis
3	10-50	3-7 times weekly	Schizophrenic reaction
110	50-600	Several times daily	Chronic intoxicated state
85	10-50	3-7 times weekly	Acute toxic reaction (multiple drug use)
112	25-200	Several times daily	Schizophrenic reaction (multiple drug use)
720	Total		

patients developed acute, toxic psychosis after the simultaneous consumption of hashish and another drug(s), and the remaining 112 patients developed persistent schizophrenic reactions following prolonged use of hashish and another drug(s). Severe hashish abusers who smoke over 50 gm per month are called "hashaholics" in the drug cult of the US Army, Europe. "Hashaholics" smoke hashish several times per day. It was possible, due to the fact that one of us (F. T.) was

TABLE 2
DATA FROM NINE SOLDIERS* OBSERVED BEFORE, DURING, AND AFTER HASHISH SMOKING

Case	Age	Period of Chronic Intoxication, mo	Monthly Dose, gm	Period of Post-Intoxication, mo	Residual Organic Symptoms
1	19	3	150	12	None
2	20	12	50	3	Intermittent episodes memory loss; confusion; (normal EEG)
3	21	8	75-100	3	None
4	20	4	200	9	Intermittent episodes memory loss; confusion; impaired calculation (normal EEG)
5	19	6	125-150	3	None
6	22	8	100	18	None
7	19	5	200-250	6	Intermittent episodes memory loss; confusion; impaired calculation (normal EEG)
8	19	6	100-125	12	None
9	20	7	50-60	6	None

*Three patients exhibited intermittent residual symptoms analogous to those of chronic brain damage after cessation of hashish consumption. All patients smoked hashish several times per day.

assigned as a unit surgeon, to identify and follow nine of the 110 severe hashish abusers prior to the time they ever smoked hashish; during the several months they severely abused hashish; and for several months after complete discontinuation of usage (Table 2). An additional 23 severe hashish abusers from this group were followed for periods ranging from six to 18 months following cessation of hashish abuse.

SHORT-TERM ADVERSE EFFECTS

Panic reactions and toxic psychosis with hashish use alone were uncommonly observed. Only those cases severe enough to require hospitalization and which gave a history of hashish consumption without concomitant ingestion of alcohol or other psychoactive drug are included. Panic reactions characterized by a feeling of impending death and/or loss of mental function occurred in five novice or first-time users and resolved with reassurance and mild sedation. Thirteen cases of toxic psychosis resulted from smoking a large amount of hashish—usually 5 to 30 gm—in a short span of a few hours. Disorientation, delusions, anxiety, depersonalization, and confusion similar to the toxic cannabis cases reported by others[3, 4] were the predominant clinical findings. Paranoia and hallucinations were observed in ten of these patients. Toxic manifestations resolved without residual effects within three days following treatment with antipsychotic agents such as chlorpromazine (Thorazine). During this three-year span, we treated an additional 85 cases of toxic, acute psychosis which occurred after simultaneous consumption of hashish and one or more hallucinogens, amphetamines, alcoholic beverages, or "downers" (ie, tranquilizers, sedatives, pain relievers).

Flashback phenomena could not be documented in any soldier whose only illegal drug consumption was hashish. Among patients who used both hashish and lysergic acid diethylamide (LSD), flashback phenomena were frequently described. A total of 15 patients recalled the hallucinations experienced on a previous LSD trip while under the influence of hashish. Weil reported similar observations in marihuana smokers.[2]

An acute psychosis analogous to an acute schizophrenic reaction occurred in 115 hashish smokers. In these instances treatment for one to three weeks with chlorpromazine did not completely result in resolution of symptoms, and the reaction progressed into a chronic phase similar to chronic schizophrenia. Although these cases became chronic, they are included in the acute category because they presented for medical treatment in the acute psychotic state. Three cases occurred following a one- to ten-day-period of high-dose hashish consumption alone. These patients exhibited hallucinations, delusions, paranoia, withdrawal, loosened associations, and inappropriate affect. All three patients required medical evacuation to the United States for long-term psychiatric hospitalization. Due to our accessible soldier population precise premorbid histories were easily obtained. In each case there was considerable evidence that latent schizophrenia probably preexisted.

Although only three psychotic episodes resembling schizophrenic reactions occurred with hashish use alone, an additional 112 psychotic reactions resembling schizophrenic reactions were associated with the concomitant consumption of hashish and hallucinogens, amphetamines, or alcoholic beverages. These patients were long-term hashish abusers who consumed 25 to 200 gm monthly for three to six months. Schizophrenic reactions occurred abruptly during their period of drug abuse and all patients at the time of admission to the hospital were psychotic enough to require restraint and observation. Premorbid histories obtained from the commanders of these patients indicated in each instance the presence of progressive psychiatric illness prior to the onset of acute symptoms. All required eventual evacuation to the United States for long-term psychiatric confinement. Psychotic reactions resembling and diagnosed by at least two psychiatrists as schizophrenic reactions have markedly increased in our soldier population since the drug era in Europe began in 1969 (Table 3). Despite the population remaining constant, the number of schizophrenic reactions has progressively risen from 18 per year in 1967 to 77 per year in 1971.

TABLE 3 PERSISTENT SCHIZOPHRENIC REACTIONS*		
Year	Schizophrenic Reactions	% Population
1967	18	.09
1968	16	.08
1969	41	.20
1970	70	.35
1971	77	.38

*The drug era in the US Army, Europe began in 1969. All cases required long-term psychiatric confinement.

LONG-TERM ADVERSE EFFECTS

In an effort to determine if long-term hashish use leads to personality and behavioral changes, we recorded hashish intake levels and maintained close follow-up of all patients which is easily accomplished in the Army community. Of the soldiers in this report, 392 limited their hashish consumption to less than 10 to 12 gm monthly. Our evaluation of these soldiers showed ostensibly they suffered no ill-effects other than occasional minor respiratory ailments such as rhinopharyngitis ("hash throat"). It was for this reason or the seeking of drug information that they even consulted us.

A total of 110 patients severely abused hashish by smoking 50 to 600 gm monthly for 3 to 12 months. These men smoked hashish several times per day. Other illegal drug usage was reported as "rare" or nonexistent in these soldiers. All 110 patients exhibited a personality disturbance which prompted psychiatric consultation at some point during their period of high-dose hashish consumption. Despite variation in overall symptomatology, all displayed symptoms of chronic intoxication similar to those found in individuals dependent on depressant-hypnotic drugs.[21] Major manifestations were apathy, dullness, and lethargy with mild-to-severe impairment of judgment, concentration, and memory. Intermittent episodes of confusion and inability to calculate occurred with high levels of chronic intoxication. Physical appearance was stereotyped in that all patients appeared dull, exhibited poor hygiene, and had slightly slowed speech. So apathetic were many patients that they lost interest in cosmetic appearance, proper diet, and personal affairs such as paying debts, job performance, etc. Although violence or overt acts of crime were rare in these patients, they were frequently in social and legal difficulties due to failure to care for their personal affairs. These manifestations have previously been described in small numbers of long-term marihuana smokers.[11-13]

It was possible to prospectively follow nine of the severe hashish abusers before, during, and after long-term, high-dose hashish abuse for periods of up to two years (Table 2). Not only was an initial examination and interview prior to severe hashish abuse accomplished in these patients, but frequent, subsequent observations were possible during the period of hashish abuse and after its discontinuation. The chronic intoxicated state described above developed after the patient smoked over 50 gm of hashish per month for two to three months. After complete discontinuation of hashish abuse, memory, alertness, concentration, and calculating ability returned to normal within two to four weeks in six of the nine patients. Three of the nine patients, however, exhibited intermittent residual symptoms analogous to those of organic brain disease. Symptoms consisted of intermittent periods of memory loss, confusion, and inability to calculate and concentrate. Episodes lasted from several hours to days, and sometimes hospitalization was required due to extreme confusion. With passage of time, these intermittent episodes became less severe and less frequent. These nine patients denied all other drug use except alcohol during their periods of observation. Twenty-three of the 110 severe hashish abusers came under our treatment during a state of chronic intoxication and then totally discontinued hashish abuse. After return to a "detoxified" state, ten of the 23 exhibited intermittent episodes of memory loss, inability to concentrate and calculate, and confusion. These 23 patients denied all other drug use except alcohol. The remaining 78 severe hashish abusers did not cease hashish consumption and continued their habit until discharge from the Army. In the vast majority (70 cases), a premature discharge was mandatory since the soldier did not adequately function in a working capacity. It is impossible to completely assess the comparative roles of hashish and underlying character-behavior disorders in these latter cases, but on clinical grounds hashish abuse appeared to play a significant deleterious role.

COMMENT

The consumption of hashish by a large, accessible, defined American soldier population in West Germany has afforded the opportunity to study the psychiatric manifestations ascribed to potent cannabis derivatives. Toxic psychosis and panic states with hashish use alone were uncommon occurrences in our patients. A total of only 18 of these acute adverse effects were observed over a three-year period among 36,000 men of which 46% reported some use of hashish. Eighty-five cases of acute toxic psychosis, however, resulted from the simultaneous consumption of hashish and alcohol or other psychoactive drugs. It is possible that other acute adverse reactions occurred but did not require hospital treatment. Flashback phenomena could only be documented in patients who simultaneously used LSD and hashish.

Hashish may induce a chronic psychosis analogous to a schizophrenic reaction in predisposed individuals. Three patients who exhibited premorbid evidence of latent schizophrenia appeared to precipitate a chronic schizophrenic reaction following high-dose hashish usage. In addition 112 patients who simultaneously abused hashish and hallucinogens, amphetamines, or alcohol developed an acute psychosis which progressed to persistent schizophrenic reactions. The dramatic rise of acute psychoses heralding persistent schizophrenic reactions in our controlled soldier population during the past five years appeared to be related to rising drug usage. There is no way of knowing, however, if this rise would have occurred regardless of the onset of the drug scene.

Our observations indicate that the occasional use of hashish under 10 to 12 gm per month if smoked in small, intermittent doses, may cause only minor respiratory ailments without ostensible adverse mental effect. Long-term hashish abuse and simultaneous consumption of hashish and other psychoactive drugs, however, may produce adverse mental effects. Compared to usual US standards of cannabis consumption, the abuse of hashish by many American soldiers in West Germany is mammoth. Soldiers who developed long-term intoxication characterized by apathy, dullness, confusion, memory loss, and decreased concentration and calculation ability consumed 50 to 600 gm of hashish per month. Assuming that the usual marihuana cigarette sold in the United States weighs .5 gm and contains 1% THC[13, 19] an equivalent THC dose would require the smoking of from at least 500 to 6,000 marihuana cigarettes per month.

Clinical observations of patients before, during, and after chronic hashish intoxication indicate that severe abuse may produce residual symptoms analogous to those of organic brain damage in some abusers; this does not at all prove the identity of such symptoms and organic brain damage. Campbell et al[22] recently reported cerebral atrophy in cannabis users; although these subjects also consumed other psychoactive drugs and the measure of atrophy used presents some problems for interpretation. Nor do we have laboratory data indicating that actual cerebral damage occurred in hashish abusers. It is emphasized, however, that carefully recorded clinical observations are required to learn the side-effects or complications of a psychoactive drug and to point to necessary laboratory investigations. Foreign investigators in India and Africa have frequently recorded observations similar to ours in long-term hashish smokers.[4, 5, 23] These foreign studies have often been disregarded in the United States since conditions of poverty, disease, and poor nutrition exist to such an extent in the indigenous populations of these countries that observations on mental changes have often been felt to be unreliable.[19, 24]

The frequency of adverse mental effects observed with hashish use in Africa, India, and among American soldiers in Europe compared to the relative lack of adverse effects with smoking marihuana obtained in the States seems to be due primarily to the extreme differences in THC potency and the quantity of consumption. In the East, however, use of the less potent cannabis products are not even considered to be a health problem; *bhang,* which is the Indian equivalent of marihuana, is not even considered to fall within the definition of cannabis by Indian authorities.[25]

Of great concern in this study has not only been the severe abuse of hashish but the simultaneous consumption of hashish with alcohol or other psychoactive drugs. A total of 112 persistent psychoses resembling schizophrenia were observed following combined drug use. Combined drug consumption and the severe hashish abuse by large numbers of American soldiers in West Germany appears relevant to the controversial issue of legalization, control, and distribution of cannabis products. Although the morale, environment, and antimilitary feelings of many American soldiers stationed in West Germany is unquestionably conducive to drug abuse, severe hashish abuse by large numbers of these young men can only be described as irresponsible. Should cannabis products become legally distributed in the United States our studies indicate to us that stringent controls and attention will be needed to prevent irresponsible abuse of the potent cannabis products.

REFERENCES

1. Bromberg W: Marihuana intoxication: A clinical study of *Cannabis sativa* intoxication. *Amer J Psychiat* 91:303–330, 1934.

2. Weil AT: Adverse reactions to marihuana: Classification and suggested treatment. *New Eng J Med* 282:997–1000, 1970.

3. Talbott JA, Teague JW: Marihuana psychosis: Acute toxic psychosis associated with the use of Cannabis derivatives. *JAMA* 210:299–302, 1969.

4. Chopra GS: Marihuana and adverse psychotic reactions: Evaluation of different factors involved. *Bull Narcotics* 23:15–22, 1971.

5. Benabud A: Psycho-pathological aspects of the Cannabis situation in Morocco: Statistical data for 1956. *Bull Narcotics* 9:1–15, 1957.

6. Keeler MH, Reifler CB, Liptzin MB: Spontaneous recurrence of marihuana effect. *Amer J Psychiat* 125:384–386, 1968.

7. Grossman W: Adverse reactions associated with Cannabis products in India. *Ann Intern Med* 70:529–533, 1969.

8. Chopra IC, Chopra RN: The use of the Cannabis drugs in India. *Bull Narcotics* 9:4–29, 1957.

9. Colbach, EM, Crowe RR: Marihuana associated psychosis in Vietnam. *Milit Med* 135:574–573, 1970.

10. Spencer DJ: Cannabis-induced psychosis. *Int J Addictions* 6:323–326, 1971.

11. Smith DE: Acute and chronic toxicity of marihuana. *J Psychedelic Drugs* 2:37–47, 1968.

12. Brill NQ, Crumpton E, Frank IM, et al: The marihuana problem. *Ann Intern Med* 73:449–465, 1970.

13. McGlothlin WH, West LJ: The marihuana problem: An overview. *Amer J Psychiat* 125:370–378, 1968.

14. Wurmser L, Levin L, Lewis A: *Chronic Paranoid Symptoms and Thought Disorders in Users of Marihuana and LSD as Observed in Psychotherapy, Problems of Drug Dependence.* Washington, DC, National Academy of Sciences–National Research Council, 1969, pp 6154–6177.

15. Kolansky H, Moore WT: Effects of marihuana on adolescents and young adults. *JAMA* 246:486–492, 1971.

16. Tennant FS Jr: Drug abuse in the US Army, Europe. *JAMA*, to be published.

17. Kouns DM: Identification of marihuana. *Naval Med School Bull* 7:12–18, 1969.

18. Kutler WP: *Methods of Analysis for Alkaloids, Opiates, Marihuana, Barbiturates, and Miscellaneous Drugs,* Bulletin 341. Internal Revenue Service Publication, 1967, pp 6–67.

19. Pillard RC: Marihuana. *New Eng J Med* 283:294–303, 1970.

20. Tennant FS Jr, Preble M, Prendergast TJ, et al: Medical manifestations associated with hashish. *JAMA* 216:1965–1969, 1971.

21. Essig C: Drug dependence of the barbiturate type. *Drug Dependence,* No. 5, pp 24–27, 1970.

22. Campbell AMG, Evans M, Thomson JLG: Cerebral atrophy in young *Cannabis* smokers. *Lancet* 2:1219–1224, 1971.

23. Soueif MI: Hashish consumption in Egypt, with special reference to psychosocial aspects. *Bull Narcot* 19:1–12, 1967.

24. Grinspoon L: Marihuana. *Sci Amer* 221:17–25, 1969.

25. Commission on Narcotic Drugs: *Report to the 20th Session, November 29-Dec 21, 1965,* E/4140, E/CN7/488. New York, United Nations, 1965.

26

Changes in Anxiety Feelings Following Marihuana Smoking

Ernest L. Abel

The psychological reaction to smoking marihuana ranges on a continuum of anxiety from sublime euphoria to acute paranoid psychosis.[1] While potency of preparations may be a factor contributing to the disparity in subject effects,[2] a more important variable would appear to be the individual himself.[3] Therefore, wherever possible, the effects of marihuana should be evaluated using the subject as his own baseline control. This is the type of design that is employed in the following study which ascertains the effects of marihuana on feelings of anxiety.

Fourteen adults, ages 22-37 served as volunteer subjects. In the marihuana condition, there were 3 men and 5 women, all of whom had had several prior experiences with marihuana. Six individuals, 2 men and 4 women, served as controls. All subjects knew beforehand whether they would be given marihuana during the study. In addition, subjects in each session knew each other and all but 2 personally knew the experimenter.

The experiment was run in 2 sessions and no less than 2 and no more than 3 subjects took part at any one time. The first session was identical

Reprinted with permission of the publisher (Longman Group Limited Journals) from the *British Journal of Addiction*, 1971, 66, 203–205.

for both groups: a copy of the Taylor Manifest Anxiety Scale (MAS)[4] being administered to each individual. The scale was modified such that statements were followed by a 7-point true-false continuum and the experimenter demonstrated how it was to be used before subjects marked their answers. The position of the trues and the falses were randomly alternated to prevent positional errors. Upon completion of the questionnaire, subjects participated in a number of tasks dealing with memory and the solution of anagrams which lasted approximately one-half hour.

The second session began immediately thereafter and was identical to the first except that following the anagrams test, subjects in the marihuana condition were given 2 marihuana cigarettes to smoke. Control subjects received no comparable treatment. Approximately 10 min after the last cigarette had been smoked, the MAS was readministered. At this time, subjects were told to fill out the questionnaire again, not because they were being tested for their consistency in answering, but because it had been previously noticed that some individuals occasionally answered some of the statements differently when retested while others did not, and the experimenter was more interested in their answers once they had had a chance to think about them.

The MAS contains a number of items designed to assess an individual's level of anxiety according to whether he answers true or false to the statements. By permitting the individual to make a quantitative judgment rather than a simple nominal answer, it is possible to determine more precisely any differences which exist between groups before treatments and to assess the effects of particular treatments on individuals in quantitative terms.

To make such an evaluation, the true and false scores were converted to numerical values ranging from +3 to −3. A +3 score indicates that the subject chose the extreme end of the true-false continuum, which corresponds to the answer given by Taylor[4] as an anxiety response. A minus score would indicate an answer opposite to that indicating anxiety. An X placed in the middle of the continuum would be scored as 0.

The scores in each session for each subject were then added with regard to sign and it was assumed that a positive score indicated the degree of anxiety while a negative score quantitatively indicated the lack of anxiety. Comparisons were made between the scores of the 2 groups in each session. In addition, each subject's answers in the first session served as a baseline control for his answers in the second session and the absolute differences in scores between the 2 sessions were also compared. The Mann-Whitney test[5] was used to determine whether any of the differences were significant.

There were no differences between the 2 groups in their anxiety scores in the first session. The means were —2·7 and —5·7 for the control and premarihuana groups respectively ($U = 15$, n.s.). Similarly, the groups did not significantly differ in their anxiety levels in the second session. The means were 0·0 and —4·7 for control and marihuana groups respectively ($U = 15$, n.s.). However, while the group differences in anxiety were not significant, there were significantly greater changes in anxiety level for subjects in the marihuana condition than for subjects in the control condition. This was determined by a comparison of the size and direction of changes from the first to the second session. Subjects in the control condition manifested a mean absolute change of 7·0 as compared to 18·0 for subjects under the influence of marihuana ($U = 5, p = 0·01$).

Since subjects in the marihuana condition showed significantly greater changes between conditions than did those in the control condition, one might have expected that given that there were no differences between the 2 groups in the first session, there should have been a difference in the second. The explanation for the failure to corroborate this expectation comes from the fact that some of the subjects with negative scores in the first session obtained positive scores in the second and vice versa, so that these changes virtually cancel each other with the result that the overall anxiety score for the group remains relatively unchanged. This hypothesis was confirmed by casting the changes from the first to the second session in a 2×2 contingency table with marihuana, no marihuana, as one of the conditions and change in sign (i.e., a change from a positive to a negative score or vice versa) versus no change, as the other condition. No subjects in the control condition changed from a positive or negative score to the other, while 4 out of 7 (the data for 1 subject was misplaced) individuals in the marihuana condition did manifest such a change. This difference as evaluated by the Fisher Exact Probability Test[5] was significant ($p = 0·043$). Thus, individuals under the influence of marihuana become highly variable in their feelings of anxiety, but such changes are not manifested when the group is examined as a whole.

The finding that marihuana leads to significant alternation in an individual's feelings of anxiety is in direct contrast to opinions which hold that rather than changing or altering personality traits, the effect of marihuana is an accentuation of existing feelings, both harmful and beneficial.[6] The data from this experiment suggest that this position is not tenable when dealing with those traits having to do with an individual's feelings of anxiety.

REFERENCES

1. C. J. Schwartz. *Can. Psychiat. Ass. J.* 14, 591 (1969); C. T. Tart, *Nature* 226, 701 (1970).

2. I. E. Waskow, J. E. Olsson, C. Salzman and M. M. Katz. *Arch. Gen. Psychiat.* 22, 97 (1970).

3. L. D. Clark and E. N. Nakashima. *Am. J. Psychiat.* 125, 379 (1968).

4. J. A. Taylor, *J. abnorm. soc. Psychol.* 48, 285 (1953).

5. S. Siegel. Nonparametric Statistics (McGraw-Hill, New York, 1956).

6. S. Allentuck and K. M. Bowman. *Am. J. Psychiat.* 99, 248 (1942-43).

27

Changes in Personality Response Ratings Induced by Smoking Marihuana

Ernest L. Abel

METHOD

Subjects. Twenty-two males and females, ages 21—30, served as volunteer subjects. Most were university students or university graduates. Prior to their agreement, subjects were told that the experimenter was interested in obtaining information regarding the effects of marihuana on memory, but that a questionnaire would also be administered during the test period.

Only subjects that had used marihuana a number of times previously and had reported feeling "high" on one such occasion, were used as experimental subjects ($N = 11$). Control subjects ($N = 11$) consisted of individuals who had and who had not previously used marihuana.

Psychological Testing. The Jackson Personality Research Form (PRF)[4] was administered to all subjects prior to any treatment. This test contains 440 items, the answers to which assess 22 personality traits such as need for achievement, aggression, impulsiveness, etc. Completing the test requires from one-half to one and one-half hours, depending on the individual's reading rate.

Reprinted with permission of the publisher (Longman Group Limited Journals) from the *British Journal of Addiction*, 1972, 67, 225–227.

Following completion of this form (AA), the subjects participated in an experiment dealing with their memory for random words. This test lasted 15 minutes. Experimental subjects were then given 1 marihuana cigarette to smoke. Control subjects were left undisturbed during this period. Twenty-five minutes after completion of the memory test, subjects were given 5 minutes to recall as many of the words from the memory test as possible. They were then asked to pick out the old words from a sheet containing both the old and a set of new words. This task required approximately 10 minutes. Following this, a second but different form (BB) of the PRF was administered to all subjects.

Thus, the interval from completion of the AA form to the beginning of the BB form was approximately 1 hour.

RESULTS

Two separate analyses were performed on the data. The first involved obtaining the difference scores from test AA to BB for each subject on each of the scales and then performing a "t" test[1] on these difference scores. This type of analysis corrects for any differences in the initial response bias between groups. The second analysis, which was supplementary, involved a comparison of scores in BB with their counterparts in AA to determine whether there had been any significant change in response tendency from test AA to BB.

The only scales for which significant differences were obtained on the first analysis were those measuring autonomy (t = 2·09, df = 20, p. < 0·05)[1], dominance (t = 3·19, df = 20, p. < 0·01), and exhibitionism (t = 2·70, df = 20, p. < 0·02). However, each of these differences arose through the operation of different factors. For autonomy (breaking away from social restraints, rebelliousness, etc.), the scores of the control subjects increased while those of the marihuana subjects decreased slightly from test AA to BB. Neither of these changes in themselves tended to be significant, but the overall pattern of change resulted in a significant separation of scores on the scale. For dominance (attempts to control one's environment, influence and direct others, etc.), the scores of the control subjects decreased significantly (t = 2·70, df = 20, p. < 0·02) from AA to BB while the slight increase in marihuana subjects was not significant. Consequently, the significant difference between the two groups arose through the fact that the marihuana-smoking subjects were not responsive to the same factors which affected control subjects. Finally, the clearest differences between the two groups emerged on the exhibitionism scale, with marihuana subjects obtaining significantly lower scores on BB than on

AA (t = 3·28, df = 20, p. < 0·01). In contrast, there was virtually no change from AA to BB for control subjects. In regard to the differences obtained on this latter scale, it is important to note that 10 out of 11 of the marihuana-smoking subjects expressed a decrease in exhibitionism as compared to only 4 out of 11 in the control group.

DISCUSSION

The data from this exploratory study of changes in subjective feelings as a result of smoking marihuana indicate that the major effect of smoking marihuana is a decrease in feelings of exhibitionism. According to Jackson's[4] definition, this means that marihuana inclines the individual to feel less like being the "center of attention" than he felt a short period before. In other words, the individual is less likely to engage in behavior that is directed at gaining the notice of others. Rather, he tends to prefer being inconspicuous and is withdrawn.

Interpretation of the scores on the other two scales where differences were obtained, however, is not as straightforward since the differences emerged as a result of changes in the control group rather than in the marihuana group. This finding is important, however, because it indicates the necessity of including a control group whenever question-naire scores are compared from one session to another, especially if the test sessions are lengthy, as in the present study. It is not sufficient to compare the premarihuana responses of subjects with their postmari-huana responses, as has been done in many studies in this area (e.g., 2, 3, 5, 7) and assume that the former condition acts as a control for the latter. In other words, it is possible that any differences which appear from one test session to the next, may be a function of the subject's reaction to being retested, rather than to any peculiar effect of a drug. This point is nicely illustrated in the present study by the observation that the dominance scores in the control group showed a significant decline from test AA to BB while there was no comparable or opposite change among marihuana subjects. This indicates that marihuana did in fact have some effect on this response tendency, but it was a stabilizing effect, and not one associated with change. Had a control group not been included for purposes of comparison, this effect would not have been indicated.

REFERENCES

1. Edwards, A. L. (1968). *Experimental Design in Psychological Research*. Holt, Rinehart and Winston, New York.

2. Hollister, L. E., Richards, R. K. and Gillespie, H. K. (1968). Comparison of tetrahydrocannabinol and synhexyl in man. *Clinical Pharmacol. and Therapeutics,* 9, 783–791.

3. Isbell, H., Gorodetzsky, C. W., Jasinski, D., Claussen, U., Spulak, F. v. and Korte, F. (1967). Effects of (—) Δ^9-Trans-Tetrahydrocannabinol in man. *Psychopharmacology,* 11, 184–188.

4. Jackson, D. N. (1967). *The Personality Research Form.* Research Psychologists Press, Goshen, N.Y.

5. *The Marihuana Problem in the City of New York.* Cattell Press, Lancaster, Pa. 1944.

6. Waskow, I. E., Olsson, M., Salzman, C. and Katz, M. M. (1970). Psychological Effects of Tetrahydrocannabinol, *Arch. General Psychiatry,* 22, 97–107.

7. Williams, E. G., Himmelsbach, C. K., Wikler, A. and Ruble, D. C. (1946). Studies on Marihuana and Pyrahexyl Compound. *Public Health Report,* 61, 1059–1083.

All tests were 2-tailed.

I thank B. Buckley for her assistance in analyzing the data. This research was conducted while the author was a post-doctoral fellow at the University of California, Berkeley, California.

28

The Behavior of Worker and Nonworker Rats Under the Influence of (—) Delta-9-Trans-Tetrahydrocannabinol, Chlorproma-zine and Amylobarbitone

Jandira Masur
Regina M. W. Märtz, and E. A. Carlini

Mowrer (1940) described an interesting pattern of social interaction among rats; when, after a previous bar pressing training, they are put in groups, one of them becomes the worker-rat performing most of the bar pressing, while the partners receive the reward without working. Recently, some of the variables involved in this interaction were studied by Oldfield-Box (1967, 1969a, 1969b, 1969c) who observed the stability of this social hierarchy. It was considered that if this stability could be disrupted by drugs, another useful tool could be added to the field of investigation concerned with the influence of drugs on social behavior of rats, in addition to the methods usually utilized, such as the common food dispenser (Heimstra and Sallee, 1965; Uyeno, 1966, 1967) and the straight runway (Work *et al.*, 1969; Masur *et al.*, 1971b).

The present work was carried out to investigate the influence of (—) Δ^9-*trans*-tetrahydrocannabinol (Δ^9-THC) on the behavior of worker and nonworker rats; this drug has been described as able to modify the

Reprinted with permission of the authors and the publisher from *Psychopharmacologia*, 1972, 25, 218—228. Copyright 1972 by Springer-Verlag.

Jandira Masur, Regina M.W. Märtz, and E.A. Carlini are all associated with the Setor de Psicofarmacologia, Departamento de Bioquimica e Farmacologia, Escola Paulista de Medicina, São Paulo, Brasil.

behavior of rats in food competition situations (Masur *et al.,* 1971b). Furthermore, our results led us to examine the influence of chlorpromazine and amylobarbitone on the same social problem.

METHODS

Experiment 1 (VI Schedule)

Drugs. Suspensions of Δ^9-THC, which was supplied by the United Nations, and a control solution were prepared according to Carlini and Kramer (1965). The biological activity of Δ^9-THC, measured by the corneal areflexia method in rabbits (Gayer test), was 0.107 ± 0.08 mg/kg.

Subjects. Forty-six Wistar male rats, 3 months old, weighing about 200 g at the beginning of the experiment were used.

Apparatus. The apparatus that was used, a modified Skinner box, was similar to that described by Oldfield-Box (1967). It consisted of a plexiglass box measuring $60 \times 30 \times 30$ cm; the water deliverer and the bar could be attached either to the same or to opposite walls.

Procedure. Initially, the rats deprived of water for 22 h were individually trained 15 min every 48 h on a variable interval schedule (VI average 34 sec) to receive 0.02 ml of water. For the first 2 trials the bar and the water deliverer were attached to the same wall, to facilitate learning; after that, they were located on opposite walls, in such a way that the animal had to press the bar and run through the apparatus to be rewarded. After reaching a stable baseline, the effect on the individual performance of 6 rats of 2.5 mg/kg of Δ^9-THC injected i.p. 45 min before the trial was studied. The remaining 40 rats were submitted to the social problem. Pairs of rats with a similar frequency of bar pressing, caged together throughout the experiment, were simultaneously introduced into the apparatus for a period of 15 min every 48 h. The frequency of bar pressing and reward obtained by each rat was recorded. After 15 paired trials, the rat which had performed at least 80% of the total amount of bar pressing performed by the pair during the last 4 trials, was classified as a worker rat, and the partner as a nonworker. Only 12 pairs reached this labor division criterion. The remaining 8 pairs reached criterion after 25 trials; however, they were not used thereafter. The 12 experimental pairs were submitted to the following treatment: 45 min before the next 6 trials, six nonworker rats were injected with 2.5 (first 3 trials) and 5.0 mg/kg (last 3 trials) of Δ^9-THC, while their partners (worker rats) received 1.0 ml/kg of control solution; for the remaining six pairs the drug treatment was reversed.

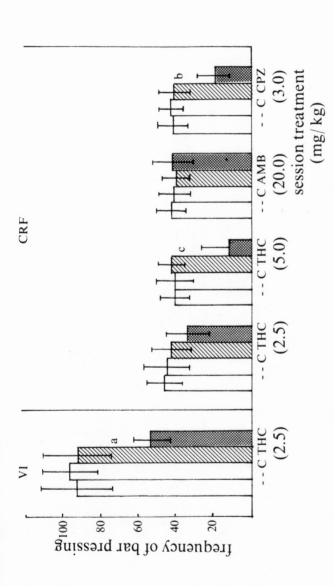

Fig. 2. *VI*: Performance of 6 male rats under a VI schedule, before drugs (white columns), after the injection of control solution (hatched columns) and of 2.5 mg/kg of Δ^9-THC (dotted columns). *CRF*: Performance of 10 male rats trained under a CRF schedule, before drugs (white columns), after control solution (hatched columns) and 2.5, 5.0, 20.0 and 3.0 mg/kg, of respectively, Δ^9-THC, Δ^9-THC, amylobarbitone and chlorpromazine (dotted columns). The vertical bars indicate the standard deviations. Significant differences are indicated by *a*, *b* and *c* which correspond to levels of, respectively, 5%, 1% and 0.1% (Student *t* test)

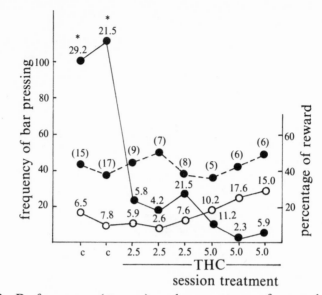

Fig. 3. Performance (●———●) and percentage of reward obtained (●– –●) by 3 worker rats, and performance (○———○) of 3 nonworker rats under the influence of control solution (C), 2.5 and 5.0 mg/kg of Δ^9-THC. The animals were rewarded under VI schedule. Standard deviations of the performances are indicated by numbers above the two curves; numbers within parenthesis indicate the total amount of reward obtained by the pairs. The asterisks indicate when bar-pressing performance of worker rats differed significantly ($p \leq 0.001$) from that of nonworkers (Student t test).

RESULTS

Individual Performance. The first part of Fig. 2 (VI) shows that in 6 rats trained under the VI schedule of reinforcement, 2.5 mg/kg of Δ^9-THC produced a significant decay of bar pressing behavior; the control solution, however, was without effect.

Paired Performance. Before drug administration, all pairs of rats achieved a stable pattern of behavior, with worker rats performing most of the labor. However, both rats of each pair were equally rewarded; as the nonworker rats did not remain all the time near the water-deliverer, probably because reward was unpredictable, the worker rat had the chance to run and reach the reward. Under the action of 2.5 or 5.0 mg/kg of Δ^9-THC, all the six worker rats showed a decrease of bar-pressing behavior. Fig. 3 shows that in 3 pairs the performance of the worker rats went down to near zero whereas that of the nonworker animals slightly increased; there was an inversion of the curves and of the criterion (nonworker rats began to perform more than 80% of the total bar-pressing) but the performance of worker and nonworker animals did not differ significantly, in contrast to that observed before drug administration. Furthermore, as shown in Fig. 3, there was no modification in the percentage of reward obtained by both groups of rats. On the other hand, for the other 3 pairs, the decrease of performance was not enough to induce a loss of the criterion as their worker rats under Δ^9-THC still performed more than 80% of the bar pressing.

Finally, the six pairs whose nonworker rats received Δ^9-THC did not show changes in their social pattern; the drug further decreased the already low (mean of 16.1 bar-pressing) performance of the nonworker rats, whereas the worker rats treated with control solution continued to press the bar at the same frequency as before.

Experiment 2 (CRF Schedule)

Drugs. Δ^9-THC, as in experiment 1; amylobarbitone sodium, dissolved in a 0.9% NaCl solution (saline); chlorpromazine hydrochloride, expressed in terms of the base, dissolved in saline.

Subjects. Thirty male Wistar rats, 3 months old, and weighing near 210 g at the beginning of the experiment were utilized.

Apparatus. The same as described in experiment 1.

Procedure. The rats were individually trained on a continuous reinforcement schedule (CRF). The rest of the procedure was identical to that of experiment 1. After reaching a stable baseline, Δ^9-THC, amylobarbitone and chlorpromazine were administered to ten rats, respectively; 45, 45 and 30 min before trials, and the individual performances recorded; the interval between drug administration was 7 days. The remaining 20 rats were paired according to their performances and each pair was trained at every 48 h for a period of 15 min under the CRF schedule. After 11 trials, 9 of the 10 pairs reached the criterion of labor division described in experiment 1; following that they were submitted to the drug treatments. The experiment was carried out during 50 days and worker rats received consecutively, control solution (saline plus Tween 80), Δ^9-THC, saline, amylobarbitone, saline, chlorpromazine, saline and Δ^9-THC, in the various dosages and time intervals as shown in the first 4 columns of Table 1. Their partners received control solution (for Δ^9-THC experiment), or saline (for chlorpromazine and amylobarbitone experiments).

TABLE 1.
Frequency of bar pressing and reward obtained by paired rats which lost the criterion of labor division when under the action of 5.0 mg/kg of Δ^9-THC and 3.0 mg/kg of chlorpromazine

Worker-rat Treatment*	Day of experiment	Dose (mg/kg)	Time between injection and training (min)	Frequency of bar pressing (mean ± SD)		Frequency of reward obtained (mean ± SD)	
				worker	nonworker	worker	nonworker
Control solution (1.0 ml/kg)	1	—	45	54.1 ± 15.6	6.8 ± 2.0[b]	7.7 ± 3.0	51.6 ± 12.5[b]
	3	—	45	51.3 ± 16.5	4.2 ± 2.5[b]	4.8 ± 2.2	51.2 ± 7.4[b]
	5	—	45	57.1 ± 11.2	3.4 ± 2.4	3.2 ± 2.2	58.8 ± 6.2[b]
Δ^9THC	7	2.5	45	50.0 ± 12.9	4.6 ± 3.3[b]	4.7 ± 2.2	48.1 ± 12.8[b]
	9	2.5	45	44.8 ± 27.2	8.3 ± 13.7[b]	7.8 ± 10.9	43.3 ± 26.6[b]
	11	5.0	45	3.0 ± 1.7	28.6 ± 7.1[b]	14.8 ± 7.6	16.6 ± 1.1
	13	5.0	45	8.6 ± 9.5	27.0 ± 12.9[a]	18.5 ± 13.3	14.6 ± 7.4
Saline (1.0 ml/kg)	18	—	15	54.2 ± 16.5	4.8 ± 3.8[b]	5.8 ± 3.7	51.7 ± 16.7[b]
	20	—	15	48.2 ± 10.4	5.5 ± 4.0[b]	8.0 ± 5.5	43.7 ± 7.0[b]
Amylobarbitone	22	10	15	63.7 ± 27.9	4.0 ± 3.4[b]	5.3 ± 4.5	71.7 ± 26.3[b]
	24	20	15	61.5 ± 16.8	2.0 ± 2.8[b]	3.3 ± 2.0	59.2 ± 16.0[b]
	26	20	45	73.6 ± 17.9	3.5 ± 2.9[b]	7.3 ± 5.2	68.3 ± 16.9[b]
	28	40	45	—	—	—	—
Saline (1.0 ml/kg)	31	—	30	74.3 ± 4.0	5.0 ± 2.6[b]	4.7 ± 2.5	74.3 ± 4.0[b]
	33	—	30	70.7 ± 4.0	4.7 ± 1.1[b]	3.0 ± 2.0	73.3 ± 5.5[b]
Chlorpromazine	35	1.5	120	70.0 ± 4.4	3.0 ± 1.0[b]	5.3 ± 1.2	67.3 ± 5.0[b]
	37	3.0	120	56.0 ± 13.0	15.0 ± 3.6[b]	5.3 ± 3.2	55.3 ± 12.3[b]
	39	3.0	30	18.3 ± 14.8	16.0 ± 6.0	16.0 ± 6.0	18.0 ± 15.4
	41	3.0	30	23.8 ± 19.9	19.3 ± 13.3	19.3 ± 13.3	23.3 ± 19.9
Control solution (1.0 ml/kg)	44	—	45	49.5 ± 19.6	2.5 ± 2.4[b]	2.8 ± 2.1	48.3 ± 18.7[b]
	46	—	45	51.7 ± 19.3	4.0 ± 5.4[b]	4.7 ± 5.5	51.0 ± 19.0[b]
	48	—	45	48.3 ± 14.7	4.6 ± 5.3[b]	4.6 ± 4.1	49.4 ± 12.4[b]
Δ^9-THC	50	5.0	45	2.6 ± 3.6	26.6 ± 12.9[a]	22.2 ± 9.0	8.6 ± 8.8[a]

*The nonworker rats received control solution at days 1, 3, 5, 44, 46, and 48 and saline during the rest of the experiment; [a] and [b] indicate significant differences between worker and nonworker groups at a level of respectively 1% and 0.1% (Student t test).

RESULTS

Individual Performance. The second part of Fig. 2 (CRF) shows the results. 2.5 mg/kg of Δ^9-THC did not significantly alter the bar-pressing behavior of rats under CRF, in contrast to that observed with VI schedule (experiment 1); however, a significant decrease was noted with 5.0 mg/kg. On the other hand, 3.0 mg/kg of chlorpromazine was also effective in decreasing performance, whereas amylobarbitone was not. In a further experiment with other rats the same negative result was obtained with 30 mg/kg of amylobarbitone.

Paired Performance. Fig. 4 summarizes part of the data obtained; it is seen that during the predrug phase, worker and nonworker rats are readily distinguishable by the frequency of bar pressing (the statistical significance is shown in Table 1). However, they were differently affected by the drugs. Thus, in six and seven pairs (respectively, parts I and IV of Fig. 4), 5.0 mg/kg of Δ^9-THC reduced the performance of worker rats to near zero; in contrast, the nonworker rats substantially increased bar pressing. As a consequence there was an inversion of the labor division criterion with the performance curves of worker and nonworker rats crossing each other. On the other hand, with three and two pairs (respectively, parts Ia and IVa of Fig. 4) Δ^9-THC did not strongly affect the bar-pressing behavior of the worker rats and there was no change in the social pattern. Furthermore, with Δ^9-THC-affected pairs there was a drastic change in the percentage of the reward obtained; under drug action the worker rats remained near the water deliverer receiving 50—70% of the reward, which contrasts with less than 10% obtained during the predrug phase. Somewhat similar results were obtained with chlorpromazine injected 30 min before trials (part III of Fig. 4); the worker rats of six pairs decreased their performance to about 20 bar pressings, from a previous level of 70, and the nonworkers increased their performance; as a consequence, worker rats began to receive near 50% of the reward. However, these changes were not sufficient to cause an inversion of the labor division criterion, with no crossing of the performance curves. In the three other pairs chlorpromazine did not alter the labor division (Fig. 4, part IIIa). Finally, Fig. 4 shows that 10 and 20 mg/kg of amylobarbitone increased the performance of worker rats with no modification of labor division in all pairs tested.

Table 1 complements Fig. 4. It shows all the results obtained with the pairs which lost criterion under drug treatment, along the 50 days of experiment. It is seen that 2.5 mg/kg of Δ^9-THC (4th and 5th rows), 10 and 20 mg/kg of amylobarbitone (10th, 11th and 12th rows), and 1.5 and 3.0 mg/kg of chlorpromazine given 2 h before trials (16th and 17th rows) did not affect the labor division. On the other hand, 40 mg/kg of amylobarbitone induced anesthesia and the data were not recorded (13th row). Furthermore, the change in the social hierarchy achieved by Δ^9-THC and chlorpromazine was reversible as once further injected with saline the pairs returned to their previous condition (8th and 9th, 14th and 15th, 20th, 21st and 22nd rows).

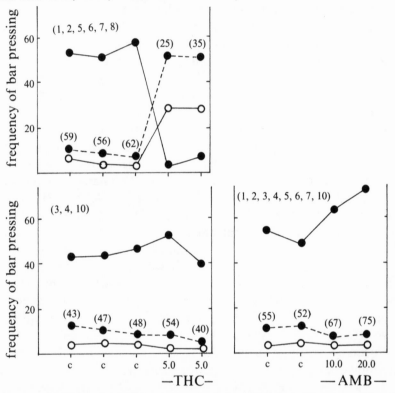

Fig. 4I—IV. Influence of drugs on the labor division of rats working in CRF schedule. (●——●) bar pressing performance of worker rats. (○——○) bar pressing performance of nonworkers. (●– – –●) percentage of reward obtained by workers; numbers above reward curve represent the total amount of reward obtained by the pairs. Upper panels refer to pairs of rats (cage number within parenthesis) which showed an inversion of labor division under THC (panels I and IV) and chlorpromazine (III). Bottom panels show pairs of rats (cage number within parenthesis) which did not respond to THC (I_a and IV_a), amylobarbitone (II_a) and chlorpromazine (III_a).

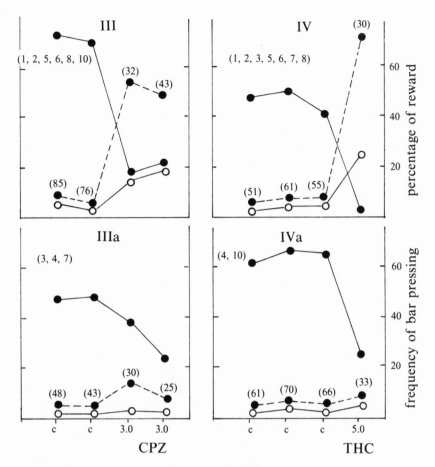

Fig. III and IV

DISCUSSION

The data of experiment 2 show that 5.0 mg/kg of Δ^9-THC was able to invert the labor division of paired rats working under CRF schedule (Fig. 4, parts I and IV; Table 1). Thus, under drug action the worker rats decreased bar-pressing performance whereas nonworker animals simultaneously increased it; in addition to stopping work, the Δ^9-THC-treated rats remained near the water deliverer and started to obtain 50—70% of the total reward. Therefore, the inversion obtained cannot be explained on the basis of a drug-induced loss of motivation, nor through motor impairment decreasing the capability of worker rats to press the bar. Although a decrease in bar pressing occurred with 2.5 and 5.0 mg/kg (Figs. 2, 3 and 4) this does not necessarily indicate a motor impairment. Thus, rats injected with the same amounts of Δ^9-THC were capable of pushing control rats through a straight runway (Masur *et al.*,

1971b) and did not show altered ambulation in an open-field arena (Masur *et al.,* 1971a).

On the other hand, the results obtained with VI schedule (exp. 1) were less clear, probably because it is less adequate than CRF for this type of study. Thus, under VI, even before Δ^9-THC, worker and nonworker rats, although pressing the bar with different frequencies, equally shared the already low amount of reward (Fig. 3). When nonworker rats received Δ^9-THC, they stopped all bar pressing but still obtained the same amount of reward as before, which again indicates an absence of Δ^9-THC effects on motivation. On the other hand, Δ^9-THC strongly decreased bar pressing performance in half of the worker-rats; however, their nonworker partners did not increase it substantially and both groups of rats continued to share the reward equally. The failure of nonworker rats to substantially increase bar pressing frequency, when their partners stopped doing the labor, could be a consequence of the VI schedule. As the reward was not contingent to every bar pressing (or to the sound of the bar being pressed), the parasitic behavior of nonworker rats was also VI rewarded, which would make it difficult to extinguish (Sidman, 1960).

On the contrary, as seen above, much clearer results were obtained under CRF (exp. 2). Thus, before drug administration the rats differed by both the amount of reward and frequency of bar pressing; Δ^9-THC action was much clearer because nonworker rats increased bar pressing 4 to 6 fold, whereas drugged animals reduced it near to zero and obtained a sharp increase of reward (Fig. 4, parts I and IV). The importance of the schedule of reinforcement to detect the effects of Δ^9-THC can also be observed when the individual (Fig. 2) or paired (Fig. 3; Table 1) performances were analysed; thus, 2.5 mg/kg of Δ^9-THC only affected significantly the rats under the VI schedule.

Another point which deserves attention is the great variability of rats' sensitivity to Δ^9-THC, which confirms previous reports (Silva *et al.,* 1968). For example, under CRF three rats in the individual situation and three other animals in the paired situation did not respond to Δ^9-THC, contrasting with the 100% of rats responding to 3 mg/kg of chlorpromazine.

The effects of Δ^9-THC were not shared by amylobarbitone. Ten, 20 and 30 mg/kg, injected 15 and 45 min before trials (Table 1), although producing ataxia, did not reduce either individual (Fig. 2) or paired performance (Fig. 4); 40 mg/kg anesthetized the animals, abolishing all activity (Table 1). On the other hand, chlorpromazine partially mimicked Δ^9-THC. Thus, 3.0 mg/kg injected 30 min before trials, reduced the individual performance and that of worker rats in the paired situation. However, it did not act as drastically as Δ^9-THC because worker rats still performed around 20 bar pressings per trial, whereas the nonworker partners increased performance to about the same value (Fig. 4, part III). On the other hand, the worker rats under chlorpromazine, as Δ^9-THC-treated rats, considerably increased the amount of reward obtained. Therefore, the effects of chlorpromazine and Δ^9-THC on this social interaction were similar, as both drugs decreased bar pressings without loss of motivation. It is interesting that they have similar effects detected by other experimental procedures. Thus, Δ^9-THC also suppresses the isolation-induced aggressiveness of mice (Santos *et al.*, 1966; Salustino *et al.*, 1966; Carlini *et al.*, 1970), decreases spontaneous motor activity of mice (Holtzman *et al.*, 1969; Carlini *et al.*, 1970), suppresses the conditioned avoidance response in rats (Grumfeld and Edery, 1969) and acutely given decreases defecation of rats in an open field arena (Masur *et al.*, 1971a). It has been suggested that the effect of Δ^9-THC could be compared to that of depressant drugs (Masur *et al.*, 1971a; Gonzalez *et al.*, 1971); however, our present results with amylobarbitone indicate that the resemblance of Δ^9-THC and CNS depressants is not shared in all situations by the barbiturate group.

Masur *et al.* (1971b) reported that rats competing for food in a T maze were "losers" when treated with a 2.5 mg/kg Δ^9-THC. They tentatively explained the results on the basis of a modification in perception, which decreased the chances of drugged animals to win the contest. In other words, a deconditioning effect could have occurred. A modification in perception was also suggested to explain some effects of LSD-25 (Uyeno, 1970). Therefore, Δ^9-THC could have induced a deconditioning effect on worker rats, due to a change in perception, resulting in a decrease of bar pressing. On the other hand, the innate behavior of drinking water was not affected, and as a consequence worker rats behaved as nonworkers. Recently, Castellano (1971) proposed a similar mechanism of action for LSD-25.

References

Carlini, E. A., Kramer, C.: Effects of *Cannabis sativa* (marihuana) on maze performance of the rat. *Psychopharmacologia* (Berl.) 7, 175–181 (1965).

— Santos, M., Claussen, U., Bieniek, D., Korte, F.: Structure activity relationship of four tetrahydrocannabinols and the pharmacological activity of five semipurified extracts of *Cannabis sativa. Psychopharmacologia* (Berl.) 18, 32—93 (1970).

Castellano, C.: Lysergic acid diethylamide, amphetamine and chlorpromazine on water maze discrimination in mice. *Psychopharmacologia* (Berl.) 19, 16—25 (1971).

Gonzales, S. C., Matsudo, V. K. R., Carlini, E. A.: Effects of marihuana compounds on the fighting behavior of siamese fighting fish *(Betta splendens). Pharmacology* 6, 186—190 (1971).

Grunfeld, Y., Edery, H.: Psychopharmacological activity of the active constituents of hashish and some related cannabinoids. *Psychopharmacologia* (Berl.) 14, 200—201 (1969).

Heimstra, N. W., Sallee, S. J.: Effects of early drug treatment on adult dominance behavior in rats. *Psychopharmacologia* (Berl.) 8, 235—240 (1965).

Holtzman, D., Lowell, R. A., Jaffee, J. H., Freedman, D. X.: 1-Δ^9-tetrahydrocannabinol: neurochemical and behavioral effects in the mouse. *Science* 163, 1464—1467 (1969).

Masur, J., Martz, R. M. W., Bieniek, D., Korte, F.: Influence of (—) Δ^9-*trans*-tetrahydrocannabinol and mescaline on the behavior of rats submitted to food competition situations. *Psychopharmacologia* (Berl.) 22, 187—194 (1971b).

— — Carlini, E. A.: Effects of acute and chronic administration of Cannabis sativa and (—) Δ^9-*trans*-tetrahydrocannabinol on the behavior of rats in an open-field arena. *Psychopharmacologia* (Berl.) 19, 388—397 (1971a).

Mowrer, O. H.: Animal studies in the genesis of personality. *Trans. N. Y. Acad. Sci.* 3, 8—11 (1940).

Oldfield-Box, H.: Social organization of rats in a "social problem" situation. *Nature* (Lond.) 213, 533—534 (1967).

— Age differences in performance between rats in two experimental social organizations. *J. Geront.* 24, 18—22 (1969a).

— Individual performance in two experimental social organizations of rats. *Amin. Behavior.* 17, 534-536 (1969b).

— The influence of specific group membership upon individual performance in a "social problem" for rats. *Psychon. Sci.* 14, 39—40 (1969c).

Salustiano, J., Hoshino, K., Carlini, E. A.: Effects of *Cannabis sativa* and chlorpromazine on mice as measured by two methods used for evaluation of tranquilizing drugs. *Med. Pharmacol.* exp. 15, 153—162 (1966).

Santos, M. S., Sampaio, M. R. P., Fernandes, N. S., Carlini, E. A.: Effects of *Cannabis sativa* (marihuana) on the fighting behavior of mice. *Psychopharmacologia* (Berl.) 8, 437—444 (1966).

Sidman, M.: The reliability and generality of data. In: *Tactics of scientific research*. New York: Basic Books, Inc. 1960.

Silva, M. T. A., Carlini, E. A., Claussen, U., Korte, F.: Lack of cross-tolerance in rats among (—) Δ^9-*trans*-tetrahydrocannabinol (Δ^9-THC), cannabis extracts, mescaline and lysergic acid diethylamide (LSD-25). *Psychopharmacologia* (Berl.) 13, 332—340 (1968).

Uyeno, E. T.: Effects of d-lysergic acid diethylamide and 2-brom-lysergic acid diethylamide on dominance behavior of the rat. *Int. J. Neuropharmacol.* 5, 317—322 (1966).

— Effects of mescaline and psilocybin on dominance behavior of the rat. *Arch. int. Pharmacodyn.* 166, 60—64 (1967).

— Lysergic acid diethylamide and a novel stimulus. *Psychon. Sci.* 18, 52 (1970).

Work, M. S., Grossen, N., Rogers, H.: Role of habit and androgen level in food-seeking dominance among rats. *J. comp. physiol. Psychol.* 69, 604—607 (1969).

Acknowledgment: The authors are grateful to Prof. J. Ribeiro do Valle for the generous gift of Δ^9-THC.
With a fellowship from Fundação de Amparo a' Pesquisa do Estado de São Paulo (FAPESP).

Part 10

Adverse Social Behavior: Aggression and Crime

In the twelfth century A.D. a secret society was organized in Arabia in which the members allegedly fortified themselves with hashish before going out into the countryside to commit various murders. The history of this society has been particularly garbled through the centuries and no responsible historians have been able to separate the facts from the legends surrounding this group, especially as concerns their use of hashish. Nevertheless, lurid tales of the nefarious deeds of this society have passed on through the centuries and have often been cited in the present-day controversy concerning the role of cannabis in criminal behavior.

In 1894, the British Army in India conducted an inquiry into the question of whether cannabis was criminogenic and concluded that there was little evidence supporting such claims: "It is instructive to see how preconceived notions based on rumor and tradition tend to preserve the impression of certain particulars while the impression of far more important features of the case are completely forgotten. In some cases, these preconceived notions seem to prevail to distort the incident altogether to create a picture in the mind of witnesses quite different from the recorded facts."

At present, two basic positions have been taken in regard to the question of cannabis and crime. On the one hand, law enforcement agencies and the press seem to accept the premise that marihuana is criminogenic; on the other, most commissions summoned by governmental officials have found little objective support for this supposed relationship between cannabis and crime.

One of the early scientifically organized investigations of this question in North America was reported in 1934 by Bromberg. Out of the 16,000 felons in the city of New York whom he examined, Bromberg reported that only 67 were marihuana users and among those, only 16 were found guilty of assault. The La Guardia Commission also failed to find any causal relationship between marihuana and crimes of violence. Again in 1946, Bromberg reported that there were only 40 out of a total of 8,280 naval and marine prisoners who were users of marihuana. In 1962, a presidential Commission investigating this question concluded that, "although marihuana has long held the reputation of inciting individuals to commit sexual offenses and other antisocial acts, evidence is inadequate to substantiate this."

In 1968, the Advisory Committee on Drug Dependence in England offered this sober conclusion, "In the United Kingdom the taking of cannabis has not so far been regarded even by the severest critics as a direct cause of serious crime."

Judging by laboratory studies of the effects of marihuana on human behavior, the overwhelming impression is that marihuana has a predominantly tranquilizing effect. This is also generally true in the case of animals, although some exceptions have been noted. For example, in a study by Carder and Olson,[1] small doses of Δ^9-THC were found to increase the incidence of fighting in rats that had been exposed to intermittent electric shock. The effect of such shock treatment has been found to elicit fighting behavior in rats and Carder and Olson reported that the drug added to the incidence of such shock-elicited fighting behavior. However, this effect is at variance with that reported by Manning and Elsmore, who point out some of the methodological problems inherent in research of this kind.

The second study by Carlini, Hamaoui and Märtz introduces two additional variables that must be considered in evaluating the relationship between cannabis and aggression in animals. As shown by Carlini and his associates, the extent to which experimental animals are deprived of food prior to being tested constitutes a variable of considerable importance in the elicitation of aggressive behavior, a phenomenon that is markedly increased if testing is done in a cold environment. Since both starvation and cold can be considered naturally stressful situations, it may be that the increases in cannabis-induced aggression shown by Carlini can only be observed when the subject is undergoing some form of comparable stress at the time of drug administration.

REFERENCES

1. Carder, B., and Olson, J. "Marihuana and Shock Induced Aggression in Rats," *Physiology and Behavior*, 1972, 8, 599–602.

29

Shock-elicited Fighting and Delta-9-Tetrahydrocannabinol

Frederick J. Manning and Timothy F. Elsmore

The relationship between marihuana use and aggression is a recurring topic in the literature on Cannabis and its by-products. Until recently the evidence has been largely anecdotal, a problem which has not tempered the vigor of the argument in the least, but it does point to a slight correlation between Cannabis use and minor asocial or antisocial behavior (U.S. Dept. of Health, Education, and Welfare, 1971; Roffman and Sapol, 1970). However, most observers appear to be reluctant to make the leap from correlation to causation without more convincing evidence. In fact, it would seem that the predominant viewpoint is that the drug not only does not lead to crime but instead acts as a deterrent, due to its sedating action (Chopra, 1969; Murphy, 1963; U.S. Dept. of Health, Education, and Welfare, 1971).

Experimental studies in animals have done little to clarify this point. Several studies have shown that cannabis extract and delta-9-tetrahydrocannabinol suppress isolation-induced fighting in mice (Salustiano, Hoshino, and Carlini, 1966; Santos, Sampaio, Fernandes, and Carlini, 1966). Delta-9-tetrahydrocannabinol(delta-9-THC), the prin-

Reprinted with permission of the authors and publisher from *Psychopharmacologia* 1972, *25*, 218–228. Copyright 1972 by Springer-Verlag.

Frederick J. Manning and Timothy F. Elsmore are affiliated with the Walter Reed Army Institute of Research, Washington, D.C.

cipal active product of the Cannabis plants (Mechoulam, 1970), also diminishes the speed and accuracy of mice in a maze task in which the opportunity to fight is used as a reward (Kilbey, Johnson, and Fritchie, 1971). On the other hand, Carlini and Kramer (1965) observed that rats given injections of cannabis extract in a study of maze learning become aggressive, attacking each other in their cages. A subsequent study by these same authors revealed that only the combination of starvation and chronic marihuana injection was capable of producing this aggressiveness (Carlini and Masur, 1969). The present study was designed to assess the effects of acute administration of delta-9-THC on fighting elicited in rats by painful electric shock.

EXPERIMENT ONE

Method. Ten male albino rats of the Walter Reed strain served as subjects. They weighed between 350 and 500 g to start and had free access to rat chow and water in individual home cages throughout the experiment[1]. All rats were visually isolated from one another except during experimental sessions. During the latter, which took place each Tuesday and Friday, the rats were paired in a random fashion and placed, one pair at a time, in a sound-attenuating metal chamber (25 cm long × 25 cm wide × 30 cm deep) with a floor of twelve stainless steel bars electrically isolated from each other. Indirect lighting was provided by two 7.5 watt bulbs and extraneous sounds were masked by continuous white noise at approximately 75 db. Fifty electric shocks were then delivered, at variable intervals, to the grid floor through a polarity scrambler. The average interval between shocks was ten seconds but the range was from one to twenty-five seconds. Each shock was a 0.4 sec pulse of 60 Hz A.C. After a short investigation of the effects of varying current intensity, a level of 2.0 ma was chosen for the duration of the experiment. This value produced fighting on about 50% of the trials, so that drug induced increases or decreases could be measured equally well. Closed circuit television was used to observe the subjects. On each trial the observer merely noted whether or not a fight had occurred, and made no attempt to characterize the behavior of the individual animals. A fight was defined as biting or repeated pawing (three or more blows) by one or both animals. The same observer was used for all sessions, but a second observer occasionally checked reliability. Such checks invariably showed near perfect agreement between the two judges.

A baseline period lasted four weeks, during which no injections were

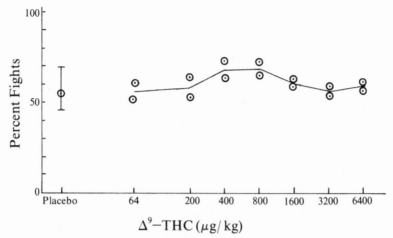

$\Delta^9-THC\,(\mu g/\,kg)$

Fig. 1. Percentage of fights elicited as a function of dosage of delta-9-tetrahydrocannabinol (Δ^9-THC)

given. Subsequently one weekly session was randomly selected and designated a THC session, and the other a placebo session. In both cases all rats received a 0.20 cc i.p. injection one hour before testing. On THC days this injection contained an ethanol solution of 95% pure delta-9-THC[2] suspended in vegetable oil, while on placebo days it contained only the ethanol and oil. Fighting was assessed twice at each of the following doses: 64, 200, 400, 800, 1600, 3200, and 6400 mg/kg, given in that order. During the last four weeks the experimenter scoring the fighting was not told whether a given day's injections were THC or placebo.

Results and Discussion. Fig. 1 shows the frequency of fighting as a function of THC dose. With the exception of the symbol above "placebo," which represents the mean range of all placebo sessions, each point is the percentage of fights seen on a single day, pooling across all five pairs of animals. The line merely connects the means. The dose-response curve is essentially flat; i.e., the effects of delta-9-THC on shock-elicited fighting were negligible in the present study.

There are of course a very large number of ways in which such results may have arisen. Accordingly we attempted to explore some of the more obvious before concluding that THC produces no change in the frequency of shock-elicited fighting. For example, despite the fact that the dose was increased a hundred-fold in the course of the experiment, it is entirely possible that striking changes in fighting might have been observed at still higher doses. Alternatively, it is possible that the time course of the drug's action is such that testing one hour after injection was inappropriate. A third possibility is that shock-elicited fighting, at least with the particular apparatus and parameters employed in this laboratory, is simply not a very sensitive measure of drug effects in our subject population. Lastly, it may be that the subjects developed a tolerance to THC, which combined with the use of an ascending series of doses to eliminate what would otherwise have been striking changes in aggression. The following experiments were directed at assessing these hypotheses.

EXPERIMENT TWO

An important consideration in any analysis of the results of the previous experiment is the relatively short duration of the test session. Each pair of animals was in the fighting chamber for only about eight minutes. In the absence of an extensive literature on absorption of delta-9-THC or the time course of its effects, it seemed possible that peak effects occurred while the animal was in his home cage, either before or after our tests for shock-elicited fighting. The present experiment investigated this possibility by varying the time elapsing between injection and testing. The vehicle in which the delta-9-THC is suspended may well play a substantial role in the time course of its effects, by affecting the rate of absorption, so this variable was also assessed.

Method. Subjects and apparatus employed were identical to those of the previous experiment, and procedures were similar in all respects but the following: dose was held constant at 6.4 mg/kg, the highest dose of Experiment One, but successive weeks involved testing at 30 min after THC in oil, 30 min after THC in propylene glycol, two hours after THC in oil, and two hours after THC in propylene glycol.

Results. Table 1 shows the percentage of fights elicited under each of the vehicle-test time combinations. Each figure is based on 250 shocks delivered to 5 pair of animals. It is clear that 6.4 mg/kg of delta-9-THC had no effect on the frequency of shock-elicited fighting, regardless of vehicle or the time elapsing between injection and testing.

TABLE 1
PERCENTAGE OF SHOCKS ELICITING FIGHTS. EACH FIGURE IS BASED ON THE BEHAVIOR OF FIVE PAIRS OF RATS, EACH RECEIVING FIFTY SHOCKS, FOR A TOTAL OF 250 SHOCKS

Injection	Time Between Injection and Test (hours)		
	0.5	1.0	2.0
Vegetable oil	53	49	55
Vegetable oil and THC	55	53	52
Propylene glycol	51	54	47
Propylene glycol and THC	48	51	50

Experiment Three

Although shock-elicited aggression has been used by a number of other investigators (e.g., Tedeschi, Tedeschi, Mucha, Cook and Fellows, 1959) for assessing the properties of psychoactive drugs, the findings of Experiment One allow for the possibility that the particular procedure employed in this laboratory is relatively insensitive to drug effects. This experiment was an attempt to rule out this explanation by use of chlordiazepoxide, a drug previously demonstrated to have significant effects on shock-elicited fighting. Christmas and Maxwell (1970), for example, have reported that this drug reduces such fighting at doses well below those required to produce analgesia or sedation.

Method. The subjects of Experiment One were used again in this study. Procedures were also identical, except that on the drug days of three successive weeks, chlordiazepoxide was given instead of THC, two hours before testing. Injections of 0.25 cc were given, intraperitoneally, of 10 mg/kg, 20 mg/kg, and 40 mg/kg, in that order. Testing and scoring were identical to that in Experiment One.

Results. Fig. 2 illustrates the dose-related depression in shock-elicited fighting seen after i.p. injections of chlordiazepoxide. The two lower doses decreased fighting from the placebo level of 54% to 44%, and the 40 mg/kg dose resulted in a session producing fights after only 20% of the 250 shocks. It should be noted that all subjects were distinctly sedated at this dose, at least in their home cages. However,

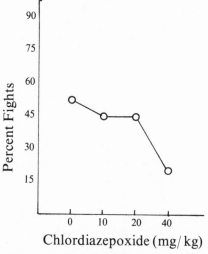

Chlordiazepoxide (mg/kg)

Fig. 2. Percentage of fights elicited as a function of dose level of chlordiazepoxide.

after 2—3 shocks all grossly observable indications of sedation had disappeared. Much activity following shock was directed at the walls of the chamber rather than at each other. At any rate the results indicated that the procedure was not insensitive to drug effects.

EXPERIMENT FOUR

A number of investigators have recently demonstrated pronounced tolerance to the behavioral effects of delta-9-THC, in the pigeon (McMillan, Harris, Frankenheim and Kennedy, 1969) and also in the rat (Carlini, 1968). In view of these findings it seemed advisable to test some naive subjects before and after a relatively large dose of delta-9-THC to assess the possible role of tolerance in Experiment One of the series, where an ascending series of doses was employed.

Method. Ten new Walter Reed male albino rats, 300—400 g in weight, served as subjects. Apparatus and testing procedures were identical to those described in Experiment One. Subjects were run for only five sessions, however, the last of which following, by one hour, intraperitoneal injections of delta-9-THC (6.4 mg/kg) suspended in propylene glycol.

Results. Although all subjects were noticeably sedated in their home cage following the injection of THC, no notable reduction in the overall frequency of shock-elicited fighting was seen in the ensuing test session. The percentage of shocks leading to fights was 39.6, 42.0, 50.4, and 43.2 in successive placebo sessions, and 41.2 in the session following drug administration. It would thus appear that the rapid development of tolerance reported by others is not a sufficient explanation for the failure of delta-9-THC to affect shock-elicited aggression.

EXPERIMENT FIVE

In Experiment One, an unsuccessful effort was made to demonstrate some effect of delta-9-THC on shock-elicited aggression by increasing dosage level from 64 μg/kg up to 6.4 mg/kg. Despite this hundredfold increase, it might still be argued that the simplest explanation of that experiment is that the range of behaviorally effective doses for our subjects was even higher than the highest doses employed by us. It is a truism that *some* level of this drug, and any other drug, will produce significant changes in shock-elicited fighting, if only due to the death of one or both fighters. However, the argument gains credence from the fact that oral LD_{50} for delta-9-THC in rats is 800—1400 mg/kg (Phillips, Turk and Forney, 1970). Thus, although Experiment One employed i.p. injections, it may be safely assumed nevertheless that the dosages never approached toxic levels. Furthermore, despite the fact that effective oral doses for humans rarely need to be over 500 μg/kg, published reports of behavioral effects in animals using less than 4 mg/kg have been rare (Grunfeld and Edery, 1969; Scheckel, Boff, Dahlen and Smart, 1968).

The following experiment was meant as a demonstration that profound behavioral effects may be seen in rats following doses well below 6.4 mg/kg, and that our inability to demonstrate changes in shock-elicited fighting at this dose level is not wholly due to the use of this relatively low dose.

Method. Six naive albino rats, of the same sex, strain, and weight as in the previous experiments, served as subjects. Their body weights were brought to 85% of that during ad libitum feeding and held at that figure for the duration of the experiment. The apparatus employed was a standard BRS-Foringer operant conditioning chamber for rats. Reinforcement consisted of three 45 mg Noyes rat food pellets. With each reinforcement, a small pilot light over the bar went out and another, over the pellet hopper, lighted. The house light and a masking noise also extinguished briefly. After shaping of the bar-pressing response was completed, each animal was run for one 60-reinforcement session on a fixed-interval three seconds schedule (FI 3″), two sessions on FI 10″, and one session on FI 20″. At this point that value of the FI was changed to 60″ (i.e., sixty seconds after delivery of reinforcement of *n*, and not until then, a bar press would produce reinforcement *n* + 1). After 15 sessions of FI 60″ the schedule was altered slightly, so that after 25% of the 60″ intervals a bar press produced all the stimuli that usually accompanied reinforcement, but the pellet feeder did not operate. The effects of such a procedure, and the modification of them by drugs, will be discussed in another report. The data relevant to this paper are merely the total number of responses in the session, and the distribution of responses within a given fixed-interval.

After twenty days performing on this modified FI 60″ schedule, all subjects were given intraperitoneal injections of 0.2 cc propylene glycol one hour before their daily sessions. This was repeated for three days, and on the fourth through the twelfth days, the injections contained 4.0 mg/kg of delta-9-THC. For reasons which will become obvious below, subjects could be run only every other day during this phase of the experiment, though injections were given daily. The experiment concluded with ten "recovery" sessions, which were not preceded by injection of any sort.

Results. In strong contrast to the experiments reported above on shock-elicited fighting, marked changes were observed in operant bar-pressing upon administration of 4 mg/kg of delta-9-THC. Panel A of Fig. 3 shows that total number of responses emitted in each daily session. THC clearly caused a profound decrease in overall responding. Two subjects failed to respond at all for 2.5 h in their first THC session, and the others all showed precipitous declines in their response rates. In two animals all three effects declined with repeated doses, but in four others the effects were essentially unchanged over the period of testing. One rat died at this point, but the other five animals quickly recovered to baseline response levels when run without THC.

A less prominent but still obvious effect of THC was seen in the temporal distribution of responses within the 60″ fixed-intervals. Panel B of Fig. 3 shows the percentage of responses occurring after the 45th second of the interval. All subjects did more responding early in the interval during THC sessions, and, unlike the more drastic decline in total responses, this effect of THC remains basically unchanged and does not disappear with repeated doses. However, like the effect on total responses, this "timing" disruption disappears quickly when THC treatment is stopped.

GENERAL DISCUSSION

The present series of experiments seems to indicate that shock-elicited fighting by rats is unaffected by a wide dose range of delta-9-tetrahydrocannabinol, the principal active compound in marihuana. Several obvious sources of artifact were ruled out by control experiments. For example, neither changes in the drug vehicle nor changes in the delay between injection and testing were effective in revealing a drug-produced change in such fighting. Similarly, our negative findings did not stem from tolerance, since rats injected once, and only once, with the highest dose of THC employed, behaved similarly to those injected many times with a variety of dosages (i.e., no changes were seen in frequency of shock-elicited fighting). Experiment Three demonstrated that our apparatus and procedure were sensitive to drug effects, since chlordiazepoxide reduced fighting in a dose-related fashion. Finally, profound behavioral effects were demonstrated in an operant conditioning experiment using doses of delta-9-THC which failed to alter shock-elicited fighting at all.

These results should be viewed in the light of an earlier observation that the isolation-induced aggression of mice (Salustiano *et al.,* 1966) and the frog-killing behavior of rats (Kilbey, Harris and Moore, 1971) is inhibited by acute administration of Cannabis extract or THC, while

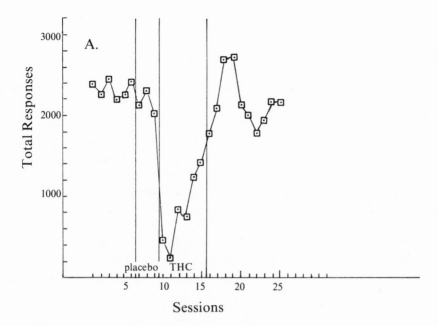

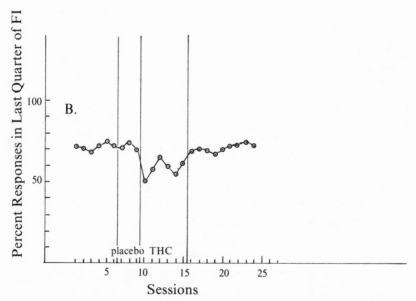

Fig. 3. (A) Total responses per daily session of bar pressing on a fixed-interval schedule of food reinforcement. (B) Percentage of these responses occurring in the final 15 sec of the fixed intervals

the spontaneous and shock-elicited aggression of starved rats is increased considerably by chronic THC administration. Taken as a whole, this group of studies suggests that the question of the relationship between marihuana and aggression is far too general to allow a single simple answer. The situations in which drug effects are seen, and the direction of those effects, are apparently highly specific. Moyer (1968) and others have anticipated this type of difficulty in suggesting that there are several kinds of aggression, distinguishable not only operationally but also in terms of their physiological substrate. For example, even considering only one type of aggression, what Moyer (1968) calls "predatory aggression," frog-killing by rats evidently does not have the same neurological basis as mouse-killing (Desisto and Huston, 1970). Such discoveries may eventually provide satisfactory resolution of the apparent discrepancies among investigations of THC and "aggression" by specifying neural systems common to those types of aggression affected by the drug in different ways. Under these circumstances it would appear that our knowledge of the effects of THC on aggression will be furthered only by systematic study of its action in all the numerous situations known to give rise to aggressive behavior.

REFERENCES

Chopra. G. S.: Man and marihuana. *Int. J. Addict.* 4, 215 (1969).

Carlini, E. A.: Tolerance to chronic administration of Cannabis sativa (Marihuana) in rats. *Pharmacology* 1, 135—142 (1968).

— Kramer, C.: Effects of cannabis sativa on maze performance of the rat. *Psychopharmacologia* (Berl.) 7, 175—181 (1965).

— Masur, J.: Development of aggressive behavior in rats by chronic administration of cannabis sativa (marihuana). *Life Sci.* 8, Pt. I, 607—620 (1969).

Christmas, A. J., Maxwell, D. R.: A comparison of the effects of some benzodiazepines and other drugs on aggressive and exploratory behavior in mice and rats. *Neuropharmacology* 9, 17—29 (1970).

Desisto, M. J., Huston, J. P.: Facilitation of interspecific aggression by subreinforcing electrical stimulation in the posterior-lateral hypothalamus. Paper presented at the Meeting of the Eastern Psychological Assoc., Atlantic City, N. J., April 1970.

Grunfeld, Y., Edery, H.: Psychopharmacological activity of the active constituents of hashish and some related cannabinoids. *Psychopharmacologia* (Berl.) 14, 200—210 (1969).

Kilbey, M. M., Harris, R. T., Moore, J. W.: Increased latency of frog-killing behavior in the rat following administration of delta-9-tetrahydrocannabinol. Paper presented at the Meeting of the Southwest Psychological Assoc., San Antonio, Tex., April 1971.

— Johnson, K., Fritchie, E.: The effect of delta-9-tetrahydrocannabinol on innate and instrumental fighting behavior in the mouse. Paper presented at the meeting of the Southwest Psychological Assoc., San Antonio, Tex., April 1971.

Mechoulam, R.: Marihuana chemistry. *Science* 168, 1159–1166 (1970).

McMillan, D. E., Harris, L. S., Frankenheim, J. M., Kennedy, J. S.: 1-delta-9-*trans*-tetrahydrocannabinol in pigeons: tolerance to the behavioral effects. *Science* 169, 501–503 (1970).

Moyer, K. E.: Kinds of aggression and their physiological basis. *Comm. Behav. Biol.* 2, Pt. A, 65–87 (1968).

Murphy, H. B. M.: The cannabis habit: a review of recent psychiatric literature. *Bull. Narcot.* 15, 15–23 (1963).

Roffman, R. A., Sopol, E.: Marihuana in Vietnam. *Int. J. Addict.* 5, 1–42 (1970).

Salustiano, J., Hoshino, K., Carlini, E. A.: Effects of cannabis sativa and chlorpromazine on mice as measured by two methods used for evaluation of tranquilizing agents. *Med. Pharmacol.* exp. 15, 153–162 (1966).

Scheckel, C. L., Boff, E., Dahler, P., Smart, T.: Behavioral effects in monkeys of race-mates of two biologically active marihuana constituents. *Science* 160, 1467–1469 (1968).

Tedeschi, R. E., Tedeschi, D. H., Mucha, A., Cook, L., Mattis, P. A., Fellows, E. J.: Effects of various centrally acting drugs on fighting behavior of mice. *J. Pharmacol. exp. Ther.* 125, 28–34 (1959).

United States Department of Health, Education, and Welfare. Marihuana and Health. Washington, D.C.: U. S. Government Printing Office, 1971.

In conducting the research described in this report, the investigators adhered to the "Guide for Laboratory Animal Facilities and Care" as promulgated by the Committee on the Guide for Laboratory Animal Facilities and Care of the Institute of Laboratory Animal Resources, National Academy of Sciences—National Research Council.

The synthesized delta-9-THC was supplied by Dr. J. A. Scigliano of the Center for Studies of Narcotic and Drug Abuse of the National Institute of Mental Health.

30

Factors Influencing the Aggressiveness Elicited by Marihuana in Food-Deprived Rats

E. A. Carlini
A. Hamaoui, and Regina M. W. Märtz

INTRODUCTION

It has been reported that chronic administration of *Cannabis sativa* extracts elicits striking fighting behaviour in rats deprived of food for 20–22 h daily (Carlini & Masur, 1969; Orsingher & Fulginiti, 1970). Further experiments carried out to determine the specificity of the effect seen with marihuana have shown that amphetamine, amylobarbitone, mescaline, LSD-25 and caffeine do not induce this behaviour alteration; (—)-Δ^9-*trans*-tetrahydrocannabinol (Δ^9-THC), however, does (Carlini & Masur, 1970). On the other hand, the aggressive behaviour displayed by the rats is only seen under the double treatment, marihuana plus food deprivation. Thus, rats fed *ad libitum* do not show it after 30–40 injections of marihuana; the aggressiveness also does not appear when food-deprived rats are chronically treated with control solution. Therefore, it seems clear that food deprivation is of paramount importance for the appearance of this effect of cannabis.

Reprinted by permission of the authors and publisher from the *British Journal of Pharmacology*, 1972, *44*, 794–804.
E. A. Carlini, A. Hamaoui, and Regina M. W. Märtz are affiliated with the Setor de Psicofarmacologia, Departamento de Bioquímica e Farmacologia, Escola Paulista de Medicina, São Paulo, Brasil.

The present work was designed to analyse this point further. It was tentatively suggested that one of the following factors, hypoglycaemia, acidosis or lack of some nutritional element, could be the factor which facilitates the induction of aggressiveness in rats by marihuana. The experiments described below were carried out to test these possibilities.

METHODS

Three hundred and seventy-eight male and female Wistar rats, ages ranging from 3 to 4 months, were housed in pairs in wire cages measuring $16 \times 30 \times 18$ cm. For each experimental condition, 3 to 7 pairs of rats were used and the groups were matched for age and sex within each experiment. After intraperitoneal injection of the marihuana extract or the control solution the animals were observed for aggressive behaviour during 2 or 3 hours. At the end of the observation period the rats were allowed 2 h of free access to food; therefore the animals were food-deprived 19–22 h daily and such animals will be referred to as either food-deprived or starved rats. In all experiments the injections of marihuana and control solution started on the first day of restricted access to food. Aggressive behaviour was timed with a stopwatch and corresponded to the time in seconds both rats of a pair assumed a stereotyped fighting position standing on their hind-legs ("boxer position") trying to bite each other. In general, aggressiveness appeared within 30-40 min after the injections and persisted for 2 to 4 hours. During this time this animals showed great irritability, vocalization, reacted violently to noise or puffs of air and vigorously attacked their cagemates. However, as stated above, only the actual fighting ("boxer position") was timed. In one experiment shock-induced aggressive behaviour was also assessed during a 10-min period beginning 50 min after the injections. For further details of the methods see Carlini & Masur (1969).

The marihuana extracts and the control solution were prepared according to Carlini & Kramer (1965). Briefly, the plant material was extracted for 12 h with petroleum ether in a reflux condenser; after getting rid of the solvent the resin obtained was suspended in alcohol and kept in darkness at 4° C. To prepare the extract the alcohol was evaporated and the residue suspended in saline with Tween-80 (3 drops of Tween-80 per 10 ml of saline). The control solution was composed of saline plus Tween-80 in the same proportions. Flowering tops of *Cannabis sativa* from Mato Grosso State (extracts Q_4 and Q_5) and Brasilia city (extract B) were employed: our thanks are due to Drs.

Orlando Rozante and Walmores V. Barbosa for the supply of these materials. Pure $(—)$-Δ^9-*trans*-tetrahydrocannabinol was used in one experiment; we are grateful to Drs. F. Korte and D. Bieniek for the gift of this compound. The potency of the three extracts and of pure Δ^9-THC as assayed by the corneal areflexia method in rabbits (Gayer test) according to Santos, Sampaio, Fernandes & Carlini (1966) was, respectively, 0.40 ± 0.12, 0.34 ± 0.09, 0.42 ± 0.19 and 0.10 ± 0.09. Unless otherwise stated the animals were fed with a commercially available food pellet diet (*normal* diet) prepared from peanut flour, soybean, meat, bone and fish with the following minimum percent composition: protein 21·8, fat 3·5, fibre 5·5, minerals 7·5, calcium 1·7 and phosphorus 0·8. One hundred and fifty mg of mineral mixture, 5,000 IU of vitamin A and 1,000 IU of vitamin D_3 were added to each kilogramme of diet.

The *balanced* diet used in some experiments had the following percent composition: casein 27, corn starch 47, soybean oil 8, sucrose 10, fibre 3·0, mineral mixture 4·0 and vitamin mixture 1·0. The *protein-free* diet was composed of 74% corn starch, 8% soybean oil, 10% sucrose, 4% mineral mixture, 3% fibre and 1% vitamin mixture. We are grateful to Dr. Sergio M. Zucas, from University of São Paulo, for the generous gift of the diets.

The following experiments were performed.

Influence of intra-peritoneal (i.p.) injections of glucose on marihuana aggressiveness (see Table 1)

Twenty-three pairs of food-deprived rats (3 months old) were treated daily with 10 mg/kg of extract Q_5 for 15 days. The experiments were carried out at room temperature, which varied from 20° to 26° C. Fierce aggressiveness beginning after the 11th day appeared in 14 pairs, which were used thereafter. After the 13th marihuana injection, fighting behaviour was scored in seconds during 30 min after it began. Then glucose (100—800 mg/kg) was injected i.p. and aggressiveness was scored again for 30 minutes. Three more injections at 30-min intervals followed: one of control solution, one of glucose, and another of control solution, respectively, during which aggressiveness continued to be measured. On the 15th day the same procedure was repeated; however, the order of the injections was control solution, glucose, control solution and glucose. On the following day (16th), glucose (800 mg/kg) and control solution were injected 5 min before the marihuana administration.

TABLE I

Influence of I.P. injections of glucose on the fighting behaviour elicited in starved rats by 10 mg/kg of cannabis extract Q_s. Glucose was injected on the 13th and 15th days after beginning of daily treatment with cannabis

Average fighting ($s \pm$ s.e.) during consecutive periods of 30 min following injections of

Day	Number of animals	No drug	Glucose (mg/kg) 100	Glucose (mg/kg) 200	Glucose (mg/kg) 400	Glucose (mg/kg) 800	Control solution (1·0 mg/kg)	Glucose (mg/kg) 400	Glucose (mg/kg) 800	Control solution (1·0 ml/kg)
13	1	360*	900	—	—	—	—	—	—	—
	1	420	—	430	—	—	135	—	—	—
	8	1,367 ± 244	—	—	1,245 ± 253	—	1,396 ± 222	1,381 ± 105	—	1,362 ± 105
	4	1,650 ± 150	—	—	—	1,616 ± 109	1,476 ± 199	—	1,386 ± 223	1,299 ± 266

Day	Number of animals	No drug	Control solution (1·0 ml/kg)	Glucose (mg/kg) 100	Glucose (mg/kg) 200	Glucose (mg/kg) 400	Glucose (mg/kg) 800	Control solution (1·0 mg/kg)	Glucose (mg/kg) 400	Glucose (mg/kg) 800	Control solution (1·0 ml/kg)
15	1	489	600	510	—	—	—	—	—	—	—
	1	760	75	—	0	—	—	—	—	—	—
	8	1,370 ± 232	1,423 ± 199	—	—	1,302 ± 277	—	—	1,562 ± 241	—	1,467 ± 252
	4	1,527 ± 107	1,583 ± 178	—	—	—	—	1,547 ± 206	—	1,259 ± 260	1,383 ± 262

*Lack of S.E. means that just one pair fought. Same in the following tables.

Influence of oral glucose on marihuana aggressiveness (see Table 2)

Five pairs of 3-month-old female rats starved 22 h daily were injected daily with cannabis extract Q_5 (10 mg/kg) for 25 days; the temperature varied from 19° to 24° C. After 13 days, aggressiveness, scored for 2 h, was evident in 4 pairs. In the following two days (14th and 15th) the rats were allowed to drink a 10% glucose solution *ad libitum;* from the 16th to the 25th days tap water was given again.

TABLE 2
INFLUENCE OF ORAL GLUCOSE ADMINISTRATION ON THE FIGHTING BEHAVIOR
ELICITED IN STARVED RATS BY 10 MG/KG OF EXTRACT Q_5

Average fighting ($s \pm$ s.e.) during 2 h after injection number and ingestion of					
12	13	14	15	20	25
water	water	glucose	glucose	water	water
$1,197 \pm 412$	$1,077 \pm 211$	0	0	0	0

Influence of temperature on marihuana aggressiveness (see Table 3)

Twenty pairs of male rats, 4 months old, were deprived of food for 22 hours. During this time, half the animals were housed in a room with temperature maintained at 27±1° C; the other 10 pairs were left in a cold room (14±1° C). Half the rats in each room were then injected with cannabis extract B (10 mg/kg) and the remaining animals with control solution. Aggressiveness was scored during the next 3 h; food was then given for a 2 h period. On the following day the same procedure was repeated. From the third to the 20th day the treatment continued only for the animals living at 27° C.

TABLE 3
INFLUENCE OF TEMPERATURE ON THE FIGHTING BEHAVIOUR ELICITED IN
STARVED RATS BY 10 MG/KG OF CANNABIS EXTRACT B

Drug	Temperature (°C)	Average fighting ($s \pm$ s.e) during 3 h after injection number			
		1	2	15	20
Cannabis	14	$4,600 \pm 1,520$	$5,041 \pm 1,981$	—	—
Extract	27	0	0	285 ± 182	217 ± 79
Control	14	0	0	—	—
Solution	27	0	0	0	0

Influence of acidifying agents on marihuana aggressiveness

Preliminary experiments with 40 rats have shown that the largest single doses of ammonium chloride and lactic acid tolerated by the animals without depression were 200 and 20 mg/kg, respectively. Acute and chronic experiments were then performed with 3-month-old rats; the temperature ranged from 20° to 26° C.

Acute experiments (see Table 4)

Thirty pairs of male rats fed *ad libitum* were used. Five pairs received 4 doses of ammonium chloride (100 mg/kg) at 6 h intervals; 30 min after the last injection, cannabis extract Q_4 (10 mg/kg) was injected and spontaneous and shock-induced aggressiveness were scored for 3 hours. Two other pairs of rats fed *ad libitum* received similar treatment, but ammonium chloride was given in 3 doses of 200 mg/kg at 4 h intervals. Pretreatment with lactic acid was as follows: two pairs of rats fed *ad libitum* received one dose of 10 mg/kg and another two pairs 20 mg/kg; 5 min later marihuana was injected. Finally, 5 pairs were injected 3 times with 10 mg/kg of lactic acid, at 3 h intervals, and 5 min after the last injection 10 mg/kg of marihuana was given.

For all groups treated with acidifying agents plus marihuana, similar groups of rats received the same number of injections of saline plus marihuana. In one control experiment the influence of lactic acid (20 mg/kg) on thiopental anaesthesia was assessed in 5 rats.

Chronic experiments (see Table 5)

Five groups of 7 pairs of 4-month-old female rats starved 20 h daily were used. Three groups were injected with saline and received 5 min later, respectively, control solution, cannabis extract Q_4 (10 mg/kg) and Δ^9-THC (2·5 mg/kg). The remaining 2 groups were pretreated with lactic acid (10 mg/kg) 5 min before the injections of extract Q_4 (10 mg/kg) and of Δ^9-THC (2·5 mg/kg) respectively. After the marihuana injections aggressiveness was scored during the following 2 hours. The treatment continued for 28 days.

Influence of corn diet on marihuana aggressiveness
(see Table 6)

Six pairs of 4-month-old male rats were used. Half the animals received corn for 2 h daily as their only diet; the other 3 pairs were fed for the same time with a normal diet of pellets. Aggressiveness was measured for 2 h daily beginning immediately after the injection of extract B (10 mg/kg). The experiment continued for 7 days during which the temperature ranged from 23° to 29° C.

Marihuana aggressiveness (see Table 7)

Nine groups of 5 pairs of 3-month-old male rats were used. Three groups were maintained in a cold room with a temperature of 16° C;

TABLE 4

Lack of influence of ammonium chloride and lactic acid injections on the aggressive behaviour elicited in rats, fed *ad libitum*, by 10 mg/kg of cannabis extract Q_4

| | Pretreatment | | | | Duration of Aggressive behaviour (s) after Marihuana | |
Drug	Number of Rats	Dose (mg/kg)	No. of Injections	Time Interval Between Injections (9h)	Shock-induced	Spontaneous
NH_4Cl	5	100	4	6	0	0
Control solution	5	1·0 ml/kg	4	6	0	0
NH_4Cl	2	200	3	4	54; 2	0
Control solution	2	1·0 ml/kg	3	4	74; 1	0
Control solution	2	1·0 ml/kg	1	—	0	0
Lactic acid	2	10	1	—	0	0
Lactic acid	2	20	1		0	0
Control solution	5	1·0 ml/kg	3	2	0	0
Lactic acid	5	10	3	2	0	0

TABLE 5

Lack of influence of 10 mg/kg of lactic acid on the aggressive behaviour elicited in starved rats by 10 mg/kg of cannabis extract Q_4 and 2·5 mg/kg of Δ^9-THC

| Pre-treatment Drug | Treatment | | Average fighting ($s \pm$ s.e.) during 2 h after marihuana injection number | | | | | | |
	Drug	Dose (mg/kg)	1	5	10	15	20	25	28
Saline	Control soln.	1·0 ml/kg	0	0	0	0	0	0	0
Saline	Cannabis	10	0	45	0	460 ± 101	0	232 ± 39	239 ± 85
Saline	Δ^9-THC	2·5	0	0	0	0	348 ± 182	21	201 ± 102
Lactic acid	Cannabis	10	123	0	15	679 ± 199	93	151 ± 39	103 ± 34
Lactic acid	Δ^9-THC	2·5	0	0	0	0	0	43	259 ± 181

TABLE 6
INFLUENCE OF NORMAL AND CORN DIETS ON THE AGGRESSIVE BEHAVIOUR ELICITED IN RATS BY 10 MG/KG OF CANNABIS EXTRACT B

Diet	Average Fighting (s ± S.E.) During 3 h After Marihuana Injection Number						
	1	2	3	4	5	6	7
Normal	0	0	2,608 ± 1,037	2,921 ± 1,112	2,608 ± 1,104	2,755 ± 985	1,201 ± 1,087
Corn	0	118	2,220 ± 1,002	2,224 ± 892	1,013 ± 801*	317 ± 218*	400 ± 114*

*Statistically significant difference (P ≤ 0·05; Mann-Witney U test).

TABLE 7
INFLUENCE OF CORN, PROTEIN-FREE AND BALANCED DIETS ON AGGRESSIVE BEHAVIOUR ELICITED IN SATIATED OR STARVED RATS WITH 10 MG/KG OF CANNABIS EXTRACT Q AND MAINTAINED AT ROOM TEMPERATURE OR IN A COLD ROOM

Diet	Daily feeding	Temperature °C	Average fighting (s ± s.e.) during 2 h after marihuana injection number						
			1	5	10	15	20	25	29
Balanced	ad libitum	19–25·5	0	1	15	0	0	0	0
Protein-free	ad libitum	19–25·5	0	13	0	0	25	0	8
Corn	ad libitum	19–25·5	0	7	28	0	0	0	0
Balanced	ad libitum	16	9	0	0	4	0	20	7
Protein-free	ad libitum	16	55	0	0	27	0	82	49
Corn	ad libitum	16	13	0	15	662 ± 294*	0	240 ± 81*	61 ± 30*
Balanced	2 h	19–25·5	0	0	2	98 ± 51	206 ± 98	723 ± 217	201 ± 64
Protein-free	2 h	19–25·5	0	0	0		510 ± 108*	1,244 ± 508*	742 ± 118*
Corn	2 h	19–25·5	0	0	0	0	222 ± 74	517 ± 181	308 ± 171

*Statistically significant difference from group fed with balanced diet (P ≤ 0·05; Mann-Whitney U test)

each of these groups received, respectively, corn, protein-free or balanced diets *ad libitum*. The other six groups were kept at room temperature which varied from 19° to 25° C; half of these animals received the diets above *ad libitum* and the other half only for 2 hours. Cannabis extract Q_5 (10 mg/kg) was injected daily for 29 days; aggressiveness was measured for 2 h after the injections.

RESULTS

Marihuana-aggressiveness and glucose

As seen in Table 1, doses of glucose up to 1·6 g/kg injected after the appearance of marihuana-induced aggressiveness were not able to counteract it. Furthermore, 800 mg/kg of glucose injected 5 min before the administration of the extract was also ineffective. A different result was obtained, however, when the rats were allowed to drink a 10% glucose solution. Thus, as shown in Table 2, after the rats were given free access to glucose for 24 and 48 h, injection of marihuana did not elicit the aggressive behaviour as it did on the two previous days; the rats drank an average of 41 ml of solution in each 24 h period. Repeating the cannabis injections for 10 more days, without further oral glucose, did not restore the aggressive behaviour.

Marihuana-aggressiveness and temperature

The food-deprived rats submitted to 14° C for 22 h showed fierce aggressiveness beginning with the first injection of marihuana (Table 3). The same result was obtained on the second day when most rats died during the fighting. In contrast, starved animals maintained at 27° C and receiving the same sample of cannabis did not show signs of aggressiveness until the 15th injection (Table 3).

Marihuana-aggressiveness and acidifying agents

Table 4 shows that neither lactic acid nor ammonium chloride was able to potentiate the aggressiveness-inducing properties of marihuana extract and Δ^9-THC. Thus, rats fed *ad libitum* and pretreated with several doses of the acidifying agents did not show spontaneous or shock-induced aggressive behaviour after the first dose of marihuana. The results with chronic treatment were also negative; thus, as seen in Table 5, aggressiveness produced by Δ^9-THC or cannabis extract was not affected by pretreatment with lactic acid during 28 days.

On the other hand, lactic acid (20 mg/kg) strongly potentiated the effects of sodium thiopental (50 mg/kg); thus, 5 control rats slept

180 ± 19 min (average $\pm$ s.d.) under thiopental, whereas 2 animals pretreated with the acid died and the other 3 slept 375 ± 65 min after receiving the barbiturate.

Marihuana-aggressiveness and diet

Rats fed exclusively on corn diet for 2 h daily showed an aggressive behaviour comparable to that of animals receiving normal diet for the same period of time (Table 6). After the 5th injection, however, aggressiveness decreased in the corn-treated animals, probably because they were weaker, weighing less than animals on a 2 h normal diet. Table 7 shows that feeding rats *ad libitum* with corn, protein-free or balanced diets, either at room temperature (first 3 rows of Table 7) or 16° C (4th to 6th rows) did not increase the aggressiveness-inducing property of marihuana. However, when the 3 diets were given only for 2 h, aggressiveness appeared as usual (last three rows) although the duration of fighting was greater in the protein-free diet group.

DISCUSSION

The results described here confirm previous reports on the aggressive behaviour elicited in food-deprived rats by chronic administration of marihuana (Carlini & Masur, 1969, 1970; Orsingher & Fulginiti, 1970). The present experiments were carried out with 3 extracts of *Cannabis sativa* and one sample of pure Δ^9-THC. The extracts possessed approximately the same potency, which was equal to one quarter of that of Δ^9-THC, as measured by the Gayer test. According to Carlini, Santos, Claussen, Bieniek & Korte (1970) this test gives a reliable measure of Δ^9-THC content in cannabis extracts. Therefore, as the extracts were used in doses 4 times greater than that of Δ^9-THC, the rats received approximately the same amount of Δ^9-THC in all experiments. The rats used were of either sex, and from 3 to 4 months of age. However, the influence of the several conditions on marihuana-aggressiveness was studied with the rats as their own controls or with the use of appropriate control groups matched for sex and age. Furthermore, Carlini & Masur (1969) have shown that marihuana-induced aggressiveness does not depend on the sex and age of rats older than 2 months. Finally, in several experiments the temperature was not kept constant (range 19 to 29° C); however, in this and in our previous work (Carlini & Masur, 1969, 1970), it was shown with appropriate control groups of rats that changes in temperature alone did not induce observable changes in behaviour.

It has been reported that food deprivation leads rats to increased excitability and aggressiveness (Davis, 1933; Moyer, 1968). In our conditions, however, aggressiveness did not appear in 288 chronically starved rats used as controls in several other experiments. These animals showed at most excitability, but vicious bitings and stereotyped fighting ("boxer position") lasting for minutes to hours, as observed in the cannabis-treated animals, have never been observed. On the other hand, as shown here and previously by Carlini & Masur (1969, 1970), marihuana does not induce aggressiveness unless the rats are starved.

Of the several conditions studied here only two, namely oral glucose and decrease of temperature, affected the aggressive behaviour induced by marihuana in starved rats. Low temperature clearly potentiated the aggressiveness. As seen in Table 3, marihuana injected in starved rats maintained at 14° C induced fierce aggressiveness in the first 2 days; at 27° C, however, it took 15 injections to achieve aggressive behaviour. This influence of temperature has been observed before (Carlini & Masur, 1969). After drinking about 40 ml of glucose solution in 24 h, which corresponded to 4 g, the animals which were previously aggressive no longer fought under marihuana (Table 2). This effect was probably not brought about simply by an elevation of blood glucose, because if that was the case then intraperitoneal administration would have given the same result. However, 800–1,600 mg/kg of glucose injected at the peak of aggressiveness or 5 min before marihuana administration did not diminish aggressiveness (Table 1). This amount of glucose corresponds roughly to 10 to 20 times the total amount of glucose in the blood of rats. On the other hand, the animals drank at the most 1·3 ml of solution in the last hour before the cannabis injection, which corresponds to about 600 mg/kg of glucose ingested, a value within the range of the intraperitoneal administration. Therefore, the inhibition of aggressive behaviour by oral glucose should not be attributed to an increase of glucose levels in blood.

Eventual changes of pH due to acidosis that may occur in food deprivation, are probably not the potentiating factor. It is known that pH changes influence the penetration of weak acids such as barbiturate into brain (Brodie & Hogben, 1957) and Δ^9-THC has a phenolic moiety in its dibenzopyran nucleus. Although no information is available concerning its dissociation properties, Δ^9-THC and other marihuana compounds might be inducing aggressiveness in starved rats through increased penetration caused by the acidosis. The results obtained, however, do not support this hypothesis. Lactic acid, which clearly potentiated thiopental, did not cause cannabis to elicit aggressiveness in rats fed *ad libitum* or to increase fighting in starved rats; the same negative results were also obtained with ammonium chloride (Tables 4 and 5).

It is also improbable that lack of a nutritional element could be the facilitating factor. Lack of tryptophan leads to a decrease in 5-hydroxytryptamine in brain (Culley, Saunders, Mertz & Jolly, 1963); an inhibitory function on central nervous system has been attributed to serotonin (Brodie & Reid, 1968; Kostowski, Giacalone, Garattini & Valzelli, 1969) and a correlation between aggression and low serotonin content in brain has been reported (Garattini, Giacalone & Valzelli, 1967; Lycke, Modigh & Roos, 1969). However, rats fed *ad libitum* exclusively on a corn diet which contains little tryptophan (Karlson, 1965) did not show marihuana-aggressiveness at room temperature (Table 7); even at 16° C there was little aggressiveness (Table 7). On the other hand, rats fed 2 h daily with corn, in two experiments at room temperature (Tables 6 and 7), showed a marihuana-aggressiveness comparable to that observed in animals fed for 2 h with normal and balanced diets.

Decrease of protein in starved animals also does not seem to be the important factor. Δ^9-THC binds to about 80-95% in plasma protein (Wahlquist, Nilsson, Sandberg, Agurell & Granstrand, 1970); thus, in hypoproteinemic animals marihuana compounds may reach the brain more easily. However, animals maintained at room temperature or at 16° C and fed *ad libitum* exclusively on a protein-free diet did not develop aggressive behaviour even after 29 marihuana injections (Table 7; 2nd and 5th rows). Typical aggressiveness appeared only when the rats were maintained on protein-free diet for 2 h daily (Table 7; 8th row).

It is interesting to analyse the failure of marihuana to induce aggressive behaviour in rats on protein-free and corn diets *ad libitum*. These rats ate a great deal but lost weight as compared with animals which fed for 2 h on normal or balanced diets; thus, these animals lost 18·1 and 17·2% of their initial weight, respectively, which did not differ significantly from the 16·4 and 20·1% losses in groups on 2 h normal and balanced diets. This indicates that they were also undernourished. However, aggressiveness appeared only in rats receiving the 2 h diets. This suggests that undernourishment *per se* is not the facilitating factor for the induction of aggressive behaviour by marihuana. On the other hand, when glucose was given by injection aggressiveness remained, whereas when rats were allowed to drink glucose aggressive behaviour was prevented. It seems therefore that if rats are allowed to eat at will, aggression as a result of injections of marihuana does not appear, even when deficient diets are furnished. These data suggest that hunger stress, rather than undernourishment, is important for facilitating marihuana-induced aggressive behaviour in the starved rat. In support of this conclusion are the data that in rats submitted at the same time to two stressful situations, food deprivation and cold, aggressiveness was more intensely and more easily elicited by marihuana (Table 3). The possibility that environmental stresses may potentiate cannabis effects has also been suggested for human beings (Talbott & Teague, 1969).

SUMMARY

1. Aggressive behaviour was elicited in rats that had been deprived of food for 20 h daily (starved), by chronic adminis-tration of *Cannabis sativa* extract or $(—)$-Δ^9-*trans*-tetra-hydrocannabinol.
2. The influence of intraperitoneal (i.p.) or oral glucose ad-ministration, cold environment, acidosis, and corn, and protein-free diets on this aggressiveness was studied.
3. Intraperitoneal injections of glucose (100–1,600 mg/ kg) did not alter the aggressiveness induced by marihuana in starved rats; glucose given orally, however, blocked this behaviour.
4. Low temperature (14° C) strongly potentiated the aggressive behaviour induced by marihuana in the starved rats.
5. Lactic acid in doses capable of potentiating thiopental anaesthesia, failed to alter the marihuana-aggressiveness of starved rats or to facilitate this effect of marihuana in rats fed *ad libitum*. The same negative results were obtained with ammonium chloride.
6. In rats fed *ad libitum* with protein-free or corn diets, marihuana administered chronically did not elicit aggressive behaviour. However, aggressiveness appeared when rats were fed for only 2 h daily on those diets.
7. The results suggest that the stress of hunger (and not hypo-glycaemia, acidosis or lack of specific nutrients due to starva-tion) is the factor that facilitates the development of aggressive behaviour by chronic administration of marihuana.

REFERENCES

Brodie, B. B. & Hogben, C. A. M. (1957). Some physical-chemical factors in drug action. *J. Pharm. Pharmac.*, 9, 345–380.

Brodie, B. B. & Reed, W. D. (1968). Serotonin in brain: functional considerations. In *Advances in Pharmacology,* ed. Garattini, S. & Shore, P. A., Vol. 6B, pp. 97–113. New York: Academic Press.

Carlini, E. A. & Kramer, C. (1965). Effects of *Cannabis sativa* (marihuana) on maze performance of the rat. *Psychopharmacologia Berl.* 7, 175–181.

Carlini, E. A. & Masur, J. (1969). Development of aggressive behaviour in rats by chronic administration of *Cannabis sativa. Life Sci.,* 8, 607–620.

Carlini, E. A. & Masur, J. (1970). Development of fighting behaviour in starved rats by chronic administration of (−) Δ^9-*trans*-tetrahydrocannabinol and cannabis extracts. Lack of action of other psychotropic drugs. *Comm. Behav. Biol.* (A), 5, 57–61.

Carlini, E. A., Santos, M., Claussen, U., Bieniek, D. & Korte, F. (1970). Structure activity relation of four tetrahydrocannabinols and the pharmacological activity of five semipurified extracts of *Cannabis sativa. Psychopharmacologia, Berl.,* 18, 82–93.

Culley, W. J., Saunders, R. N., Mertz, E. T. & Jolly, D. H. (1963). Effect of a tryptophan deficient diet on brain serotonin and plasma tryptophan level. *Proc. soc. exp. Biol. Med., N.Y.,* 113, 645–648.

Davis, F. C. (1933). The measurement of aggressive behaviour in laboratory rats. *J. Genet. Psychol.,* 43, 213–217.

Garattini, S., Giacalone, E. & Valzelli, L. (1967). Isolation, aggressiveness and brain 5-hydroxytryptamine turnover. *J. Pharm. Pharmac.,* 19, 338–339.

Karlson, P. ('1965). In *Introduction to Modern Biochemistry,* 2nd Edition, p. 382. New York: Academic Press.

Kostowski, W., Giacalone, E., Garattini, S. & Valzelli, L. (1969). Electrical stimulation of midbrain raphe: biochemical, behavioural and bioelectrical effects. *Eur. J. Pharmac.,* 7, 170–175.

Lycke, E., Modigh, K. & Roos, B. E. (1969). Aggression in mice associated with changes in the monoamine metabolism of the brain. *Experientia,* 25, 951–953.

Moyer, K. E. (1968). Kinds of aggression and their physiological basis. *Comm. behav. Biol.* (A), 2, 65–87.

Orsingher, O. A. & Fulginiti, S. (1970). Effects of *Cannabis sativa* on learning in rats. *Pharmacology,* 3, 337–344.

Santos, M., Sampaio, M. R. P., Fernandes, N. S. & Carlini, E. A. (1966). Effects of *Cannabis sativa* (marihuana) on the fighting behaviour of mice. *Psychopharmacologia, Berl.*, 8, 437—444.

Talbott, J. A. & Teague, J. W. (1969). Marihuana psychosis. *J. Amer. med. Ass.*, 210, 299-302.

Walhquist, M., Nilsson, I. M., Sandberg, F., Agurell, S. & Granstrand, B. (1970). Binding of Δ^1-tetrahydrocannabinol to human plasma proteins. *Biochem. Pharmac.*, 19, 2579—2584.

This work was supported by research grants from Fundação de Amparo à Pesquisa do Estado de São Paulo (FAPESP).

Part 11

Summary

The last paper in this collection represents an attempt by Leo Hollister, one of the leading authorities in the area of marihuana research, to summarize the evidence dealing with the effects of marihuana on humans that has appeared in the last few years. As Hollister is quick to point out, much of the present work is merely a rediscovery of facts that had been known at one time. Nor is it likely that we are going to discover something new about a drug that has been used for over five thousand years. What is becoming clear from these studies, however, is that cannabis is capable of contributing to dramatically different effects on behavior depending upon the potency of the material consumed. This finding could account for much of the controversy surrounding the claims about cannabis.

31

Marihuana in Man: Three Years Later

Leo E. Hollister

Few drugs have been used so long and by so many people as that derived from *Cannabis sativa*. Until the spectacular resurgence of use of marihuana by Western society during the past decade, scientific interest had been largely dormant. During the past 3 years, in particular, this interest has been rekindled, in part because of the social importance of the drug, in part because of the possibility of doing more precise studies, and in relatively small part because research funds became available. After a slow start while legal hobbles were being ameliorated, the rate of increase in scientific inquiry into the effects of marihuana has risen in almost an exponential manner. It may soon be impossible to keep current with the rapidly growing literature. It seems propitious, therefore, to assess accomplishments in regard to marihuana's effects in man during the past 3 years, comparing these with those of the past, as well as taking inventory of what still needs to be done.

Reprinted with permission of the author and publisher from *Science*, 1971, *172*, 21–29. Copyright 1972 by the American Association for the Advancement of Science.

Leo E. Hollister, M.D., is Medical Investigator with the Veterans Administration Hospital in Palo Alto, California, and Associate Professor of Medicine at Stanford University School of Medicine, Stanford, California.

MARIHUANA IN MAN: PAST

Customarily, those of us engaged in research with marihuana deplore the ignorance that existed about the drug before we came along. Much of the work of the past, to be sure, was based on descriptions of effects by individuals exposed to uncertain doses of the drug. Still, much of the newer work with marihuana involves the rediscovery of phenomena known for a long time, sometimes camouflaged by coining new names for old phenomena or by elegantly proving the obvious. Looked at in its historical context, the present flurry of experimentation may have contributed less that is really new than we like to believe.

Baudelaire, an avid member of the hashish cult fashionable in Paris during the middle of the 19th century, provided an elegant description of its clinical effects. He may either have used more than a little poetic license or have taken enormous doses of the drug[1]. If we brush aside much of his rhetoric, we find that he clearly described such phenomena as euphoria, uncontrollable laughter, paresthesia and weakness, perceptual disorders affecting time, space, and hearing, mental disorganization with flight of ideas and incoherence, hallucinations, and depersonalization. His account of his experience with hashish is strongly reminiscent of later accounts of the effects of psychotomimetics. That higher doses of the drug were psychotomimetic was recognized by his contemporary, the psychiatrist, Moreau de Tours, who not only took the drug himself, but encouraged its use by his students so that they could gain insights into mental disturbances[2].

Similar descriptive accounts, which have hardly been improved upon today, are found in the monograph by Lewin: Anxiety and restlessness; euphoria, hilarity; faintness and weakness; perceptual distortions; flight of ideas and mental confusion; and finally, sleep. Like effects of the drug are described in two reports from India, both of which were primarily concerned with sociological questions revolving about the widespread social use of the drug[3].

Concern about the social use of marihuana in the United States stimulated some investigations in the early 1940's under the auspices of the La Guardia commission[4]. These were quasipharmacological studies in which measured quantities of marihuana were both orally administered and smoked. Measures of dose were usually in milliliters of an alcoholic extract of marihuana or milligrams of marihuana leaves, both of unknown composition, so that pharmacologic precision was somewhat illusory. Effective doses were obtained, however, and clinical effects resembled those described before. As always, euphoria was prominent, as was difficulty in concentrating or maintaining attention; floating sensations or feelings of heaviness and lightness; dryness of mouth; blurring of vision; palpitation and tachycardia; and increased appetite. Laboratory studies were usually within normal limits. Electroencephalographic studies were thought to show a correlation between euphoria and increased alpha activity. Performance tests, such as static equilibrium, hand-steadiness, tapping speed, and complex reaction time were impaired. Users of the drug were more tolerant of impairment and less likely to experience initial anxiety or excitement than were nonusers. Tests of various intellectual functions showed some impairment at higher doses, but many tests remained unimpaired by the modest doses used. The wavelike character of the syndrome, with waxing and waning, as well as the development of frank hallucinations in some subjects, was noted when somewhat higher doses were used. Studies of a synthetic homolog, synhexyl, revealed similar findings[5-6].

Thus, by the late 1950's, many of the phenomena of marihuana intoxication had been described. It was not until another 10 years had passed and a marked change in the patterns of use of the drug had occurred in American society that interest in clinical studies was again revived.

MARIHUANA IN MAN: PRESENT

The availability of synthetic *trans*-Δ^1-tetrahydrocannabinol (monoterpinoid numbering system; tetrahydrocannabinol is henceforth referred to as THC) as well as chemical techniques for quantifying its content in marihuana has made possible for the first time pharmacological studies which provide some precision in dose[7]. When the material is smoked, a still uncertain and variable fraction of THC is lost by smoke escaping into the air or exhaled from the respiratory dead space. Relatively little is lost by pyrolysis, as it is likely that the cannabinoid is volatilized in advance of the burning segment of the cigarette. The efficiency of the delivery of a dose by smoking has been estimated from 20 to 80 percent, but with most experienced smokers it should approximate 50 percent[8]. Synthetic THC and marihuana extracts are also active by mouth, but doses equivalent in effect to those from smoking are about threefold larger[9]. Undoubtedly, some THC may be inactivated within the gastrointestinal tract or during its passage through the intestinal mucosa and liver. As no method for the quantitative estimation of THC concentration in plasma or urine is available with usual chemical techniques, the actual doses of THC obtained by various routes are still unknown.

When smoked, THC is rapidly absorbed and effects appear within seconds to minutes. If marihuana is of low potency, effects may be subtle and brief[10]. Seldom do they last longer than 2 to 3 hours after a single cigarette, although users prolong effects by repeated smoking. Oral doses delay the onset of symptoms for 30 minutes to over 2 hours. Because synthetic THC, as well as marihuana extracts, requires nonpolar solvents, even the administration of accurate doses to animals for pharmacological studies has been a problem. Intravenous doses of drug are preferable to intraperitoneal doses in animals, as the latter may be poorly absorbed.

Because of the dual route of administration, as well as the still unsettled problem of whether natural marihuana materials have activity different from synthetic THC, we shall consider each type of clinical study separately. Very likely most pharmacological activity is determined by the quantity of THC, the main difference being the route of administration.

Studies of Oral Doses of Synthetic THC

Three groups including our own at Veterans Administration Hospital, Palo Alto, have now published on the effects of oral doses of synthetic THC in man. The group at the Addiction Research Center, U.S. Public Health Service Hospital, Lexington, Kentucky, employed doses of 10 to 30 milligrams, or 120 to 480 micrograms per kilogram of body weight. We used doses of 30 to 70 milligrams, or 341 to 946 micrograms per kilogram. A group from the National Institute for Mental Health (NIMH) used a single dose of 20 milligrams, not specifying the weight of the subjects. Between the three groups, however, a rather wide range of dose was explored[9, 11]. It should be emphasized that, even if we account for the lesser potency of the material when given orally as compared to smoking, most doses were beyond those which might be obtained from smoking an ordinary marihuana cigarette. If one assumes that an average cigarette may consist of 500 milligrams of marihuana containing 1 percent THC, and that delivery is 50 percent efficient, the dose delivered would be 2.5 milligrams of THC, equivalent perhaps to 7.5 milligrams of THC given orally. The experimental doses might be more comparable to those obtained from smoking several cigarettes of reasonable quality, or from smoking hashish.

1) *Physiological effects:* No changes in pupil size, respiratory rate, or deep tendon reflexes were observed. We found no change in oral temperature of any consequence, but the NIMH group reported a slight but consistent decline. All observers have commented on the constant increase in pulse rate, often one of the first effects of the drug. Blood pressure tends to fall slightly or remains unchanged; at higher doses, we observed two instances of orthostatic hypotension. Conjunctival reddening is also constantly observed, and in this case is clearly not an artifact produced by irritation from smoke. Both this symptom and the increased pulse rate correlate quite well in time with the appearance and duration of psychic effects of the drug. We measured muscle strength with the finger ergograph and could demonstrate muscle weakness objectively.

2) *Perceptual and psychic changes:* Euphoria was most pronounced in our subjects, who were graduate students. It was less marked in the Lexington series, which used imprisoned former drug addicts, or in the NIMH group of subjects, who were prisoners at a correctional institution. Sleepiness was constantly observed, and often deep sleep followed the higher doses. Time sense was altered, hearing was less discriminant, vision was apparently sharper with many visual distortions. Depersonalization, difficulty in concentrating and thinking, and dreamlike states were prominent. Many of these symptoms were similar to those produced by psychotomimetics such as lysergic acid diethylamide (LSD), mescaline, or psilocybin. On self-reporting mood scales, our subjects became more friendly initially, but less so with the passage of time; less aggressive, especially late in the course; less clear-thinking persistently; sleepy, especially after 3 hours; euphoric persistently; and dizzy persistently. The NIMH group found only increased sleepiness and less clear-thinking with the same scale, but their comparisons were made against controls who received placebos rather than against their own baseline and were ratings by others rather than by the subjects themselves.

3) *Psychometric tests:* We used repetitive psychometric tests of arithmetic ability or freehand drawing, both of which were impaired in different ways. The arithmetic test, a familiar and simple task, showed a slowing of performance against time, with maintained accuracy. The drawing test, less familiar and more difficult, showed reduced accuracy with no slowing of performance, probably indicating some loss of finer

judgment. The NIMH group found that accuracy of serial addition was impaired, but that the drug had no effect on ability to count backwards, to say the alphabet, or to repeat digits forwards or backwards.

4) *Biochemical tests:* We were the only group to attempt these measures. Amounts of free fatty acids in the plasma remained unchanged, unlike the case with drugs such as LSD where sharp elevations are observed. Glucose concentrations in the blood were also unchanged, despite previous reports indicating that marihuana produces hypoglycemia. The lack of change in plasma glucose values has now been verified on numerous occasions. Both creatinine and phosphorus clearance were temporarily decreased, a phenomenon which has been observed with LSD[12].

5) *Comparisons with other THC homologs and other materials:* We compared synthetic THC with the synthetic Δ^3THC homolog, synhexyl, both given orally. The latter compound has been studied rather extensively for possible clinical utility [6, 13]. On the whole, the changes reported above were also produced by synhexyl, but synhexyl was approximately one-third as potent as THC. The onset of the effects of synhexyl was delayed by about 1 hour, but lasted longer in equivalent doses.

The Lexington group compared the effect of taking THC orally with its effects when smoked (known quantities were added to cigarettes). They estimated that potency is increased approximately threefold by smoking as compared with taking the same material by mouth[9]. As might be expected, effects appeared sooner, but were of briefer duration, when the material was smoked. They also compared the effects of smoked THC (75 to 225 micrograms per kilogram) with those of LSD given intramuscularly in doses of 0.5 to 1.5 micrograms per kilogram[14]. Subjective effects between the two drugs were not readily distinguished, but objective differences were marked: LSD elevated body temperature, increased systolic and diastolic blood pressure, and exaggerated deep tendon reflexes and dilated pupils whereas THC had none of these effects. We made a retrospective comparison of the effects of LSD and THC taken orally and came to similar conclusions regarding the objective differences[15]. Subjectively, we thought that THC produced less total impairment with more euphoria and dreamlike states than did LSD at comparable doses and that, unlike the latter drug, sedation was a prominent feature with THC, with most subjects falling asleep. In general, we have seen fewer psychotomimetic effects from THC than did the Lexington group.

Studies of Oral Doses of Marihuana Extracts

We have completed several experiments with extracts of marihuana, gauging doses on the basis of THC content. We used doses ranging from 5 to 60 milligrams, and compared these to each other and to the placebo extract. At the smaller doses, appreciable clinical effects were usually observed as compared with placebo; at the larger doses, psychotomimetic effects were observed. In general, one had the impression that the effects produced by these extracts were comparable to those which would have been produced by similar doses of synthetic THC.

Tests comparing the effects of doses of marihuana extract containing the equivalent of 20, 40, and 60 milligrams of THC with the effects of placebo indicated that whereas long-term memory (tested by subtraction of serial sevens) was maintained, short-term memory (tested by the span of forward and backward remembered digits) was impaired. Along with this was an impairment of a more complex task, goal-directed serial alternation, in which successive subtractions and additions had to be made to reach a specified end number. The latter task requires the retention, coordination, and serial ordering of memories relevant to a specific goal which must also be kept in mind. Disturbance of this type has been termed temporal disintegration. Both confusion and depersonalization are prominent clinical features of the intoxication from marihuana[16].

We also compared marihuana extracts with ethanol and dextroamphetamine in regard to their effects on mood and mental functions[17]. Marihuana and ethanol were most alike in their effects; they caused decreased activity and had a tendency to impair performance on certain psychometric tests as well as performance on the simple reaction-time test. Marihuana was distinctly different from the other two drugs in regard to effect on time estimation and production, with subjective time being slowed.

A group at the University of Utah has also used marihuana extracts in clinical studies. They, too, have been impressed with the disruptive effects of marihuana on sequential thought, which suggests impairment of rapid decision-making and short-term memory. They have noted, as have others, a great variability in performance during marihuana intoxication, which may be related to the fact that subjects go "in-and-out," the effects seeming to come and go. A later study by this same group used doses of marihuana extract containing 0.3 milligrams of THC per pound (0.66 mg/kg) of body weight. Performance was impaired in complex reaction time, digit-code memory, time estimation, hand-steadiness, and reading comprehension. Once again, the sporadic nature of the experience was noted, with lapses in response while attention waned. Thus, impairment was explainable by loss of selective attention, immediate recall, and systematic thinking. They suggested that prolongation of time estimates might be a secondary phenomenon[18].

Studies with Smoked Marihuana

As marihuana is more commonly smoked than taken orally, some investigators feel that proper studies can be done only by utilizing this particular route of administration. The major argument is that smoking native marihuana may include other active materials present in the plant which are not found in synthetic THC or extracts, or that the process of combustion may create new active materials. No proof for either assertion is at hand. The disadvantages are great: the dose, even when one knows the amount in the cigarette, is impossible to judge as variations in technique of smoking may create tremendous variations in delivery of the dose.

The first such study provided marihuana in cigarettes, the putative doses being 4.5 and 18 milligrams, which were compared with a placebo smoke[10]. Naive smokers experienced few subjective effects, although they showed an increased heart rate and reddening of the whites of the eyes. Experienced smokers of marihuana reported a typical "high," not much elaborated upon. Performance on the digit-symbol substitution test and the pursuit-rotor test was unchanged. No changes in blood sugar were found. In general, the effects of the drug smoked in this fashion were relatively mild and innocuous, which led the investigators to take a sanguine view of the social use of the drug. It seems possible, in retrospect, that the doses in this study were far less than assumed, both on the basis of another investigator's experience with aged natural material (see below) and studies of synthetic THC.

Another study tested driving skill, with a driving simulator, in subjects 30 minutes after smoking two marihuana cigarettes over a 30-minute period and 1 hour after consumption of large doses of ethanol, as well as after no treatment. Under marihuana conditions, speedometer errors were increased, which suggests that the subjects did not monitor the speedometer as carefully as they might have normally, but driving was otherwise little impaired. As might have been expected, marked impairment was observed from the high doses of alcohol, which were intended to approximate concentrations of 100 milligrams per 100 milliliters of blood. Such highly controversial findings have elicited criticism because the doses of the two drugs were disproportionate, because a dose-response curve was not obtained, and because simulated driving might not be an adequate model for real life[19]. Other objections are that smoking delivers an uncertain dose of drug and that most marihuana users tend to titrate their rate of smoking to a desired clinical "high," which in this case might have been lower than usual due to the subjects' bias in favor of marihuana over ethanol. The earlier study of smoked marihuana found that most effects dissipated by the end of 1 hour, so that the testing may have missed some impairment. Although the authors were careful not to state that the marihuana did not affect one's ability to drive a car, it is unfortunate that many lawyers and courts may draw this conclusion. Sometimes it is better not to be so scientific. Since our first experiments, we simply asked subjects when they were "high," "Do you think you could drive a car now?" Without exception the answer from those who had really gotten "high" has been "No!" or "You must be kidding!"

Ten experienced marihuana smokers who smoked two to three cigarettes containing a putative dose of 3.9 milligrams of THC each, had only minimum effects. Besides reporting a feeling of being "high," they showed a slight decrease in intellectual efficiency, some excess jocularity, and a slight loosening of associations. Neurological examination revealed a slight improvement in vibratory sense. The electroencephalogram showed slight slowing in the alpha band with more peaking of frequencies. Subsequent assays of the materials smoked in the above study revealed an almost tenfold decrease in its reported strength, emphasizing the difficulties in using the unextracted natural product, which seems to have a relatively short shelf-life. Ethanol extracts of marihuana, especially if kept cold and in the dark, maintain stability very well[20].

The electroencephalographic effects reported in the above study were similar to those we found following oral doses of marihuana extract that contained the equivalent of 32 milligrams of THC. However, the changes resembled those of drowsiness and were not readily distinguishable from those from the same subjects under placebo conditions, where some drowsiness also occurred[21]. Others have reported somewhat different electroencephalographic effects, which reemphasizes the difficulty in corroborating such effects of various drugs.

Eight subjects smoked both placebo cigarettes and those containing marihuana extract in an amount equivalent to 10 milligrams of THC[8]. Prior testing suggested that, even when smoked with maximum efficiency, only 50 percent of the dose in cigarettes was delivered, so the results were construed as representing an effective dose of 5 milligrams of THC. As compared with placebo, marihuana impaired performance on a pursuit meter, as well as on five of nine performance tests done under conditions of delayed auditory feedback. Subjects reported many more symptoms from marihuana than from placebo and were able to identify the active cigarettes without error; half the group thought the placebo cigarette was also active, once again confirming the unreliability of subjective identification, which may be biased by the procedure of smoking, the taste and smell of the smoke, and conditioning from past experience. A subsequent study by the same group, with similar doses of marihuana combined with a dose of ethanol calculated to produce concentrations of 50 milligrams per 100 milliliters of plasma, revealed evidence of an additive effect in regard to impaired functioning[22].

Ordinary cigarettes were dosed with marihuana extract equivalent to 12 milligrams of THC, placebo marihuana extract, Δ^3THC (15 milligrams), and synhexyl, a Δ^3THC homolog (15 milligrams) and were smoked in blind fashion by subjects habituated to nicotine. Even the placebo cigarettes produced an evanescent high, which testifies to the effect of the smoking process itself in contributing to some placebo responses. The cigarettes containing the active materials were clearly distinguishable on the basis of subjective effects, which resembled those well described for marihuana. Both Δ^3THC and synhexyl were somewhat less potent than THC in the extract, being from one-third to one-sixth as active[23].

Studies with Both Oral and Smoked Marihuana

Ten heavy users of marihuana smoked active marihuana and marihuana from which all active material had been removed (placebo), and they ingested active and placebo extracts of marihuana and ethanol[24]. Doses were the equivalent of 9 milligrams of THC for the active smokes, the equivalent of 90 milligrams of THC for active orally ingested material, and 0.95 grams of ethanol per kilogram. Not only did these subjects show little effect from the rather large acute dose of ethanol, but they were scarcely able to distinguish active smoked marihuana from the placebo. They uniformly distinguished the active oral dose, which was considerably stronger than the active smoke as measured by the symptom reports. Both forms of marihuana increased pulse rate and time estimation; they had no effect on time production, the rod-and-frame test, and digit-symbol substitution. Ethanol had an opposite effect on time estimation, decreasing it. The electroencephalographic changes were described as increased low-voltage fast activity, decreased alpha activity, and slight slowing of the alpha frequencies. Because of the remarkable tolerance of these subjects to ethanol, as well as to a monumental dose of marihuana (if the putative oral dose was correct), the possibility of some cross-tolerance between alcohol and marihuana was raised.

Metabolism in Man

Until recently, very little was known regarding the fate of THC in man. We attempted to measure unchanged THC in plasma with gas-liquid chromatographic techniques without any success. Others with techniques of even greater sensitivity (detection of 600 picograms of THC) have also failed. A relatively simple technique for measuring the excretion of metabolites of marihuana in urine used thin-layer chromatographic techniques[25]. The possible use of this test forensically is limited by the persistence of some of the new spots that appear after marihuana was smoked or ingested for periods far longer than the span of drug effect; we have found some present for 2 weeks after the last dose. With thin-layer techniques, we have not found measurable amounts of unchanged THC in urine, even when this was the sole substance given in very large amounts. Others have reported no cannabinoids as present in urine after marihuana smoking[7]. Recently a 7-hydroxy metabolite of THC has been described, which also has pharmacological activity[26]. Thus, it seems possible that the drug may exert its action through an active metabolite. The prolonged latent period following ingestion of synhexyl led us to propose that it must be converted to an active metabolite. On the other hand, conversion of THC to any active metabolite, if this is necessary for its action, must be swift, as effects of potent preparations are noticeable within minutes after smoking.

By use of tracer doses of THC (5.6 to 7.9 micrograms per kilogram) labeled with carbon-14, the disposition of an intravenous dose was determined in man. A two-phase biological half-life was found in the plasma, the rapid phase lasted about 30 minutes during which redistribution of the drug occurred and was followed by a slow phase of about

56 hours. As the rapid phase correlated reasonably well with the expected span of clinical effects of THC similarly administered, pharmacologically active doses of the drug might be handled in a similar fashion. Metabolites of THC appeared in plasma within 10 minutes, but during the first hour most THC in plasma was unchanged. The 7-hydroxy metabolite constituted only a relatively small fraction of material in plasma but other presently unidentified materials might represent further metabolites derived from it. Less than 1 percent of THC was excreted in urine unchanged[27]. Intravenous injection of tritiated THC in rabbits revealed a shorter half-life, ranging from 7 to 16 minutes, with disappearance of most unchanged THC over a 30-minute period. In vitro studies showed that THC is bound to lipoproteins in human plasma to the extent of 80 to 95 percent. Thus, assumption of prolonged binding in tissues, as indicated by the prolonged half-life after redistribution of the drug, is quite reasonable[28].

Relevance of Laboratory Experiments
to Social Use

One must always be concerned when one studies in the laboratory drugs that affect the mind lest the constraints of an experiment alter what one is measuring (the uncertainty principle in the behavioral sciences). Implicit in all research with these drugs are the influences due to the types of subjects, their expectations and past life experiences, the attitudes of the experimenters, and the setting in which the experiment takes place, all of which may alter the drug effects which are observed. Past experience with laboratory experiments involving psychotomimetic drugs indicates that such extraneous influences have been given undue emphasis. With proper information-gathering techniques, a basic group of clinical signs and symptoms can be delineated for various drugs that correlate well with those reported from their social use[29].

It is rather heartening, therefore, that the clinical syndromes described for marihuana in the laboratory correspond closely to those reported by street users (with the exception of those which are too personal or metaphysical to be measured). With a questionnaire technique and a sampling method that allowed distribution of the questionnaire until it reached a respondent who was a user of marihuana, clinical aspects of the social use of the drug were described[30]. The most common symptoms and signs reported were: paresthesia, floating sensations, and depersonalization; weakness and relaxation; perceptual changes (visual, auditory, tactile); subjective slowing of time; flight of ideas, difficulty in thinking and loss of attention; loss of immediate memory; euphoria and silliness; sleepiness. Other common symptoms which are not verifiable in the laboratory were claims of increased insight and perception, as well as increased sexual desire, performance, and enjoyment.

On the basis of these data, one would assume that at least the respondents to this questionnaire had explored most of the range of marihuana dosage that has been studied in the laboratory. The resemblance of many of the effects reported to those previously reported from hallucinogenic drugs suggests that some of the doses of marihuana which are used socially are fairly high. In any case, laboratory experiments can be contrived which are highly relevant to the effects of these drugs as they are used socially.

Part of the problem in relating social use of marihuana to laboratory studies may be due to the fact that adulterated drug may be encountered in social use. Adulterants have included oregano, *Stramonium* leaves, methamphetamine, cocaine, LSD, and, allegedly, heroin, although use of the latter scarcely makes economic sense. Atypical reactions from marihuana use, at least those which seem to be unexplainable by laboratory studies of its pharmacological effects, might be better explained by the presence of a different drug.

Marihuana in Man: Future

Social Use of Marihuana

Much has already been written about the problem of the rapid spread of marihuana usage, especially among younger Americans and Western Europeans[31]. Unfortunately, we lack many important facts for making a proper judgment about the desirability or undesirability of accepting this drug into our culture. Here are some important, but not fully answered, questions. Most of these are not answerable by laboratory experiments.

Is marihuana to be equated with alcohol as a social drug? This assertion is often made by its proponents, who view it as a desirable substitute. In terms of its extraordinary low acute toxicity, as compared with alcohol, marihuana would appear preferable. The fact that it is noncaloric is another advantage, as many medical complications of alcohol stem from the fact that it is an inadequate food. On the other hand, the degree of impairment from casual or continued use seems to be about equal for either drug, assuming that equivalent mind-altering doses are taken. One of the great present difficulties is that the dose of marihuana is exceedingly difficult to gauge in its presently available forms, whereas that of alcoholic beverages is most precise. This disadvantage might be overcome in part by synthetic THC's, which afford a rather precise, but not nearly so palatable, method of titrating dose. Unlike alcohol, which is almost totally absorbed, oral doses of THC are absorbed to a far lesser extent. Delivery of a dose of drug by smoking is even more uncertain. The greatest problem is the assumption that marihuana would supplant alcoholic beverages for a great number of people. Past history suggests that the drug would simply be added to the use of alcoholic beverages by many, or even be used by sizable numbers of people who ordinarily might not take social drugs at all.

Another aspect of the comparison between marihuana and alcoholic beverages has to do with the ostensible reasons for using them. Few people admit to taking a drink to get "stoned" (in the old days this term was applied to the effects of overdoses of alcohol), but rather because they enjoy the various highly palatable forms in which beverage alcohol is available or the various social occasions at which its use is socially sanctioned. Marihuana, on the other hand, can be used only for its drug effects. The smoke is hardly enjoyable in its own right, much less the rigorous method of smoking, and the noxious taste of orally administered forms of the drug is virtually impossible to disguise. Whatever esthetic benefits marihuana may provide must be attributed to the drug effect and not to the process of taking the drug. Thus, in considering the social use of marihuana one must justify drug-taking in its own right without the various social conventions surrounding the use of alcohol, nicotine, or caffeine, as these drugs are presently used socially.

How serious is the dependence problem with marihuana? Psychological dependence has been well-documented, but physical dependence manifested by withdrawal reactions is unknown. To this extent, one might assume that marihuana might be easier to give up than are alcohol or sedatives. Nonetheless, where the drug is freely available despite legal restraints (such as in Egypt, not to mention the United States), many people use it repetitively. A study of such users in Egypt revealed that the amount of use varied from 5 to 50 times monthly, that most users started before the age of 20 years, and that the principal reasons for starting were to be socially conforming, to satisfy curiosity, and to attain euphoria and sexual stimulation. Although two-thirds of the users expressed a wish to discontinue, their habituation to the euphoriant and soothing effects, as well as their continuing need to conform to a now-expected social pattern, made them continue use of the drug[32]. A similar pattern seems to be emerging in the United States.

Does marihuana use lead to opiate addiction? This point is highly controversial, and it may be too early to provide an adequate answer. In many parts of the United States, especially the northern urban centers, opiate addiction is related to prior use of marihuana[33]. Yet, it is also apparent that only a small number of all marihuana users follow such a progression. If anything is clear, it is that the availability of a drug is directly related to its nonmedical use and that such use of any drug increases the likelihood of multiple drug use. As the phenomenon of widespread use of marihuana by youth in our country is still comparatively recent, it remains to be seen whether the number of persons in their early 20's who are dependent upon narcotics will increase during the early 1970's, when such a phenomenon might be expected to occur if there is progression from marihuana to more potent agents. During the past 2 years, it appears that multiple drug use among our youth has led many to become heroin addicts. The present pattern of heroin use by white, middle-class, native-born, suburban youth contrasts sharply with the pattern of use by poor, culturally unassimilated, central city residents which had been stable for the previous 25 years.

What are the immediate and remote dangers of marihuana use? As more reports come in, it appears that the immediate dangers are almost identical with those from LSD, probably because at higher doses many of the same mental and emotional reactions are obtained. Manic or elated excitement, panic states, precipitation of schizophrenic-like or depressive illnesses, and frank deliriums are infrequent complications encountered among users[34]. What is more disturbing are reports of subtle effects on the personality associated with prolonged use—loss of a desire to work, loss of motivation, and loss of judgment and intellectual functions[35]. It may well be argued that individuals with these manifestations may have developed them in the absence of drug use, but available evidence does not allow this assertion. In view of the fact that many drug users are recruited from segments of our youth most favored with intelligence and opportunity, the future loss of a large number of these individuals from productive society could be of considerable social consequence.

Should marihuana be legalized? Again the example of alcohol is cited. This seductive solution would have several immediate benefits: it would reduce the number of possible crimes one can commit, it would provide a legal source of pleasure, it would provide another source of taxation, and it might serve to reduce tensions between races and generations. Arguments for legalization of marihuana have been extensively set forth and are superficially quite convincing[36]. A distinction should be made between legalization and making something "less illegal" as by eliminating penalties for possession for personal use. Legalization of marihuana would require the government to take over the licensing and control of the production, manufacture, distribution, and sale of marihuana products. The same enormous bureaucracy which is required to control alcoholic beverages would have to be duplicated or expanded. Control of marihuana might be far more difficult to achieve than control of alcoholic beverages. No one feels constrained to watch over every field of corn, but would anyone dare leave a field of marihuana unguarded? And no one can produce a potable alcoholic beverage easily from that corn, but the weed comes ready to use. Bootlegging of beer and wine is possible, but not especially easy; anyone with a window box can bootleg marihuana. What legalization might very well produce is the same type of disrespect for the law deplored by those who object to the present marihuana laws. Increasingly it is becoming apparent that the criminal law is not a suitable means to control the problem of drug abuse; it has failed in virtually every instance[37]. What may be more immediately appropriate would be to eliminate penalties for possession of marihuana for personal use, not to establish a new body of law that might prove to be as difficult to enforce as the one we have. Other countries are coming to similar conclusions about the amelioration of marihuana laws[38].

Pharmacological Questions

Undoubtedly, the next few years will see a rapid expansion of our pharmacological knowledge about marihuana. Many talented people have entered the field, for a variety of reasons. It is unlikely that pharmacological answers will provide answers to the social questions about the drug. In this instance, as in all others regarding nonmedical drug use, the problem has many dimensions.

The true potency of THC has not been fully explored as yet. As techniques for administering the material by inhalation improve, it seems to be more potent than originally believed. Very likely an acceptable form for intravenous use, binding drug to species-specific albumin, will soon be available. Even now, the potency of THC, either as a hypnotic or as a hallucinogen, is substantial in comparison to other drugs. Whether or not THC is the major active material in marihuana should become clearer soon, as it becomes possible to test separately other cannabinoids for pharmacological effects. Although there seems to be no question that Δ^6THC is also an active material, it constitutes such a small fraction of cannabinoids in the natural plant that its contribution must be negligible. Alkaloids may be found in the plant, but it remains to be seen whether these are pharmacologically active or present in significant quantity. Finally, the possibility exists that other materials in the plant, even though inactive in themselves, may interact with THC to make it more active, or may be converted to active materials within the body. These questions should be settled equally well by tests of the materials given orally as well as by smoking; to date there is little evidence that pyrolysis creates any new or greater amount of active materials than was originally present in the plant.

If THC should prove to be the major active natural constituent, it may still not be the active material in man or animals. Active metabolites have been described for both THC isomers, representing hydroxy-derivatives of the free methyl group[26]. It is still uncertain that these metabolites constitute an important product of the metabolism of the drug in man.

To date, not much study of various THC isomers and homologs has been accomplished in man. Both THC and Δ^3THC are active when smoked, but the latter is far weaker; it has about the same potency as synhexyl, a Δ^3THC homolog with a somewhat longer side chain[23]. Other isomers are possible, but have not been explored, although it is likely that Δ^6THC will soon be tested in man. Side chain variants may selectively single out specific types of pharmacological effects; the dimethylheptyl side chain configuration has the strongest hypotensive effects. Homologs containing nitrogen have also been prepared and have shown pharmacological activity in animals. Consequently, we may expect to see an increasing number of marihuana analogs and homologs developed during the next several years. Relationships of structure to activity should become clearer as these are studied in man.

The question of tolerance, or possibly "reverse" tolerance, is of some interest. The only study of chronic dosage of marihuana, as well as synhexyl, in man indicated that tolerance in the usual sense occurred[39]. It was not of great degree and no definite withdrawal symptoms were encountered. Recent work indicates that tolerance can be produced in two animal species[40]. On the other hand, pharmaco-kinetic considerations would lead one to believe that any drug with such a prolonged secondary biological half-life (56 hours) as THC should show increasing effects with repeated doses, or so-called reverse tolerance. This will depend upon whether or not the secondary biological half-life really applies to THC or other active materials, rather than inactive metabolites. The notion of reverse tolerance undoubtedly includes some learned effects about the proper method of smoking and what symptoms may be anticipated, as well as the placebo effect which chronic use of marihuana seems to develop. Perhaps this learned sensitization minimizes true pharmacological tolerance of mild degree, so that chronic users do not feel constrained to increase their dose to maintain desired effects.

Interactions between marihuana and other drugs used socially will undoubtedly be studied soon. Among the lore of the street, it is a common practice to drink sweet, fortified wines while smoking marihuana to enhance its effects. From what we know of the effects of these two drugs, they have much in common, so the practice seems to be well-based. One might expect some degree of additive effects with barbiturates, but a more complex, mixed pattern with amphetamines and hallucinogens. Curiously, such combinations, other than that mentioned for alcohol, are seldom used socially.

Elucidating the mechanism of action of drugs is the holy grail of pharmacologists, but it is seldom achieved. In view of the current emphasis on the action of psychoactive drugs on brain biogenic amines, one might expect a great deal of work on this area. Preliminary studies have been rather ambiguous, due in part to the difficulty in administering doses of drugs to animals, as well as experimental constraints in man[41]. Some of these difficulties should be overcome, and with increased supplies of drug, an abundance of studies of the mechanism of action will soon ensue.

Therapeutic Potential

One of the most prominent pharmacological effects of marihuana or THC is its sedative-hypnotic action. As such drugs are extremely popular, it is likely that some attempts may be made to exploit this effect therapeutically. Several difficulties seem evident. First, the onset of the action of oral doses of THC is often rather slow, contrary to that of conventional sedative-hypnotics. When the drug is smoked, the onset is rapid, but the duration is relatively short. Thus, it seems impossible with current methods of administration to attain both a rapid onset and long duration of action. Second, doses high enough to produce a marked hypnotic effect are almost always accompanied by some degree of psychotomimetic-like perceptual disorders, which many patients might find disagreeable. Third, the fine titration of dose required to provide sedative effects is likely to be difficult. Finally, the drug does not have novel effects compared with other sedative-hypnotics. Because of the frequent report of dreamlike states during marihuana intoxication, we tested its effect in the sleep laboratory. The effect on rapid eye movement sleep was similar to that of more conventional hypnotics, in that a mild dose caused a tendency to decrease time spent in rapid eye movement sleep[42].

Analgesic effects from *Cannabis* have been described for a long time. They are also demonstrable in animal screening tests, such as the rat tail-flick test. Whether such analgesic effects are secondary to the hypnotic effects, or more similar to those of opiates, is still unsettled. In any case, the place of opiates or opioids for treating severe pain or even that of codeine for treating milder pain will be difficult to challenge, either in terms of rapidity of onset, duration of action, or presence of tolerable side effects.

Despite some superficial similarity of the effects of marihuana to those of barbiturates or opiates, it is likely that this drug is not a pharmacological equivalent of either of the latter. Thus, it would seem to be an unlikely candidate for treating withdrawal reactions to alcohol, barbiturates, or opiates. Clinical trials for this purpose were undertaken a number of years ago, but despite some initially favorable reports, this use did not catch on[6, 43]. In view of the present abundance of drugs which are satisfactory for treating withdrawal reactions, marihuana is not likely to offer any compelling advantages.

The sedative and euphoriant effects of marihuana might seem valuable for treating depression, where anxiety and sadness are often the rule. Past attempts to treat depression with marihuana did not attract much interest, but it could be that the times were prejudicial to its wider use[44]. As sedative drugs may be of value in treating common types of depression mixed with anxiety, marihuana could be useful, but probably no more so than the conventional sedatives so widely available. The actions of tricyclic antidepressants, which are clearly the drugs of choice for endogenous or retarded depressions, are quite different from marihuana, which would not supplant these agents in these more severe depressive syndromes.

Street lore has long had it that one's appetite becomes ravenous and one's appreciation of food sublime after use of marihuana. A recent attempt to study this appetite-stimulating effect in the laboratory gives some support to this idea, although it is by no means a constant phenomenon[45]. As it has not been studied in patients whose appetite is poor, but only in subjects with normal appetite, one cannot draw conclusions about its clinical utility. Further, to be truly useful in the clinic, this effect would have to be sustained over time.

The hypotensive effects, both of THC and especially of homologs such as the dimethylheptyl derivative, have engendered hopes that some derivative might be a useful therapeutic agent for essential hypertension. Hypotensive effects have only been attainable with doses of THC which have severe mental effects. Although the mechanism of its hypotensive action has not been worked out, it may be due to blocking of compensatory mechanisms for maintaining blood pressure in the erect posture. As this mode of action is perhaps the least desirable mechanism for lowering blood pressure of the several available, and many other available drugs work in this way, the possible therapeutic use of some THC derivatives as an antihypertensive drug is doubtful.

Other uses which have been proposed for marihuana include the treatment of epilepsy, as prophylaxis for attacks of migraine or facial neuralgia, or as a sexual stimulant. These are more speculative in nature, but because suitable drugs are lacking for at least the last two uses, they will probably bear some investigation.

SUMMARY

The past 3 years of renewed research on the effects of marihuana in man has added little not previously known about the clinical syndromes produced by the drug. The major advance has been a quantification of dose in relation to clinical phenomena, and a beginning of an understanding of the drug's metabolism. The crucial clinical experiments in regard to the social questions about marihuana, such as the possible deleterious effects from chronic use, cannot be answered by laboratory experiments. These must be settled by close observations made on those who experiment on themselves. It should be possible, within a relatively short time, to determine whether marihuana has any medical utility, but the future would appear to be no more promising than the past in this regard. The mechanisms by which marihuana alters mental functions are not likely to be answered in man, nor even answered soon by animal studies. As marihuana may be unique among drugs in that more experimentation has been accomplished in man than in animals, it may be necessary to look to additional animal studies to provide leads for pertinent future studies in man.

REFERENCES AND NOTES

1. D. Ebin, Ed., *The Drug Experience. First Person Accounts of Addicts, Writers, Scientists and Others* (Orion, New York, 1961).

2. J. Moreau, *Du hachisch et de l'alienation mentale. Etudes psychologiques. 34: Libraire de Fortin* (Masson, Paris, 1845).

3. L. Lewin, *Phantastica, Narcotic and Stimulating Drugs* (Dutton, New York, 1964); *Indian Hemp Drugs Commission Report* (Simla, India Government Printing Office, 1893–1894) (reprinted by Jefferson, Silver Spring, Md., 1969); R. N. Chopra and G. S. Chopra, *Ind. Med. Res. Mem. Mem. No. 31* (July 1939), p. 119.

4. Mayor's Committee on Marihuana, *The Marihuana Problem in the City of New York—Sociological, Medical, Psychological, and Pharmacological Studies* (Cattell, Lancaster, Pa., 1944).

5. F. Ames, *J. Ment. Sci.* 104, 972 (1958).

6. C. K. Himmelsbach, *South. Med. J.* 37, 26 (1944).

7. R. Mechoulam, *Science* 163, 1159 (1970).

8. J. E. Manno, G. F. Kiplinger, I. F. Bennett, S. Haine, R. B. Forney, *Clin. Pharmacol. Ther.* 11, 808 (1970).

9. H. Isbell, G. W. Gorodetsky, D. Jasinski, U. Claussen, F. Spulak, F. Korte, *Psychopharmacologia* 11, 184 (1967).

10. A. T. Weil, N. E. Zinberg, J. M. Nelson, *Science* 162, 1234 (1968).

11. L. E. Hollister, R. K. Richards, H. K. Gillespie, *Clin. Pharmacol. Ther.* 9, 783 (1968); I. E. Waskow, J. E. Olsson, C. Salzman, M. M. Katz, *Arch. Gen. Psychiat.* 22, 97 (1970).

12. L. E. Hollister and B. J. Sjoberg, *Compr. Psychiat.* 5, 170 (1964).

13. C. S. Parker and F. Wrigley, *J. Ment. Sci.* 96, 276 (1950).

14. H. Isbell and D. R. Jasinski, *Psychopharmacologia* 14, 115 (1969).

15. L. E. Hollister and H. K. Gillespie, in *Drugs and Youth,* J. R. Wittenborn, H. Brill, J. P. Smith, S. A. Wittenborn, Eds. (Thomas, Springfield, Ill., 1969).

16. F. T. Melges, J. R. Tinklenberg, L. E. Hollister, H. K. Gillespie, *Science* 168, 1118 (1970); *Arch. Gen. Psychiat.* 23, 204 (1970); J. R. Tinklenberg, F. T. Melges, L. E. Hollister, H. K. Gillespie, *Nature* 226, 1171 (1970).

17. L. E. Hollister and H. K. Gillespie, *Arch. Gen. Psychiat.* 23, 199 (1970).

18. L. D. Clark and E. N. Nakashima, *Amer. J. Psychiat.* 125, 379 (1969); L. D. Clark, R. Hughes, E. N. Nakashima, *Arch. Gen. Psychiat.* 23, 193 (1970).

19. A. Crancer, Jr., J. M. Dille, J. C. Delay, J. E. Wallace, M. D. Haykin, *Science* 164, 851 (1969); H. Kalant, *ibid.* 166, 640 (1969).

20. E. A. Rodin, E. F. Domino, J. P. Porzak, *J. Amer. Med. Ass.* 213, 1300 (1970); C. H. Song, S. L. Kanter, L. E. Hollister, *Res. Commun. Chem. Pathol. Pharmacol.* 1, 375 (1970).

21. L. E. Hollister, S. L. Sherwood, A. Cavasino, *Pharmacol. Res. Commun.,* in press.

22. J. E. Manno, G. F. Kiplinger, N. Scholz, R. B. Forney, *Clin. Pharmacol. Ther.,* in press.

23. L. E. Hollister, *Nature* 227, 968 (1970).

24. R. T. Jones and G. C. Stone, *Psychopharmacologia* 18, 108 (1970).

25. J. Christiansen and O. J. Rafaelsen, *ibid.* 15, 60 (1969).

26. I. M. Nilsson, S. Agurell, J. L. G. Nilsson, A. Ohlsson, F. Sandberg, M. Wahlquist, *Science* 168, 1228 (1970); S. H. Burstein, F. Menezes, E. Williamson, R. Mechoulam, *Nature* 225, 87 (1970); R. L. Foltz, A. F. Fentiman, Jr., E. G. Leighty, J. L. Walter, H. R. Drewes, W. E. Schwartz, T. F. Page, Jr., E. B. Truitt, Jr., *Science* 168, 844 (1970).

27. L. Lemberger, S. D. Silberstein, J. Axlerod, I. J. Kopin, *Science* 170, 1320 (1970).

28. S. Agurell, in *Botany and Chemistry of Cannabis,* S. H. Curry and C. R. B. Joyce, Eds. (Churchill, London, 1970), pp. 175–191.

29. L. E. Hollister, *Chemical Psychoses: LSD and Related Drugs* (Thomas, Springfield, Ill., 1968).

30. C. T. Tart, *Nature* 226, 701 (1970).

31. Leading article, *Lancet* 1963-II, 989 (1963); "Dependence on *Cannabis* (Marihuana)," *J. Amer. Med. Ass.* 201, 368 (1967); G. Edwards, *Practitioner* 200, 226 (1968); A. Wikler, *Arch. Gen. Psychiat.* 23, 320 (1970).

32. M. I. Soueit, *Bull. Narcotics* 19, 1 (1967).

33.. J. C. Ball, C. D. Chambers, M. J. Ball, *J. Criminal Law Criminol. Police Sci.* 59, 171 (1968).

34. F. G. Wilkins, *Brit. Med. J.* 2, 496 (1967); J. A. Talbott and J. W. Teague, *J. Amer. Med. Ass.* 210, 299 (1969).

35. E. Tylden, *Brit. Med. J.* 2, 502 (1967).

36. J. Kaplan, *Marihuana—The New Prohibition* (World, Cleveland, 1970).

37. L. E. Hollister, and J. Kaplan, *J. Clin. Pharmacol.* 9, 345 (1969).

38. *Home Office Report by the Advisory Committee on Drug Dependence, Cannabis* (Her Majesty's Stationery Office, London, Eng., 1968).

39. E. G. Williams, C. K. Himmelsbach, A. Wikler, B. J. Lloyd, Jr., *Pub. Health Rep.* 61, 1059 (1946).

40. E. A. Carlini, *Pharmacology* 1, 135 (1968); D. E. McMillan, L. S. Harris, J. M. Frankenheim, J. S. Kennedy, *Science* 169, 501 (1970).

41. D. Holtzman, R. A. Lovell, J. H. Jaffe, D. X. Freedman, *Science* 163, 1464 (1969); L. E. Hollister, F. Moore, S. L. Kanter, E. Noble, *Psychopharmacologia* 17, 354 (1970).

42. T. Pivik, V. Zarcone, L. E. Hollister, W. Dement, *Psychophysiology* 6, 261 (1969).

43. L. J. Thompson and R. C. Proctor, *N. Carolina Med. J.* 14, 523 (1953).

44. G. T. Stockings, *Brit. Med. J.* 1, 918 (1947); D. A. Pond, *J. Neurol. Neurosurg. Psychiat.* 11, 271 (1948).

45. L. E. Hollister, *Clin. Pharmacol. Ther.* 12, 44 (1971).

Supported in part by NIH grant MH–03030.

Dr. Ernest Lawrence Abel is a noted research scientist who has been active in the study of drugs. He has participated in many of the experiments on the effects of marihuana use described in this book.

A Canadian, he attended the University of Toronto from which he received his bachelor's, master's and doctoral degrees. He has also been a post doctoral fellow at the School of Medicine of the University of North Carolina in Chapel Hill.

His previous published works include *Drugs and Behavior,* published in 1974, *Ancient Views on the Origins of Life,* and *The Roots of Antisemitism.*

He has contributed articles to *Science, Nature, British Journal of Pharmacology, CIBA Symposium, Journal of Comparative and Physiological Psychology.*

Dr. Abel is a member of the New York Academy of Science, the American Society for Experimental Pharmacology and Therapeutics, and the American Psychological Association.